WEBSTER'S NEW WORLD

Spanish Grammar and Exercises

Grammar Compiled by
LEXUS
with
Hugh O'Donnell
and
Marjory O'Donnell

Macmillan ■ USA

INTRODUCTION

The Grammar section of this book has been written to meet the demands of language teaching in schools and colleges. The essential rules of the Spanish language have been explained in terms that are as accessible as possible to all users. Where technical terms have been used then full explanations of these terms have also been supplied. There is also a full glossary of grammatical terminology on pages 3–9. While literary aspects of the Spanish language have not been ignored, the emphasis has been placed squarely on modern spoken Spanish. This grammar, with its wealth of lively and typical illustrations of usage taken from the present-day language, is the ideal study tool for all levels—from the beginner who is starting to come to grips with the Spanish language through to the advanced user who requires a comprehensive and readily accessible work of reference.

The Grammar section is further divided into two main parts:

THE FUNCTIONS OF SPANISH explains how to use Spanish to refer to things and actions, to express conditions, emotions and the like. This list of functions does not claim to be exhaustive, but it does contain those most likely to cause difficulties for the English-speaking learner.

THE FORMS OF SPANISH explains the formation of all the principal elements of the language. Here you can check the formation of tenses or any unknown form you may come across in your reading.

A considerable effort has been made to explain not only *how* Spanish operates in different contexts, but, more importantly, to explain *why* it operates the way it does. This is an essential aspect of the book, because experience shows that what the learner of a foreign language *really* requires is not so much rules, as understanding.

Experience also shows that the pattern of errors among learners of Spanish is by and large predictable. Most make essentially the same mistakes in the same proportions. To help you to avoid these pitfalls, any aspect of Spanish which is traditionally a cause of frequent errors has been highlighted in the Grammar by the symbol △. These are areas where special attention is required.

Hugh O-Donnell

The Exercises section has been conceived to help you assess your knowledge of the essential grammar points of the Spanish language. It includes 26 chapters, each of which concentrates on a particular grammatical point. The exercises have been designed to consolidate and extend your understanding of Spanish grammar.

Every chapter focuses on a precise point of Spanish grammar, and within the chapter the exercises take you gradually through various levels of grammatical difficulty. Answers to every exercise are given at the end of the book. After every test a score is given, which allows you to assess your level.

We have tried to vary as much as we could the types of the exercises and the themes used. We hope that this will make your study both enjoyable and stimulating. The vocabulary used in the book is based on contemporary written and spoken Spanish.

The obtained score for each test enables you to assess your level accurately. Do not worry if you do not obtain a good score the first time. If you have too many difficulties with a test or a chapter and if, despite the answers, some points remain unclear, we advise you to go back to the Grammar section and to redo the test or the chapter in question later on.

If your score is:

- between 90 and 100% your knowledge is excellent;
- between 80 and 90% you have a good level;
- between 60 and 80% your level is not bad but we would recommend that you redo the test or the chapter after a while and that you review the particular points in the Grammar section;
- under 60%: don't be discouraged, work quietly on the weak points using the Grammar and redo the tests several times if necessary

We wish you good luck and hope that you will make good progress with your Spanish and will enjoy working with this book.

CONTENTS

Part I

Grammar

GLOSSARY OF GRAMMATICAL TERMS

ABSTRACT NOUN

An abstract noun is one which refers not to a concrete physical object or a person but to a quality or a concept. Examples of abstract nouns are *happiness, life, length*.

ACTIVE

The active form of a verb is the basic form as in *I remember her*. It is normally opposed to the passive form of the verb as in *she will be remembered*.

ADJECTIVAL NOUN

An adjectival noun is an adjective used as a noun. For example, the adjective *young* is used as a noun in *the young at heart*.

ADJECTIVE

A describing word telling us what something or someone is like (e.g. *a **small** house, the **Royal** Family, an **interesting** pastime*).

ADVERB

Adverbs are normally used with a verb to add extra information by indicating **how** the action is done (adverbs of manner), **when, where** and **with how much intensity** the action is done (adverbs of time, place and intensity), or **to what extent** the action is done (adverbs of quantity). Adverbs may also be used with an adjective or another adverb (e.g. *a **very** attractive girl, **very** well*).

AGREEMENT

In Spanish, words such as adjectives, articles and pronouns are said to agree in number and gender with the noun or pronoun they refer to. This means that their form changes according to the **number** of the noun (singular or plural) and its **gender** (masculine or feminine).

APPOSITION
A word or a phrase is said to be in apposition to another when it is placed directly after it without any joining word (e.g. *Mr Jones*, **our bank manager**, *rang today*).

ARTICLE
See DEFINITE ARTICLE and INDEFINITE ARTICLE.

AUGMENTATIVE
An augmentative is added to a noun to indicate largeness or awkwardness, e.g. *un hombrón, una mujerona*.

AUXILIARY
Auxiliary verbs are used to form compound tenses of other verbs, e.g. **have** in *I have seen* or **will** in *she will go*. The main auxiliary verbs in Spanish are **haber, estar** and **ser**.

CARDINAL
Cardinal numbers are numbers such as *one, two, ten, fourteen*, as opposed to **ordinal** numbers (e.g. *first, second*).

CLAUSE
A clause is a group of words which contains at least a subject and a verb: *he said* is a clause. A clause often contains more than this basic information, e.g. *he said this to her yesterday*. Sentences can be made up of several clauses, e.g. *he said / he'd call me / if he were free*. See SENTENCE.

COLLECTIVE
A collective noun is one which refers to a group of people or things but which is singular in form. Examples of collective nouns are *flock* or *fleet*.

COLLOQUIAL
Colloquial language is the sort of language that can be used in everyday informal conversation but is avoided in formal writing such as legal contracts etc.

COMPARATIVE
The comparative forms of adjectives and adverbs are used to compare two or more things, persons or actions. in English, *more . . . than, -er than, less . . . than* and *as . . . as* are used for comparison.

COMPOUND
Compound tenses are verb tenses consisting of more than one element. In Spanish, the compound tenses of a verb are formed by the **auxiliary** verb and

the **present** or past participle: *estoy hablando, han llegado.*

COMPOUND NOUNS

Compound nouns are nouns made up of two or more separate words. English examples are *goalkeeper* or *dinner party.* Spanish compound nouns are normally linked by *de*, e.g. *un muro de piedra.*

CONDITIONAL

This mood is used to describe what someone would do, or something that would happen if a condition were fulfilled (e.g. *I **would come** if I was well; the chair **would have broken** if he had sat on it*). It also indicates future in the past, e.g. *he said he **would come**.*

CONJUGATION

The conjugation of a verb is the set of different forms taken in the particular tenses and moods of that verb.

CONJUNCTION

Conjunctions are linking words (e.g. *and, but, or*). They may be coordinating or subordinating. Coordinating conjunctions are words like *y, o, pero*; subordinating conjunctions are words like *que, si, aunque.*

DEFINITE ARTICLE

The definite article is *the* in English and *el, la, los, las* in Spanish.

DEMONSTRATIVE

Demonstrative adjectives (e.g. *this, that, these*) and pronouns (e.g. *this one, that one*) are used to point out a particular person or thing.

DIMINUTIVE

A diminutive is added to a noun (or occasionally to an adjective) to indicate smallness or a favorable attitude by the speaker, e.g. *mesita, hijito.*

DIRECT OBJECT

A noun or a pronoun which in English follows a verb without any linking preposition, e.g. *I met **a friend**.* Note that in English a preposition is often omitted, e.g. *I sent him a present—him* is equivalent to *to him—a present* is the direct object.

ENDING

The ending of a verb is determined by the **person** (1st/2nd/3rd) and **number** (singular/plural) of its subject.

EXCLAMATION	Words or phrases used to express surprise, annoyance etc. (e.g. *what!*, *wow!*; *how lucky!*, *what a nice day!*). Exclamations in Spanish begin with an upside-down exclamation mark, e.g. *¡caramba!*
FEMININE	See GENDER.
GENDER	The gender of a noun indicates whether the noun is **masculine** or **feminine**. In Spanish, the gender of a noun is not always determined by the sex of what it refers to, e.g. *la víctima (the victim)* is a feminine noun.
IDIOMATIC	Idiomatic expressions (or idioms), are expressions which cannot normally be translated word for word. For example, *it's raining cats and dogs* is translated by *está lloviendo a cántaros*.
IMPERATIVE	A mood used for giving orders (e.g. *stop!*, *don't go!*) or for making suggestions (e.g. *let's go*).
INDEFINITE	Indefinite pronouns are words that do not refer to a definite person or thing (e.g. *each*, *someone*).
INDEFINITE ARTICLE	The indefinite article is *a* in English and *un, una* in Spanish.
INDICATIVE	The form of a verb normally used in making statements or asking questions, as in *I like, he came, we are trying*. It is opposed to the subjunctive, conditional and imperative.
INDIRECT OBJECT	A pronoun or noun which follows a verb sometimes with a linking preposition (usually *to*), e.g. *I spoke to **my friend/him**, she gave **him** a kiss*.
INFINITIVE	The infinitive is the form of the verb as found in dictionaries. Thus *to eat, to finish, to take* are infinitives. In Spanish, all infinitives end in **-r**: *tomar, beber, vivir*.
INTERROGATIVE	Interrogative words are used to ask a **question**. This may be a direct question (***when** will you arrive?*) or an indirect

question (*I don t know **when** he'll arrive*). See QUESTION.

MASCULINE See GENDER.

MOOD The name given to the four main areas within which a verb is conjugated. See INDICATIVE, SUBJUNCTIVE, CONDITIONAL, IMPERATIVE.

NEUTER There are no neuter nouns in Spanish. Only the definite article *lo*, the pronoun *ello* and the demonstrative pronouns *esto, eso* and *aquello* have a neuter form. The article *lo* is used with adjectives, e.g. *lo bueno* (that which is good, the good thing), the demonstratives refer to an entire situation, e.g. *no acepto eso*.

NOUN A word which refers to living creatures, things, places or abstract ideas, e.g. *postman, cat, shop, passport, life*.

NUMBER The number of a noun indicates whether the noun is **singular** or **plural**. A singular noun refers to one single thing or person (e.g. *boy, train*) and a plural noun to several (e.g. *boys, trains*).

OBJECT See DIRECT OBJECT, INDIRECT OBJECT.

ORDINAL Ordinal numbers are *first, second, third, fourth* etc.

PASSIVE A verb is used in the passive when the subject of the verb does not perform the action but is subjected to it. In English, the passive is formed with a part of the verb *to be* and the past participle of the verb, e.g. *he was rewarded*.

PAST PARTICIPLE The past participle of a verb is the form which is used after *to have* in English, e.g. *I have **eaten**, I have **said**, you have **tried***.

PERSON In any tense, there are three persons in the singular (1st: *I* . . . , 2nd: *you* . . . , 3rd: *he*/*she* . . .), and three in the plural (1st: *we* . . . , 2nd: *you* . . . , 3rd: *they* . . .). See also ENDING.

PERSONAL PRONOUNS   Personal pronouns stand for a noun. In English they are words like *I, you, he/she/it, we, they* or *me, you, him/her/it, us, them*.

PLURAL   See NUMBER.

POSSESSIVE   Possessives are used to indicate possession or ownership. They are words like *my/mine, your/yours, our/ours*.

PREPOSITION   Prepositions are words such as *with, in, to, at*. They are normally followed by a noun or a pronoun.

PRESENT PARTICIPLE   The present participle is the verb form which ends in **-ing** in English (**-ndo** in Spanish).

PROGRESSIVE   The progressive is formed in English by the verb *to be* + **present participle**, e.g. *I am speaking, he is writing*. In Spanish it is formed by **estar** + **present participle**, e.g. *estoy hablando, está escribiendo*.

PRONOUN   A word which stands for a noun. The main categories of pronouns are:

- **Personal pronouns** (e.g. *you, him, us*)
- **Possessive pronouns** (e.g. *mine, yours, his*)
- **Reflexive pronouns** (e.g. *myself, himself*)
- **Interrogative pronouns** (e.g. *who?, what?, which?*)
- **Relative pronouns** (e.g. *who, which, that*)
- **Demonstrative pronouns** (e.g. *this, that, these*)
- **Indefinite pronouns** (e.g. *something, none*)

QUESTION   There are two question forms: **direct** questions stand on their own and require a question mark at the end (e.g. *when will he come?*); **indirect** questions are introduced by a clause and require no question mark (e.g. *I wonder when he will come*). Direct questions begin in Spanish with an upside-down question mark, e.g. *¿qué haces?*

REFLEXIVE

Reflexive verbs 'reflect' the action back onto the subject (e.g. *I dressed myself*). They are always found with a reflexive pronoun and are more common in Spanish than in English. Verbs are also used reflexively in Spanish with a passive meaning.

SENTENCE

A sentence is a group of words made up of one or more clauses (see CLAUSE). The end of a sentence is indicated by a punctuation mark (usually a full stop, a question mark or an exclamation mark).

SINGULAR

See NUMBER.

STEM

See VERB STEM.

SUBJECT

The subject of a verb is the noun or pronoun which performs the action. In the sentences *the train left early* and *she bought a record, the train* and *she* are the subjects.

SUBJUNCTIVE

The subjunctive is a verb form which is rarely used in English (e.g. *if I were you, God save the Queen*). It is very much more common in Spanish.

SUPERLATIVE

The form of an adjective or an adverb which, in English, is marked by *the most ..., the -est* or *the least ....*

TENSE

Verbs are used in tenses, which indicate when an action takes place, e.g. in the present, the past, the future.

VERB

A 'doing' word, which usually describes an action (e.g. *to sing, to work, to watch*). Some verbs describe a state (e.g. *to be, to have, to hope*).

VERB STEM

The stem of a verb is its 'basic unit' to which the various endings are added. To find the stem of a Spanish verb remove **-ar**, **-er** or **-ir** from the infinitive. The stem of *hablar* is *habl*, of *beber*, *beb*, of *vivir*, *viv*.

VOICE

The two voices of a verb are its active and passive forms.

Functions

1. REFERRING TO THINGS: THE NOUN

The word 'thing' is used here not just to refer to objects—books, houses, cars etc, also known as *inanimate* nouns—but also to people and animals—*animate* nouns—and to what are known as *abstract* nouns. Abstract nouns refer not to things which you can touch or see, but only to ideas which you can think about—justice, peace, democracy and so on.

A. USES OF THE DEFINITE AND INDEFINITE ARTICLES

For the formation of the definite and indefinite articles, see page 137.

There is a considerable degree of agreement between Spanish and English as to when a noun is used with a definite or an indefinite article. However, some important differences also occur.

The traditional terms 'definite article' ('the' in English) and 'indefinite article' ('a', 'an' in English) are to some extent misleading, since it is not necessarily the case that the definite article refers to a specific object (or idea) and the indefinite article does not. For example, in the sentences:

> **la casa es vieja**
> the house is old

and

> **hemos comprado una casa en el campo**
> we have bought a house in the country

both nouns refer to a specific house.

Moreover, there are in fact *three* different cases to consider:

> cases where the noun is used with a definite article
> cases where the noun is used with an indefinite article
> cases where the noun is used with no article at all

As you will see later, *truly* indefinite nouns are in fact used without any article in Spanish.

12

1. Nouns which are used to represent *all* of the thing or things they are referring to—*all* butter, *all* wine, *all* Spaniards and the like— are preceded by the definite article in Spanish:

> **me gusta la cerveza, pero no me gusta el vino**
> I like beer (all beer, beer in general), but I don't like wine (wine in general)

> **los españoles beben mucho vino**
> Spaniards (all Spaniards) drink a lot of wine

If the noun is used with an adjective or an adjectival phrase, it will still take the definite article if it refers to all of the thing or things indicated by the noun and the adjective or phrase:

> **no me gusta el vino tinto**
> I don't like red wine

el vino tinto does not represent all wine, but it does stand for all red wine:

> **los granjeros del sur de España cultivan muchas frutas**
> farmers in the south of Spain grow a lot of fruit

This refers to all farmers in the south of Spain.

2. Abstract nouns take the definite article in Spanish, since they also refer to the idea as a whole:

> **la justicia es necesaria si la democracia va a sobrevivir**
> justice is necessary if democracy is to survive

> **la inflación está subiendo**
> inflation is going up

If the abstract noun is used with an adjective, then in some cases it can take the indefinite article:

> **me miró con una curiosidad creciente**
> he looked at me with growing curiosity

3. Names of languages take the definite article:

> **el español es muy interesante, pero no me gusta el francés**
> Spanish is very interesting, but I don't like French

However, no article is used after **en**, **de** and the verbs **hablar** and **estudiar**:

> **¿hablas español?**
> do you speak Spanish

> **el libro está escrito en español**
> the book is written in Spanish

Again, if a particular example of the language is being referred to rather than the language as a whole, the indefinite article is used:

John habla un español excelente
John speaks excellent Spanish (i.e. the particular Spanish that
he speaks is excellent)

4. Names of academic subjects follow the same pattern as in 3:

   no me gustan las matemáticas, prefiero la física
   I don't like math, I prefer physics

   but no article is necessary in the following cases:

   he comprado un libro de química
   I've bought a chemistry book

   estudia matemáticas
   he is studying mathematics

   es licenciado en física
   he has a degree in physics

5. Illnesses and diseases

   These usually take the definite article, unless the idea of 'a case
   of' is clearly meant, in which case no article is used:

   ¿tiene algo contra la laringitis?
   do you have anything for laryngitis?

but:

   tengo laringitis?
   I have laryngitis

6. Parts of the body used in general physical descriptions take the
   definite article:

   tiene el pelo castaño y los ojos verdes
   she has brown hair and green eyes

   However, if the description highlights how one person's eyes etc.
   are different from everyone else's, the indefinite article is used:

   tiene unos ojos azules que nadie puede resistir
   she has blue eyes which no one can resist

   When the part of the body is the subject of the verb the
   possessive adjective is normally used:

   sus ojos son azules como el mar
   her eyes are blue like the sea

7. **Where English uses the possessive adjective, Spanish uses
   the definite article (sometimes together with the indirect
   object pronouns for greater precision) to indicate possession
   in relation to parts of the body and items of clothing:**

   levantó la cabeza
   he lifted his head

me duele la cabeza
I have a headache

su madre le lavó la cara
his mother washed his face

se puso la chaqueta y salió
he put on his jacket and went out

8. For reasons of style the definite article is frequently omitted in lists of words, even where you might expect it to appear:

necesitarás entusiasmo e interés
you will need enthusiasm and interest

B. CASES IN WHICH NO ARTICLE IS USED

1. In general, no article is used with the noun if:

the noun does not refer either to the thing as a whole or to a specific example of the thing in question:

me llamó ladrón
he called me a thief

the noun refers to an indefinite amount of or number of the thing(s) in question:

no bebo cerveza
I don't drink beer

2. No article is used with general statements of profession or occupation, political or religious conviction, and the like:

mi padre es médico y mi tía es enfermera
my father is a doctor and my aunt is a nurse

ella es católica; él es comunista
she is a Catholic; he is a communist

However, if the noun is made more precise by being used with an adjective, then the indefinite article is indeed used:

su padre es un cirujano conocido
his father is a well known surgeon

Not all surgeons are famous.

3. Frequently (though not always) when a noun is dependent on a negative or a question:

¿tienes coche? — no, no tengo coche
have you got a car? — no, I don't have a car

Again, this is not a reference to any particular car. If you did wish to refer to a particular car, you would use the indefinite article:

¿tienes un coche rojo?
do you have a red car?

4. When the noun is used with one of a small number of adjectives. These are otro (other), and tal, semejante and parecido (all meaning such), and cierto (certain, some):

¿me das otro libro, por favor?
would you give me another book, please? (i.e. any other *undefined* book)

semejante situación nunca se había producido antes
such a situation had never arisen before (a situation of this general kind)

estoy de acuerdo contigo hasta cierto punto
I agree with you up to a point (an *undefined* point)

5. After qué and vaya in exclamations:

¡qué lástima!
what a shame!

¡vaya sorpresa!
what a surprise!

¡vaya paliza!
what a bore!

Note that any adjective used in such an exclamation is usually preceded by **tan** or **más**:

¡qué día más magnífico!
what a magnificent day!

This **más** is not considered comparative (see page 34), and does not become **mejor** or **peor** when used with **bueno** or **malo**:

¡qué idea más buena!
what a good idea!

6. After **como** in expressions such as the following:

te hablo como amigo
I'm speaking to you as a friend

I am speaking to you not as a particular friend, but as any friend would.

mándenos diez cajas como pedido de prueba
send us ten boxes as a trial order

Compare this with the following:

ya hemos recibido un pedido de prueba de esa empresa
we have already received a trial order from this firm

This is a reference to a specific trial order.

7. When expressing indefinite quantities:

¿tienes mantequilla?
do you have (any) butter?

no quiero vino, siempre bebo cerveza
I don't want (any) wine, I always drink beer

Compare this with **la cerveza** earlier, which meant 'all beer', 'beer in general'.

buen número de personas no querían aceptar eso
a good number of people did not want to accept this

parte/buena parte/gran parte del dinero se invirtió en el proyecto
part/a good part/a large part of the money was invested in the project

tengo cantidad/infinidad de preguntas que hacerte
I've got loads/masses of questions to ask you

8. With nouns in apposition:

vive en Madrid, capital de España
he lives in Madrid, the capital of Spain

C. NAMES OF PERSONS, COUNTRIES, ETC.

A proper noun is invariably the name of a person, country, continent, organization or the like. Most proper nouns, including virtually all feminine names of countries, are used without any article in Spanish (see page 138 for a list of names of countries which do take the article):

Alemania es un país mucho más rico que España
Germany is a much richer country than Spain

However, the article is used in the following cases:

1. When a person's name is preceded by a title of some kind:

el señor Carballo no estaba
señor Carballo wasn't in

el general Olmeda ya se había marchado
General Olmeda had already left

The exceptions to this are:

- the titles **don** and **doña**
- when the title is used in direct address
- foreign titles

¿qué piensa de esto, señor Carballo?
what do you think of this, señor Carballo?

Lord Byron era un poeta inglés muy conocido
Lord Byron was a very famous English poet

2. When the noun is used with an adjective:

el pobre Juan no sabía qué hacer
poor Juan didn't know what to do

esto ha ocurrido muchas veces en la historia de la Europa occidental
this has happened many times in the history of Western Europe

However, **Gran Bretaña** and **Estados Unidos** have come to be regarded as proper nouns in their own right, so that the definite articles are no longer used in these cases:

Gran Bretaña votó en contra de la propuesta
Great Britain voted against the proposal

3. Acronyms

An acronym is a name consisting of the initial letters of a series of words. Known as **siglas**, these are very widely used in Spanish. With the exception of certain names of political parties, **siglas** always take the definite article, and their gender is determined by the gender of the first noun in their expanded form.

A few common acronyms:

la CEE	La Comunidad Económica Europea	The EEC
la OTAN	La Organización del Tratado del Atlántico Norte	NATO
el INI	El Instituto Nacional de Industria	Government Department in charge of nationalized industries
el INEM	El Instituto Nacional de Empleo	Department of Employment
el PSOE	El Partido Socialista Obrero Español	Socialist party
AP	Alianza Popular	Conservative party

España ingresó en la CEE en 1986
Spain joined the EEC in 1986

España sigue siendo miembro de la OTAN
Spain is still a member of NATO

Even those acronyms which are not proper names take the definite article:

el SIDA	**El Síndrome de Immuno-Deficiencia Adquirida**	AIDS
el IVA	**El Impuesto sobre el Valor Añadido**	VAT
el PVP	**El Precio de Venta al Público**	Retail price

el SIDA es la enfermedad más grave de nuestra época
AIDS is the most serious illness of our time

D. THE NEUTER ARTICLE lo

1. Abstract nouns

The neuter article **lo** is used almost exclusively with adjectives and adverbs. When used with an adjective, it transforms it into an abstract noun based on the meaning of that adjective. For example **lo bueno** means 'that which is good'. The translation of such 'nouns' varies according to their context (e.g. adjective + 'thing'):

lo esencial es que todos estemos de acuerdo
the essential thing is for all of us to agree

lo verdaderamente importante es que todos lo acepten
what's really important is for everyone to accept it

lo más absurdo es que él no sabía nada
the most absurd part of it is that he knew nothing

2. 'how'

lo + adjective expresses the idea of 'how' in constructions such as the following. Note that in these constructions the adjective agrees with the noun it describes. If there is no noun, the neuter form is used:

no me había dado cuenta de lo caros que son
I hadn't realized how expensive they are

¿no ves lo inútil que es?
can't you see how pointless it is?

E. USING A VERB AS A NOUN

A verbal noun is a verb used as the subject or object of another verb. In Spanish the *infinitive* is used to express the verbal noun, whereas in

English we use the present participle. When used as the subject of a verb, the infinitive is sometimes preceded by the definite article **el**, though it is more common without:

> **fumar es peligroso para la salud**
> smoking is dangerous for your health

> **detesto tener que hacer esto**
> I hate having to do this

⚠ Under *no* circumstances can a present participle be used as a verbal noun in Spanish as it is in English. Note in particular that the infinitive is the *only* form of the verb which can come after a preposition in Spanish:

> **tomó un café antes de salir**
> he had coffee before leaving

> **se sintió mejor después de dormir un rato**
> he felt better after sleeping a while

F. SITUATING SOMETHING IN PLACE OR TIME: DEMONSTRATIVES

This function is carried out in Spanish by the demonstrative adjectives and pronouns (see page 139). The difference between the three demonstrative adjectives in Spanish is as follows:

1. Used to denote place

este	refers to something which is close to the speaker
ese	refers to something which is close to the listener
aquel	refers to something which is remote from both speaker and listener

> **¿me das ese libro?**
> will you give me that book? (ie the one near you)

> **tomo esta caja**
> I'll take this box (ie this one I'm holding, pointing to etc)

> **aquellas flores son muy hermosas**
> those flowers are very beautiful (those over there)

2. Used to denote time

este is used, as in English, if the *noun* refers to present time:

> **esta semana fuimos a la playa**
> we went to the beach this week

Both **ese** and **aquel** can be used to refer to past time with little difference in meaning, though **aquel** may suggest that the action is more remote:

en esa época no se permitían los partidos políticos
at that time political parties were not allowed

en aquella época la población de Madrid era de sólo un millón de personas
at that time the population of Madrid was only one million

3. 'those who', 'those of'

Note that 'those who' is expressed in Spanish as **los que** or **las que**. The actual demonstratives are not used:

los que piensan eso se equivocan
those who think that are wrong

Likewise, 'that of', 'those of' are expressed as **el de, la de, los de, las de. el** takes the same contractions as it does when it is used as a definite article—ie **a** + **el** becomes **al** and **de** + **el** becomes **del** (see page 137):

preferimos las mercancías de Vds. a las de sus competidores
we prefer your goods to those of your competitors

prefiero el coche de Luis al de Paco
I prefer Luis's car to Paco's (to that of Paco)

4. The demonstrative pronouns

For the formation of the demonstrative pronouns, see page 139. The demonstrative pronouns denote time and place in the same way as the demonstrative adjectives. Note, however, the use of **éste** and **aquél** to express the idea of 'the former' and 'the latter':

éste es más difícil que aquél
the former is more difficult than the latter

The neuter demonstrative pronouns **esto, eso** and **aquello** are used to represent an unknown object, a general situation, an entire idea.

⚠ They can *never* be used to represent a specific noun whose identity is known to the speaker:

¿qué es esto?
what's this? (unknown object)

no puedo aceptar esto
I can't accept this (this situation)

Compare this with:

no puedo aceptar esta situación
I can't accept this situation

G. LINKING NOUNS

For a list of coordinating conjunctions, see page 216.

1. The simplest way of linking nouns is by using the conjunctions **y** (and) and **o** (or). Note that **y** is replaced by **e** if the pronunciation of the next word begins with the vowel **i**. It is the pronunciation that is important, not the way the noun is spelled:

   padres e hijos
   parents and children

   Likewise, **o** is replaced by **u** if the next word begins with the sound **o**:

   siete u ocho
   seven or eight

   In the Spanish press, **o** is frequently written **ó** between numbers to avoid confusion with the number **0**:

   60 ó 70
   60 or 70

2. Expressing 'both'

   'both' + plural noun

   When 'both' is followed by a *single* plural noun, **los dos** or **las dos** is used, depending on the gender of the noun. In more formal Spanish, the adjective **ambos** may be used:

   los dos hermanos vinieron/ambos hermanos vinieron
   both brothers came

   comí las dos tartas/comí ambas tartas
   I ate both cakes

   ⚠ Neither *los/las dos* nor *ambos* may be used to express the idea of 'both ... and ...' in Spanish.

   'both' + two adjectives

   'both' used to link two adjectives referring to the same noun is **a la vez**:

   encuentro este libro a la vez divertido e interesante
   I find this book both entertaining and interesting

   'both' + two nouns or pronouns

   By far the commonest way of expressing 'both ... and ...' linking two dissimilar things in Spanish is **tanto ... como...** . Since **tanto** is used as an adverb in this construction, it never changes; no matter what the number or gender of the nouns involved:

   tanto tú como yo queremos resolver este problema
   both you and I want to solve this problem

2. RELATIONSHIPS BETWEEN THINGS

A. PREPOSITIONS

The commonest way of expressing relationships between nouns is by the use of prepositions. For a detailed list of both simple and compound prepositions and their uses, see pages 150–159. However, the following deserve special mention:

por and para

As well as having a variety of other meanings, both **por** and **para** can be used to express the ideas of 'for' and 'by' in Spanish. Their uses in these meanings can be summarized as follows:

Meaning 'for'

1. In a general sense, it can be said that **por** refers to *causes*, whereas **para** refers to *aims* or *objectives*.

   The following short examples, both of which mean 'I am doing it for my brother', may clarify the difference:

   lo hago por mi hermano

   Here the emphasis is on what *caused* the speaker to decide to do what he is doing. He is doing it because his brother asked for it to be done, or because his brother needed help in some way.

   lo hago para mi hermano

   para here indicates that the action is being done in order to secure some advantage for the brother in the future.

   Likewise, the question **¿por qué hiciste esto?** asks for an explanation of what caused the action to be done, whereas the question **¿para qué hiciste esto?** asks for an explanation of the future objectives.

   Other examples showing the distinction between **por** and **para** (note that, although the basic ideas remain unchanged, 'for' is not always the best translation in English):

   lo hizo por necesidad
   he did it out of necessity

cometió el error por cansancio
he made the mistake through tiredness

lo dejaron para otro día
they left it for another day

estamos estudiando para un examen
we're studying for an exam

2. If there is any idea of an exchange, **por** is always used:

pagué diez mil pesetas por esta radio
I paid ten thousand pesetas for this radio

voy a cambiar mi viejo coche por otro más moderno
I am going to exchange my old car for a more modern one

3. To express the idea of 'as regards', 'as far as it concerns', use **para**:

este libro es demasiado difícil para mí
this book is too difficult for me

tal situación sería inaceptable para España
such a situation would be unacceptable for Spain

Meaning 'by'

1. When introducing the person or thing by whom an action was carried out (the passive mood), **por** is always used:

el edificio fue inaugurado por el rey Juan Carlos
the building was inaugurated by King Juan Carlos

2. When 'by' refers to a future deadline, **para** is used:

necesitamos las mercancías para finales de octubre
we need the goods by the end of October

a and en

Basically **a** indicates motion *towards* a thing or place, whereas **en** indicates position *in* or *on* a thing or place. The difference is usually clear in English, but problems can arise when translating the preposition 'at'. If 'at' indicates position *in* or *on*, **en** must be used:

Juan está en casa
Juan is at home

vi este ordenador en la feria de muestras
I saw this computer at the exhibition

antes de, delante de, antes

1. **antes de** refers usually to time:

llegamos antes de medianoche
we arrived before midnight

Colloquially, it may also refer to place, though the idea of 'before you arrive at …' is usually involved:

la iglesia está antes del cruce
the church is before the junction

2. **delante de** refers to physical position:

el buzón está delante de Correos
the mailbox is in front of the Post Office

3. **ante** refers to mental position, and is usually used with abstract nouns. It expresses roughly the same idea as the English expressions 'in the presence of', '(when) faced with' and the like:

el gobierno no sabía como reaccionar ante este problema
the government did not know how to react when faced with this problem

There are a few set expressions where **ante** may refer to physical position, but these are very limited and refer often to legal contexts:

compareció ante el juez
he appeared before the judge

B. POSSESSION

For the formation of the possessive adjectives and pronouns, see pages 140–141.

The weak forms of the possessive adjectives, which are *by far* the commonest, are placed before the noun. The strong forms go after the noun.

1. The weak possessive adjectives

⚠ **It is important to note that, like any other adjective, the possessive adjective agrees in gender and number with the noun it describes. The 'owner' of the things described is irrelevant from this point of view:**

¿dónde están nuestras maletas?
where are our suitcases?

nuestras is in the feminine plural form because **maletas** is feminine plural. The owners ('we') could be either male or female:

los chicos hablaban con su abuelo
the boys were speaking with their grandfather

las chicas ayudaban a su madre
the girls were helping their mother

su is singular because both **abuelo** and **madre** are singular. The fact that there were a number of boys or girls does not alter this in any way.

2. **The strong possessive adjectives**

In contemporary Spanish, the strong forms of the possessive adjectives are for all practical purposes restricted to forms of direct address, or to expressing the idea 'of mine', 'of yours' etc:

esto no es posible, amigo mío
this is not possible, my friend

unos amigos míos vinieron a verme
some friends of mine came to see me

3. **The possessive pronouns**

For the formation of the possessive pronouns, see pages 140–141.

The possessive pronouns take the definite article unless they are used with the verb **ser**:

¿quieres el mío?
do you want mine?

esta radio no es tuya, es nuestra
this radio isn't yours, it's ours

su casa es mucho más grande que la mía
his house is much bigger than mine

4. **Cases where confusion might arise**

On occasions, confusion may arise with the use of the form **su** and the pronoun **suyo**. These forms can mean 'his', 'her(s)', 'your(s)' (singular), 'their(s)', 'your(s)' (plural). In most cases the context will make it clear which meaning is involved. However, if confusion is likely to arise, the following forms can be used instead:

his	**de él**
her(s)	**de ella**
your(s) (singular)	**de Vd.**
their(s)	**de ellos, de ellas**
your(s) (plural)	**de Vds.**

María no ha perdido su propia maleta, ha perdido la de ellos
María has not lost her own suitcase, she has lost *theirs*

¿es de ella este coche?
is this car hers?

5. **Possession in general**

There is no equivalent of 's' in Spanish. Possession is expressed in various ways, the most common being the use of the preposition

de. The order in which the nouns are expressed is the exact opposite of English:

el amigo de mi padre
my father's friend

Note that **de** + **el** becomes **del**:

el primo del amigo del profesor
the teacher's friend's cousin

6. Expressing 'whose'

'whose' in a question is **¿de quién?**

¿de quién es este lápiz?
whose is this pencil?

In an adjectival clause, 'whose' is expressed by the adjective **cuyo**, which agrees with the thing owned:

el hombre cuya ventana rompieron está furioso
the man whose window they broke is furious

la mujer cuyos hijos se fueron
the woman whose children went away

7. The verb **pertenecer**

Possession of objects can sometimes be expressed by the use of the verb **pertenecer** (to belong). However, this is rather formal and is much less common than the use of **de**:

¿a quién pertenece esto? — pertenece al profesor
whose is this? — it's the teacher's

The more common meaning of **pertenecer** is 'belong' in the sense of 'be a member of':

pertenece al partido socialista
he belongs to the socialist party

8. With parts of the body and items of clothing

When used as the object of a verb, parts of the body and items of clothing take the definite article, not the possessive adjective as in English. The 'owner' is often indicated by means of the indirect object pronoun:

su madre le lavó la cara
his mother washed his face

se quemó la mano
he burned his hand (i.e. his own hand)

27

C. COMPOUND NOUNS

A compound noun consists of a group of nouns which go together to express a more complex idea, e.g. kitchen table, bedroom carpet.

1. Using **de**

   In Spanish, the elements of a compound noun are usually joined by a preposition, which will in most cases be **de**:

   una pared de piedra
   a stone wall

   un portavoz del ministerio de energía
   an energy department spokesman

   Note that the order in which the nouns are expressed is again the opposite of English, and that the gender of the compound noun in Spanish is based on the gender of the first noun:

   un sombrero de paja viejo
   an old straw hat (**viejo** agrees with **sombrero** and not with **paja**)

2. Other compounds

   In recent years a number of compound nouns have appeared in Spanish which do not have a preposition of any kind. The two nouns simply appear side by side, or are joined by a hyphen. Such nouns take the gender of the first noun, and are also made plural by making the first noun plural:

un coche-bomba	**coches-bomba**
a car bomb	car bombs
la fecha límite	**fechas límite**
the closing date	closing dates
un retrato robot	**retratos robot**
an identikit portrait	identikit portraits

   You should beware of inventing your own compound nouns of this type. Use only those you know for certain to exist. Otherwise always use the construction with **de** as described above.

3. DESCRIBING THINGS

A. AUGMENTATIVES AND DIMINUTIVES

For the formation of augmentatives and diminutives, see pages 142–143.

A particular characteristic of Spanish is to suggest a different view of something by adding either an augmentative or a diminutive to the end of the noun. Both augmentatives and diminutives can have a simply physical meaning, or they can introduce more subjective elements into the way in which the noun is presented.

Both augmentatives and diminutives require a certain amount of care in Spanish, and the learner should beware of inventing his own at random. Use only those of whose connotations you are sure.

Diminutives

Diminutives are widely used in spoken Spanish, though they are much less common in formal written Spanish, and would be frequently out of place there. They may express mainly size, but they more often suggest a favorable/unfavorable attitude of the speaker towards what he is describing. There is often no simple translation for a diminutive used in this way.

1. Size

   un momentito, por favor
   just a moment, please

   había una mesita en el rincón
   there was a small table in the corner

2. Favorable attitude

   This is expressed primarily the diminutive -**ito**, which is the commonest of all the diminutives:

   me miraba con la carita cubierta de lágrimas
   he looked at me with his face covered in tears

   'hola', me dijo con su vocecita encantadora
   'hello', she said in her charming little voice

3. Unfavorable attitude

This is expressed by the diminutive **-uelo** which is comparatively rare:

> **pasamos por dos o tres aldehuelas sin interés**
> we passed through two or three uninteresting little villages

Augmentatives

Augmentatives indicate mostly size, though sometimes the idea of clumsiness or even ugliness may also be implied:

> **llegó un hombrón y se puso a trabajar**
> a big fellow arrived and started to work

> **un hombrote, un hombrazo, un hombracho**
> a big brute of a fellow

> **una mujerona**
> a big strong woman

Some augmentatives and diminutives have now become words in their own right and no longer have any of the connotations mentioned above:

el sillón	armchair
la tesina	dissertation
el gatillo	trigger

B. THE ADJECTIVE

1. Agreement

For the formation of the feminine and plural of adjectives, see pages 145–146.

All adjectives in Spanish must agree both in gender and number with the noun they are describing:

> **las paredes eran blancas, y el suelo era blanco también**
> the walls were white, and the floor was white as well

If a single adjective refers to a mixture of masculine and feminine nouns, it takes the masculine form:

> **las paredes y el suelo eran blancos**
> the walls and the floor were white

If a plural noun is followed by a series of adjectives each of which refers to only one of the things mentioned in the noun, each adjective may take the singular form:

> **los partidos socialista y communista votaron en contra de la ley**
> the socialist and communist parties voted against the bill
> (there is only one socialist party and one communist party)

2. Lists of Adjectives

A number of adjectives may be used to describe the same noun in Spanish as in English. Those adjectives considered most important should be placed closest to the noun. This will usually result in an order of adjectives which is the exact opposite of English:

un diputado socialista español conocido
a well known Spanish socialist congressperson

la política agraria común europea
the European common agricultural policy

3. Choice of position

Although most adjectives usually follow the noun (see page 144), they can be placed in front of the noun for emphasis. This option is widely used in contemporary written Spanish, though it is less common in spoken Spanish:

este equipo da una fiel reproducción del sonido original
this equipment gives a faithful reproduction of the original sound

This is very much a question of style, and should be used with caution unless you have seen or heard the particular example you wish to use.

C. THE INDEFINITE ADJECTIVES

For the forms of **alguno** and **cualquiera** see page 144.

1. 'some'

In the singular, the adjective **alguno** means 'some' in the sense of 'some ... or other':

compró el libro en alguna librería
he bought the book in some bookshop (or other)

In the plural it simply means 'some'. In this case it can be replaced without change of meaning by the appropriate form of **unos/unas**:

vinieron algunos/unos hombres y se pusieron a trabajar
some men turned up and started to work

2. 'any'

Both the adjective **alguno** and the adjective **cualquiera** can be translated into English as 'any', and the difference between the two is often difficult for the English-speaking learner to grasp.

alguno in this sense appears mostly in questions, and is used to find out whether a specific thing or group of things actually exists. **cualquiera**, on the other hand, refers in a completely indefinite way to things which are known to exist. It expresses much the same idea as the English phrases 'any at all', 'any whatsoever'.

Compare the following:

¿hay alguna librería por aquí?
are there any bookshops around here?

This question is asked to see if any bookshops exist: ie are there any actual bookshops? (Note that *in a question* **alguno** is almost always used in the *singular* in Spanish, even when a plural would normally be used in English).

puedes encontrar este libro en cualquier librería
you can find this book in any bookshop

i.e., you can buy it in any bookshop whatsoever. This statement assumes that there are indeed bookshops.

In other cases, the logic of the statement will require one adjective to be used rather than the other:

cualquier mecánico podría hacer eso
any mechanic could do that

i.e., any mechanic at all. **algún** would not make any sense in this context.

Note that very often English 'any' is not translated into Spanish:

¿tiene mantequilla?
do you have any butter?
no tenemos plátanos
we don't have any bananas

The order of 'indefiniteness' in Spanish is as follows:

alguna librería	some bookshop (or other)
algunas/unas librerías	some bookshops
cualquier librería	any bookshop whatsoever
librerías	bookshops

D. VARYING THE FORCE OF AN ADJECTIVE

1. Diminutives and Augmentatives

It is possible to add diminutives, and in a small number of cases augmentatives, to certain adjectives. The connotations involved are as for nouns. This feature requires extra special care. Use only those you know to exist and about which you feel confident:

el agua está calentita hoy
the water is nice and warm today

¿qué tontita eres!
how silly you are!

el niño está muy grandón
the child is very big (for his age)

2. Adverbs

A whole range of adverbs can be used to vary the force of an adjective. For the formation of adverbs, see page 165. A list of adverbs of intensity can be found on pages 168–169.

Any adjective modified by an adverb in this way *must* go after the noun, even if the simple form normally precedes the noun:

me dió un libro sumamente interesante
he gave me an extremely interesting book

⚠ **It is essential to remember that adverbs are invariable, in other words, they *never* change their form, no matter what the gender or number of the adjective they modify.**

3. Increasing the force of the adjective

encuentro todo esto muy aburrido
I find all of this very boring

muy cannot be used on its own. If there is no adjective to follow it, it is replaced by **mucho**. In this case **mucho** is used as an adverb and never changes its form:

¿encontraste interesante la revista? — sí, mucho
did you find the magazine interesting? — yes, very

este libro es sumamente (*or* extremamente *or* extremadamente) interesante
this book is extremely interesting

4. Decreasing the force of the adjective

The adverb **poco** is used to lessen or even *negate* the force of an adjective:

me parece poco probable que venga
it seems unlikely to me that he will come

⚠ *poco* must not be confused with *un poco*, which means 'a little'. *la sopa está poco caliente* (the soup is not very hot) is clearly not the same as *la sopa está un poco caliente* (the soup is a little hot).

E. COMPARING THINGS: THE COMPARATIVE AND THE SUPERLATIVE

THE COMPARATIVE

For the formation of comparatives, see page 147.

Simple comparison

1. The comparison of equality (one thing is as good, as interesting etc. as another)

   If the comparison is based on an adjective, it is expressed by **tan** + adjective + **como**:

   > **Juan es tan alto como su hermana**
   > Juan is as tall as his sister

   > **Luisa no es tan trabajadora como su hermana**
   > Luisa isn't as hard-working as her sister

   If the comparison is based on a noun i.e. it is one of quantity - 'as much as', 'as many as'), it is expressed by **tanto** + noun + **como**. **tanto** is used as an adjective here and therefore agrees with the noun:

   > **yo tengo tantos discos como tú**
   > I have as many records as you

2. The comparison of superiority (one thing is better, longer etc. than another)

   When the comparison is based on an adjective, the construction **más** + adjective + **que** is used (see page 147 for irregular comparatives):

   > **María es más inteligente que su hermano**
   > María is more intelligent than her brother

   If the comparison is one of quantity, the construction **más** + noun + **que** is used:

   > **ellos tienen más dinero que nosotros**
   > they have more money than us

   If the comparison is made with a specific number or amount, **de** is used instead of **que**:

   > **vinieron más de cien personas**
   > more than one hundred people came

   > **esperamos más de media hora**
   > we waited for over half an hour

3. The comparison of inferiority (one thing is less good, less interesting than another)

The comparison of inferiority is expressed by **menos**. It follows the same patterns as the comparison of superiority:

> **esta revista es menos interesante que aquélla**
> this magazine is less interesting than that one

> **tú haces menos errores que yo**
> you make fewer mistakes than me

> **pagué menos de mil pesetas**
> I paid less than a thousand pesetas

4. Note that, whereas English uses the terms 'ever' and 'anyone' in a comparison, Spanish uses the corresponding *negative* terms:

> **la situación es más grave que nunca**
> the situation is more serious than ever

> **él sabe más que nadie**
> he knows more than anyone

Other indefinite comparisons are usually expressed using the adjective **cualquiera** (see page 144):

> **Isabel es más inteligente que cualquier otro estudiante**
> Isabel is more intelligent than any other student

Comparison with a clause

When the comparison is being made not with a noun but with a clause, **que** is replaced by more complex forms.

1. Comparison based on an adjective

When the comparison is based on an adjective, the clause is introduced by **de lo que**:

> **la situación es más compleja de lo que piensas**
> the situation is more complex than you think

> **el problema era más difícil de lo que habían dicho**
> the problem was more difficult than they had said

2. Comparison based on a noun (i.e. comparison of quantity)

In this case, the appropriate form of **del que, de la que, de los que, de las que** is used. The form chosen must agree in gender and number with the noun:

> **vinieron más personas de las que esperábamos**
> more people came than we expected

> **surgieron más problemas de los que habíamos previsto**
> more problems arose than we had foreseen

The **los** in **de los que** agrees with **problemas**, which is masculine:

gasté más dinero del que ahorré
I spent more money than I saved

The **el** in **del que** agrees with **dinero**.

Other phrases of comparison

1. 'more and more' is expressed in Spanish by the phrase **cada vez más**:

   encuentro su comportamiento cada vez más extraño
   I find his behavior more and more odd

   vez may be replaced by another word indicating time without the idea of 'more and more' being lost:

   la situación se pone cada día más grave
   the situation is becoming more and more serious every day

   'less and less' is **cada vez menos**:

   encuentro sus explicaciones cada vez menos verosímiles
   I find his explanations less and less plausible

2. 'the more/less ... the more/less ...'

   'the more/less ... the more/less ...' is expressed by **cuanto** + comparative ... **tanto** + comparative ... . **cuanto** is invariable if used with an adjective or adverb, but agrees in comparisons of quantity (i.e. with nouns).

   In all cases the **tanto** can be omitted, and it is in fact more common to omit it:

   cuanto más fáciles son los ejercicios, más le gustan
   the easier the exercises are, the more he likes them

   cuanto más dinero tiene, más quiere
   the more money he has, the more he wants

   cuantos menos problemas tengamos, más contento estaré
   the fewer problems we have, the happier I'll be

3. 'all the more' + adjective + 'because' is expressed in Spanish as **tanto** + comparative + **cuanto que**. This construction is limited to very formal Spanish:

   esto es tanto más importante cuanto que nos queda poco tiempo
   this is all the more important because we don't have much time

THE SUPERLATIVE

For the formation of superlatives, see page 149.

The relative superlative

1. The relative superlative is used to express one thing's superiority over all others of its kind:

   el español es la asignatura más interesante de las que estudio
   Spanish is the most interesting subject I study

   Luisa se puso su mejor traje
   Luisa put on her best suit

2. The scope of the superlative

   The preposition **de** is used to introduce the scope of the superlative, whereas in English we use 'in':

   es el hombre más rico de la ciudad
   he's the richest man in town

   Estados Unidos es el país más poderoso del mundo
   The United States is the most powerful country in the world

3. Order of superlatives

   A descending order of superlatives ('the second oldest man', 'the third richest woman') is expressed as follows:

   el segundo hombre más viejo
   the second oldest man

   la tercera mujer más rica
   the third richest woman

The absolute superlative

It is important to distinguish clearly in Spanish between the relative superlative used to compare one thing with others, and the absolute superlative which refers only to one thing without reference to others (for the formation of the absolute superlative see page 149):

> **eso es rarísimo**
> that's most unusual

No comparison is involved here—the statement is simply that something is *very* unusual.

The absolute superlative can also be expressed by one of the adverbs of intensity:

> **encuentro esto sumamente interesante**
> I find this most interesting

F. ADJECTIVAL PHRASES

Spanish, like English, can use a wide range of adjectival phrases to describe a noun. Such phrases are often the only way to translate certain compound adjectives into Spanish. They consist mostly of nouns introduced by the preposition **de** though other prepositions do occur:

> **un hombre de dos metros de altura**
> a man two meters tall
>
> **una mujer de pelo rubio y ojos azules**
> a fair-haired, blue-eyed woman
>
> **refugiados sin casa ni dinero**
> homeless, penniless refugees

G. ADJECTIVAL CLAUSES

Adjectival clauses are used to describe things. The thing being described is referred to as the 'antecedent'. Like all clauses, an adjectival clause *must* contain a verb.

The Relative Pronoun

For the formation of the relative pronouns, see page 160.

> ⚠ **Unlike English, *all* adjectival clauses in Spanish must be introduced by a relative pronoun. Failure to use a relative pronoun will result in a failure to communicate successfully with your listener or reader.**

1. The relative pronoun **que**

   In most cases, the simple relative pronoun **que** can be used:

   > **los hombres que están charlando son españoles**
   > the men who are chatting are Spanish
   >
   > **¿viste la película que pusieron ayer?**
   > did you see the movie (that/which) they put on yesterday?

2. Adjectival clauses with prepositions

   > ⚠ **Note that a preposition can *never* appear at the end of an adjectival clause in Spanish. Such a construction is meaningless to a Spaniard. Any preposition *must* be placed before the relative pronoun:**

   > **los muchachos con quienes jugaba se han marchado**
   > the boys he was playing with (with whom he was playing) have gone away
   >
   > **la carta en que leí esto por primera vez está en la mesa**
   > the letter I read this in for the first time (the letter in which I read this ...) is on the table

If the antecedent is a *person*, **que** may not be used. It is usually replaced by **quien** (or plural **quienes**), though the appropriate forms of **el que** or **el cual** are also sometimes used:

el hombre con quien hablaba es mi tío
the man I was speaking with is my uncle.

los turistas a quienes vendí mi coche
the tourists I sold my car to

If the antecedent refers to a *thing*, the following rules apply:

If the relative pronoun is preceded by a compound preposition (i.e. one consisting of more than one word), one of the compound forms of the relative pronoun must be used. You must choose the form of **el que** or **el cual** which agrees in number and gender with the antecedent:

la casa detrás de la cual se encuentra el lago
the house behind which the lake is to be found

el árbol debajo del cual nos besamos por primera vez
the tree under which we first kissed

Since the **el que** and **el cual** forms are in fact forms of the definite article followed by **que** or **cual**, the usual contractions occur (see page 137):

el edificio delante del cual esperábamos
the building we were waiting in front of

preferimos tu nuevo coche al que tenías antes
we prefer your new car to the one you had before

After the simple prepositions **de, en, con** etc. **que** may be used, though in more formal Spanish the compound forms are often preferred in such cases:

la casa en que vivimos es muy vieja
the house we live in is very old

3. **lo que, lo cual**

If the antecedent does not refer to an identifiable thing or things, but refers instead to an entire situation or idea, then the neuter forms **lo que** or **lo cual** *must* be used. They are interchangeable:

Juan insistió en acompañarnos, lo que no me gustó nada
Juan insisted on coming with us, which did not please me at all

What displeased you was not Juan, but the fact that he insisted on coming along:

María se negó a hacerlo, lo que no entiendo
María refused to do it, which I don't understand

Again, it is not María that you do not understand, but the fact that she refused to do it.

Adjectival clauses with an indefinite or negative antecedent

An adjectival clause has an indefinite antecedent if the noun being described refers to something (object/person/idea) which may or may not exist.

The antecedent is negative if the noun being described refers to something which does not exist.

⚠ **In both these cases, the verb in the adjectival clause *must* be put into the subjunctive.**

For the formation of the subjunctive see pages 180–190. Use the present or the imperfect subjunctive, depending on which is more logical in the context.

1. Indefinite antecedents

   busco a alguien que hable español
   I am looking for someone who can speak Spanish

   This person may not exist—you may not find him or her.
   Compare this with **busco a un hombre que habla español**, where the use of the indicative **habla** indicates that you know a specific gentleman who in fact speaks Spanish, but you just cannot find him at the moment:

   los que no quieran participar pueden irse ahora
   those who don't wish to take part can leave now

   There is no way of telling how many people will not want to take part. In fact everyone might want to take part.

   This construction is frequently used with adjectival clauses which refer to the future:

   los que no lleguen a tiempo no podrán entrar
   those who don't arrive on time will not be allowed in

   Obviously, everyone might arrive on time.

   In formal Spanish, **quien** is used on its own as an indefinite relative pronoun meaning 'someone', 'anyone'. It can be either the subject or the object of the adjectival clause:

   busco quien me ayude
   I am looking for someone to help me (who can help me)

   quien diga eso no entiende nada
   anyone who says that understands nothing

2. Negative antecedents

   no hay nadie que sepa hacerlo
   there is no one who knows how to do it

   no tengo libro que te valga
   I haven't got any books which would be any use to you

   no conozco ningún país donde permitan eso
   I don't know any country where they allow that

4. REFERRING TO ACTIONS: THE VERB

The word 'actions' is used here not just to refer to actions as they are normally understood. It also includes mental activities such as 'thinking', 'considering' and the like, as well as states such as 'being', 'seeming', 'appearing' and so on.

A. WHO IS PERFORMING THE ACTION?: THE SUBJECT

1. The subject pronoun

For the subject pronouns, see page 161.

a) *Cases where the subject pronoun is not stated*

In English, the subject of the verb is either explicitly stated – 'my friend went back to Spain yesterday' – or it is replaced by a pronoun – 'he went back to Spain yesterday'.

However, the ending of the verb in Spanish usually makes it clear who the subject is – or example **hablo** can only mean 'I speak', **hablamos** can only mean 'we speak'. Consequently, it is also possible in Spanish to use the verb on its own without a subject pronoun:

¿qué piensas de todo esto?
what do you think of all this?

iremos a la playa mañana
we'll go to the beach tomorrow

This is in fact more common than using the subject pronoun with the verb. However, **Vd.** and **Vds.** are used more frequently than other pronouns. This is to avoid confusion with, for example, **él, ella** and **ellos, ellas** since the verb endings are the same.

¿por qué estudia Vd. español?
why are you studying Spanish?

Note that the subject pronoun is also not used in constructions such as the following:

los norte americanos preferimos la cerveza
we North Americans prefer beer

los españoles bebéis mucho vino
you Spaniards drink a lot of wine

b) *Use of the subject pronouns*

However, the subject pronouns *are* expressed (1) for emphasis or (2) where obvious confusions would arise:

¿qué piensas tú de todo esto?
what do *you* think of all this?

él salió al cine, pero ella se quedó en casa
he went out to the movie theater, but she stayed at home

If the pronouns were not expressed here, it would not be clear who did what.

Remember that **nosotros, vosotros** and **ellos** have feminine forms which must be used if only girls or women are involved:

María y Carmen, ¿qué pensáis vosotras de esto?
Maria and Carmen, what do you think of this?

Note also the difference between Spanish and English in constructions such as the following:

¿quién es? - soy yo/somos nosotros
who is it? - it's me/it's us

soy yo quien quiere hacerlo
it's me who wants to do it

As can be seen, the verb **ser** agrees here with its expressed subject.

c) *ello*

ello is a *neuter* pronoun in Spanish and can *never* be used to refer to a specific object. It is used to refer to an entire idea or situation. Its use as a genuine subject is rare and is by and large restricted to a few constructions in formal Spanish:

todo ello me parece extraño
all of that seems very strange to me

ello here refers to a situation which has just been described:

por ello decidió no continuar
he therefore decided not to continue

d) *Emphasizing the subject pronoun*

The subject pronouns are emphasized by using the appropriate form of the adjective **mismo**:

lo hice yo mismo
I did it myself

A woman saying this would obviously say **lo hice yo misma**.

me lo dijeron ellos mismos
they told me so themselves

e) *tú and usted*

Traditionally, **tú** has been reserved for close friends and relatives, and children, **usted** being used in any more formal situation. However, there is little doubt that the use of **tú** has increased dramatically in Spain in recent years, and any young person going to Spain can confidently expect to be automatically addressed as **tú** by people his or her own age, and should also respond using **tú**.

Even the not-so-young will find themselves addressed as **tú** by people they have never spoken to before. However, a certain amount of caution is still required. When addressing an older person, or someone in authority, for the first time, **usted** is certainly to be recommended. In general, you should take your lead from the Spaniards you are talking to. If everyone is using **tú**, it would be silly (and unfriendly) to persist with **usted**.

2. The indefinite subject

In colloquial English, the indefinite subject is expressed as 'you' and less frequently as 'they'. In more formal spoken and written English, it is expressed as 'one'. In Spanish it can be expressed in the following ways:

a) *Use of tú*

In colloquial Spanish the **tú** forms of the verb can also be used to express an indefinite subject:

bajas por esta calle y tomas la primera a la izquierda
you go down this street and you take the first on the left

Like its English equivalent, this is not a reference to the person addressed, but is a truly indefinite subject.

In formal spoken and in written Spanish, however, this construction would be out of place. Two alternative constructions are available, as follows.

b) *Reflexive use of the verb*

> **se dice que los precios en España son muy bajos**
> they say that prices are low in Spain

> **se cree que habrá menos turistas este año**
> they think there will be fewer tourists this year

c) *The use of* **uno** *or* **la gente**

> **uno no puede por menos de reírse**
> one cannot help laughing

> **la gente no cree todo lo que dice el gobierno**
> people don't believe everything the government says

Either **uno** or **la gente** is obligatory if the verb itself is used reflexively:

> **a la larga uno se acostumbra a todo**
> you can get used to anything in the long run

3. Agreement of subject and verb

The verb in Spanish *must* agree in number and person with the subject.

⚠ **Remember in particular that nouns such as *la gente*, *el gobierno* and phrases such as *todo el mundo* are grammatically *singular*. They may be logical plurals (i.e. they refer to a number of people), but they are singular nouns and *must* take a singular verb:**

> **la gente no quiere que el gobierno haga eso**
> people don't want the government to do that

> **todo el mundo lo sabe**
> everyone knows it

la mayoría and **la mayor parte** (both meaning 'the majority', 'most') take a singular verb. However, if they are followed by a second plural noun, the verb is usually plural:

> **la mayoría votó en contra de la propuesta**
> the majority voted against the proposal

> **la mayoría de los diputados votaron en contra de la propuesta**
> most of the congresspersons voted against the proposal

On the other hand, there are a small number of plural nouns which are perceived as referring to a singular object, and which are regularly followed by a singular verb:

> **Estados Unidos ha expresado su desacuerdo con esta decisión**
> the United States has expressed its disagreement with this decision

Estados Unidos is treated here simply as the name of a country. This also occurs with the name of the trade union **Comisiones Obreras**.

> **Comisiones Obreras se opuso a la política del gobierno**
> Comisiones Obreras opposed the government's policy

However, if the article were used, the verb would indeed be plural:

> **los Estados Unidos no están de acuerdo**
> the United States are not in agreement

Note also that if the verb **ser** is followed by a plural noun, it is itself plural, even if its apparent subject is singular:

> **el problema son los elevados precios del petróleo**
> the problem is the high prices of oil

B. TO WHOM IS THE ACTION BEING DONE?: THE OBJECT

1. Direct and indirect objects

If the action of a verb applies *directly* to a person or thing, that person or thing is the *direct object* of the verb.

If the action does not apply directly, but the idea of 'to someone or something' or 'for someone or something' is involved (even if this idea is not explicitly expressed) then the person or thing is the *indirect object* of the verb.

A verb can have both a direct and an indirect object at the same time:

> **le escribí una carta a mi hermano**
> I wrote a letter to my brother

In this sentence **carta** is the direct object since it is the letter which is written, and **hermano** is the indirect object since it is the brother that the letter is written *to*.

a) *'to' or 'for'*

This can sometimes be confusing for an English-speaking learner of Spanish because the difference between direct and indirect objects is not always clear in English, whereas it must *always* be clearly signalled m Spanish. Take the following examples.

I gave the dog to my brother
I gave the dog a bone

In the first sentence, 'the dog' is the direct object of the verb 'give', since the dog is actually what you gave. 'brother' is the indirect object, since you gave the dog to your brother.

In the second sentence, 'the dog' is no longer the direct object, since here you are not giving the dog at all. What you are giving is 'a bone', and 'bone' is now the direct object. You gave the bone to the dog, so that 'the dog' is now the *indirect* object. Although 'the dog' has changed from being the direct to the indirect object, there is nothing in the words used in English to indicate this change.

This is not the case in Spanish. An indirect object is *always* clearly marked in spanish by being preceded by the preposition **a**. Consequently the Spanish translation of the sentences given above is:

le di el perro a mi hermano
le di un hueso al perro

(For the use of the pronoun **le** here, see page 47). As can be seen, if both nouns are expressly Stated in Spanish (as opposed to being replaced by pronouns), the direct object precedes the indirect object.

b) *'from'*

Unlike English, Spanish uses an indirect object to indicate the person 'from' whom something is taken, stolen, bought or hidden:

le compré el coche a mi padre
I bought the car from my father

le robó el dinero a su madre
he stole the money from his mother

trataron de ocultar la verdad al profesor
they tried to hide the truth from the teacher

2. The personal *a*

If the direct object of a verb is a particular person or a particular group of people, it is *essential* to precede it in Spanish by the preposition *a*.

⚠ **It must be clearly understood that this *a* does not transform the direct object into an indirect object. This *a* is not translated in English:**

veo a mi hermano
I can see my brother

encontré a mi padre
I met my father

If the direct object is a person but is not a *particular* person, the **a** is not used:

buscamos un médico
we are looking for a doctor

Not a particular doctor, but any doctor at all.

The personal **a** is also used with certain pronouns referring to people, even though these may not always refer to specific people:

conozco a alguien que puede ayudarte
I know someone who can help you

no veo a nadie
I can't see anyone

The personal **a** is also used with animals if it is a specific animal which is being referred to:

llevé a mi perro a dar un paseo
I took my dog for a walk

3. The object pronouns

The function of a pronoun is to stand for a noun. For example, in the sentence 'John wanted the book, so I gave it to him', 'it' stands for 'the book', and 'him' stands for 'John'. For the forms of the object pronouns, see pp. 161–162.

a) *Direct and indirect object pronouns*

The direct object pronoun can only stand for the direct object of a verb as explained above. If there is *any* idea of 'to' or 'for', the indirect object pronoun *must* be used in Spanish, even though the words 'to' or 'for' may not actually be used in the equivalent English expression. This does not apply with verbs of motion - for example *ir a* - or where the idea of 'to' or 'for' is contained in the verb - for example *buscar*, meaning 'to look for' (for a list of such verbs, see page 206):

le dí el dinero
I gave him/her the money (I gave the money to him/her)

les ofreció diez mil pesetas
he offered them ten thousand pesetas (he offered ten thousand pesetas to them)

le mandé una carta ayer
I sent her a letter yesterday (I sent a letter to her)

In both spoken and written Spanish, the third person indirect object pronoun is almost always used even when the indirect object is explicitly stated:

le dí el libro a mi amigo
I gave the book to my friend

él se lo dio a su hermano
he gave it to his brother

b) *le and lo as direct object pronouns*

Strictly speaking, **le** is used as the direct object referring to a man or boy (a masculine *person*), whereas **lo** is used as the direct object referring to a masculine *thing*:

¿ves a mi hermano? – sí, sí, le veo
can you see my brother? – yes, yes, I can see him

¿ves el libro? – sí, sí, lo veo
can you see the book? – yes, yes, I can see it

However, in spoken Spanish, and occasionally also in written Spanish, these forms are often mixed up, giving rise to what is known as **loísmo** (the use of **lo** for **le**):

¿ves a mi hermano? – sí, sí, lo veo
can you see my brother? – yes, yes, I can see him

leísmo - the use of **les** for **los** in the plural – also occurs:

¿tienes los libros? – sí, les tengo
have you got the books? – yes, I've got them

You will almost certainly come across these at some point, though it is probably best not to imitate them.

4. The neuter pronoun *lo*

The neuter pronoun **lo** can never refer to an identifiable person or thing. It refers only to a whole idea or situation:

¿sabes que ha llegado Juan? – sí, ya lo sé
do you know that Juan has arrived? – yes, I do (I know it)

What you know is that 'Juan has arrived'. **lo** in this sense often translates 'so' in English:

tú mismo me lo dijiste
you told me so yourself

lo can also be used after either of the verbs 'to be' (**ser** and **estar**). In this case it usually refers back to the last adjective, though in the case of **ser** it can also refer back to a noun.

Remember that **lo** never changes its form, no matter what the gender or number of the adjective or noun to which it refers:

ellos están cansados, y nosotros lo estamos también
they are tired, and so are we

lo here refers back to **cansados**.

su padre es médico, y el mío lo es también
his father is a doctor, and so is mine

lo here refers back to the noun **médico**.

5. The strong object pronouns

For the forms of the strong object pronouns, see page 162. The strong pronouns are used after prepositions:

¿este dinero es para mí? – no, es para ellos
is this money for me? – no, it's for them

The strong pronouns are also used with the preposition **a** to lend emphasis to direct or indirect pronouns which are stated in the same sentence:

me dio el libro a mí, no a ti
he gave the book to *me*, not to you

te veo a ti, pero no la veo a ella
I can see you, but I can't see her

This emphasis can be further heightened by placing the strong pronoun before the verb:

a mí no me gusta nada
I don't like it at all

C. EMPHASIZING THE ACTION

In English all verb tenses have two forms – the standard form ('I read') and the progressive form ('I am reading'). As well as this, the present and past tenses have an emphatic form ('I do read', 'I did read'), which is used to give special emphasis to the verb, or to ask questions. In Spanish, only the standard and progressive forms of the verb are available.

If you wish to emphasize the verb, other constructions must be used, for example:

sí que te creo; te aseguro que te creo
I *do* believe you

ella sí que no vendrá; seguro que ella no vendrá
she definitely won't come

Occasionally an action is emphasized by using first the infinitive and then the appropriate part of the verb:

¿tú bebes? – beber no bebo, pero fumo mucho
do you drink? – I don't drink, but I smoke a lot

D. NEGATING THE ACTION

1. Simple negation

In simple negation, **no** is placed in front of the verb:

no leo muchas revistas, no me gustan
I don't read many magazines, I don't like them

no le vi porque no vino
I didn't see him because he didn't come

2. Compound negation

With negatives other than **no**, two possibilities are usually available:

a) **no** is placed in front of the verb and the other negative is placed after the verb. In most cases this construction is preferred:

no conozco a nadie aquí
I don't know anyone here

no sabe nada
he doesn't know anything

Note that this does *not* constitute a 'double negative' as in English. This applies even when the second negative is in a different clause:

no quiero que hables con nadie
I don't want you to speak to anyone

no es necesario que hagas nada
it isn't necessary for you to do anything

b) **no** is omitted and the negative is placed before the verb on its own. By and large this construction is usually confined to uses of **nadie** as subject of the verb, and to **tampoco**, **nunca** and **jamás**:

nadie sabe adonde ha ido
no one knows where he has gone

Luisa nunca llega a tiempo
Luisa never arrives on time

a mí tampoco me gusta
I don't like it either

⚠ Note that *también no* is not used in Spanish.

3. Other negatives

The phrases **estar sin** + infinitive and **estar por** + infinitive negate the action in a way which can suggest that it has *not yet* been done:

la puerta está todavía sin reparar
the door hasn't been repaired yet

este problema está todavía por resolver
this problem has still to be solved

estar can be replaced by **quedar**:

queda mucho trabajo por hacer
there's still a lot of work to do

4. Negatives after prepositions

Note that the prepositions **sin** and **antes de** are followed by
negatives whereas in English they are followed by the
corresponding positive term:

salió sin hablar con nadie
he went out without speaking to anyone

decidió comer algo antes de hacer nada más
he decided to eat something before doing anything else

5. More than one negative

A number of negatives may be used together in Spanish as in
English. In English, however, only the first term is negative. In
Spanish, *all* terms are negative:

nadie sabe nunca nada
no one ever knows anything

no hablo nunca con nadie
I never speak to anyone

6. Emphasizing the negative *(nouns)*

With nouns, the negative can be emphasized by using the
negative adjective **ninguno** (see page 144). **ninguno** is seldom
used in the plural:

no me queda ningún dinero
I have no money left

For added emphasis, the appropriate form of **alguno** may be
placed *after* the noun:

no tiene miedo alguno
he's not the least bit afraid

In colloquial Spanish, **nada de** can also be used before the noun:

no me queda nada de dinero
I have no money left at all

The order of 'negativeness' in Spanish is:

no tengo miedo	I'm not afraid
no tengo ningún miedo	I'm not at all afraid
no tengo miedo alguno/	I'm not the slightest bit afraid
no tengo nada de miedo	

Note also the following:

no tengo ni idea/	I haven't the slightest idea
no tengo ni la menor idea/	
no tengo la más mínima idea	

7. Emphasizing the negative (*adjectives*)

In the case of an adjective, the negative can be emphasized by placing **nada** before the adjective. **nada** is invariable:

no encuentro sus libros nada interesantes
I don't find his/her books at all interesting

8. Emphasizing the negative (*verbs*)

nada can also be used as an emphatic negative rather than meaning 'nothing', though this construction is seldom used if the verb takes a direct object:

la película no me gustó nada
I didn't like the film at all

no he dormido nada
I haven't slept at all

If the verb has an object, a phrase such as **en absoluto** may be used:

no entiendo esto en absoluto
I don't understand this at all

Note that, on its own, **en absoluto** means '*not* at all':

¿me crees? - en absoluto
do you believe me? - not at all

E. ASKING QUESTIONS

As was the case with negations, questions are formed using the standard or progressive forms of the verb, as appropriate.

1. Simple questions

Simple questions do not begin with an interrogative word. They can have the subject after the verb as in English:

4 REFERRING TO ACTIONS : THE VERB

¿está aquí tu hermano?
is your brother here?

However, they can sometimes be identical in form to statements, though this tends to suggest that the speaker expects the answer **sí**. In this case, the fact that they are questions is conveyed to the listener by the speaker's tone of voice:

¿el agua está fría?
is the water cold?

The idea of 'isn't it?' etc. is expressed in Spanish by **¿no es verdad?**, **¿verdad?**, or more colloquially, simply **¿no?**. These expressions are all invariable:

tú le diste el dinero, ¿verdad?
you gave him the money, didn't you?

te gusta hablar español, ¿no?
you like speaking Spanish, don't you?

éste está mejor, ¿no es verdad?
this one's better, isn't it?

2. Interrogative pronouns and adjectives

A preposition can *never* be placed at the end of a question in Spanish. Any preposition present must be placed in front of the interrogative pronoun or adjective. A Spanish speaker will not connect a preposition placed anywhere else in the question with the interrogative word, and will consequently not understand the question:

¿a quién le diste el dinero?
who did you give the money to? (to whom did you give the money?)

¿con quién fuiste al cine?
who did you go to the movie with?

Note that **cuál** is an interrogative pronoun. If the noun is expressed, **cuál** must followed by **de**:

¿cuál de los coches prefieres?
which of the cars do you prefer?

¿cuál te gustó más?
which did you like best?

qué is used (1) as an indefinite interrogative pronoun or (2) as an interrogative adjective immediately in front of a noun:

¿qué quieres?
what do you want?

53

¿qué libro te gustó más?
which book did you like most?

Note that **qué** is invariable.

3. Indirect questions

Indirect questions are introduced either by the conjunction **si** (whether), or by an interrogative pronoun or adjective. The tenses used are identical to those used in English:

me preguntó si había visto la película
he asked me if I had seen the movie

no sé cuál de los coches prefiero
I don't know which of the cars I prefer

Again, any preposition *must* precede the pronoun or adjective:

se negó a decirme can quién había salido
he refused to tell me who he had gone out with

F. REFLEXIVE USES OF THE VERB

1. The reflexive pronouns

A verb is used reflexively if the subject of the verb performs the action on himself/herself/itself. The verb is made reflexive in Spanish by using it with the appropriate form of the reflexive pronoun (see page 161).

In English, a number of verbs can be used either with or without the reflexive pronoun without changing their meaning. For example, there is no real difference between 'I wash' and 'I wash myself', between 'he shaves' and 'he shaves himself'. This freedom to choose is not available in Spanish. If a particular action is perceived as reflexive, the reflexive forms of the verb *must* be used.

The number of actions which are perceived as reflexive is much greater in Spanish than in English:

se levantó, se lavó, se vistió y salió
he got up, washed, got dressed and went out

The indirect reflexive pronouns express the idea of 'for oneself':

se compró un elepé
he bought himself an LP

The reflexive pronouns are also essential with actions done to parts or one's own body or one's own clothes. Where English would use the *possessive adjective*, the noun is preceded by the *definite article* in Spanish:

se rompió la pierna
he broke his leg

se puso la chaqueta
he put on his jacket

2. The prefix *auto-*

In contemporary Spanish a number of reflexive verbs also have the prefix **auto-** (meaning 'self') joined to them to emphasize the reflexive nature of the action. However, such verbs should be used with care. Use only those you have seen and know to exist:

se autoexcluyeron
they opted out (they excluded themselves)

estos grupos se autoubican en la izquierda
these groups claim to be (place themselves) on the left

This prefix is also found in a large number of nouns: **autodominio** (self-control), **autocrítica** (self-criticism) etc.

3. Reciprocal action

A verb can be used reflexively not only to express the idea of doing an action to oneself, but also to express the idea of doing the action 'to each other'. In such cases the verb is invariably plural:

nos encontramos en la calle
we met each other in the street

nos vemos mañana
see you tomorrow (we'll see each other tomorrow)

If the verb is itself reflexive, the reciprocal action may be indicated by the use of **uno a otro**, though this also may be omitted if the context makes it clear that reciprocal action is involved.

se felicitaron uno a otro
they congratulated each other

If the verb takes a preposition before its object, this preposition will replace the **a** of **uno a otro**:

se despidieron uno de otro
they said goodbye to each other

se despidieron would simply mean 'they said goodbye'.

In very formal language, **uno a otro** can be replaced by the adverbs **mútuamente** or **recíprocamente**:

se ayudan mútuamente
they help each other

4. Other meanings

A number of verbs can be used reflexively in Spanish with little or
no true reflexive meaning, and with very little difference in meaning
from the non-reflexive forms. The commonest of these are:

caer, caerse	to fall
morir, morirse	to die

Others change their meanings in largely unpredictable ways:

comer	to eat	**comerse**	to eat completely
dormir	to sleep	**dormirse**	to go to sleep
ir	to go	**irse**	to go away
llevar	to carry	**llevarse**	to take away
quedar	to remain, to be left	**quedarse**	to stay

G. GIVING COMMANDS

For the formation of the imperative, see page 183. For the
position of pronouns with imperatives, see page 163.

It is important to remember that the imperative proper is
used only for positive commands addressed either to **tú** or
vosotros/vosotras. In *all* other cases (positive commands
addressed to **Vd.** and **Vds.**, and *all* negative commands) the
appropriate form of the subjunctive is used:

no leas esa revista, lee ésta
don't read that magazine, read this one

**tenéis que escribir la carta en español, no la escribáis
en inglés**
you have to write the letter in Spanish, don't write it in English

vengan mañana, no vengan hoy
come tomorrow, don't come today

The subjunctive is also used for third person imperatives, which
are usually preceded by **que**:

¡qué lo hagan ellos mismos!
let them do it themselves!

First person imperatives (i.e. 'we') may be formed either by the
subjunctive, or by **vamos a** followed by the infinitive of the verb.
The use of the subjunctive implies a more committed attitude to
the action in question:

vamos a ver
let's see

vamos a empezar
let's start

hagamos eso ahora mismo
let's do it right now

H. THE PASSIVE

1. *ser* plus the past participle

The passive is formed in Spanish by **ser** plus the past participle.
It must be borne clearly in mind that the passive is used
exclusively to express an *action*. If you are not referring to an
action but are describing a state, then **estar** will be used.

In this construction the past participle *always* agrees with the
subject, i.e. with the thing or person to whom the action was done:

el palacio fue construido en el siglo XV
the palace was built in the 15th century

This is a reference to the castle actually being built. Compare
also the following:

la ventana fue rota por la explosión
the window was shattered by the explosion

cuando entré en la sala vi que la ventana estaba rota
when I went into the room I saw that the window was broken

The first of these sentences refers to an action which occurred at
a precise moment in time. The second describes a state. The
corresponding action took place some time before you entered
the room - you are now describing the *state* the window was in
when you entered the room.

⚠ *ser* **+ past participle cannot be used to express the idea
of 'to' or 'for' as the equivalent construction can be in
English – there is no direct Spanish equivalent of 'I was
given a book' (a book was given *to* me). If you have to
express such an idea in Spanish, a different construction
must be used (see below).**

2. Use of the reflexive

An alternative method of expressing the passive in Spanish is to
put the verb into the reflexive form. This is not a way of 'avoiding'
the passive. On the contrary, this construction is interpreted as a
genuine passive by Spaniards. On hearing the sentence:

el palacio se construyó en 1495
the palace was built in 1495

no Spaniard believes, even for the merest fraction of a second,
that the palace actually built itself.

se dice con frecuencia que España es un país atrasado
it is often said that Spain is an underdeveloped country

las mercancías pueden mandarse por vía aérea
the goods can be sent by air freight

This construction can be used to express the idea of 'to' or 'for' by combining it with the appropriate form of the indirect object pronoun. However, this is very formal, and the construction using the third person plural of the active form would normally be preferred:

se me concedió un libro como premio/me concedieron un libro como premio
I was given a book as a prize

3. Use of the active forms of the verb

Although by no means rare, the passive forms are rather less used in Spanish than in English. It is always possible to use the active forms of the verb instead, and indeed this construction is necessary in certain circumstances. For example, 'I was given a book by the teacher' must be expressed in Spanish as **el profesor me dio un libro**.

el vendedor me ofreció un descuento del diez por ciento
I was offered a ten percent discount by the salesman

If no agent is expressed, the third person plural form of the verb is used:

construyeron la central hace dos años
the power station was built two years ago

suprimirán todos los derechos de aduana
all customs duties will be abolished

5. SITUATING ACTIONS IN TIME

A. EXPRESSING TIME THROUGH VERBAL PHRASES

Verbal phrases of time are extremely useful in that they can be applied to any time, present, past or future, without any change in their form.

1. Preposition + infinitive

a) *Prepositions of time + infinitive*

Most verbal phrases of time are formed by a preposition of time followed by a verb in the infinitive. This construction is most often used when the subject of the infinitive is the same as the subject of the main verb of the sentence:

tomé un café antes de salir
I had coffee before leaving

después de terminar mis deberes, escucharé la radio
after finishing my homework, I'll listen to the radio

In rather literary style, it is possible for the infinitive to have a different subject from the main verb, but this subject must be placed *after* the infinitive:

me cambié de ropa antes de llegar mis amigos
I changed before my friends arrived

b) **al** + *infinitive*

This is a very useful construction in Spanish, though it is more common in the written than in the spoken language. The closest English equivalent is 'on' + present participle. It expresses simultaneous actions in present, future or past time. It may even take its own subject which can be different from that of the main verb in the sentence:

al entrar vieron los otros salir
when they came in (on coming in) they saw the others leaving

al aparecer el cantante, el público aplaudió
when the singer appeared, the audience applauded

This construction can also have a causal meaning:

al tratarse de una emergencia, llamamos a un médico
since it was an emergency, we called a doctor

2. Preposition + past participle

In literary Spanish, both **después de** and **una vez** can be used with the past participle to form a phrase of time, though this construction is never used in the spoken language. The past participle agrees with the subject of the phrase:

después de terminadas las clases, volvimos a casa
after classes had finished we returned home

pagaremos la factura una vez entregadas las mercancías
we shall pay the invoice once the goods have been delivered

B. EXPRESSING PRESENT TIME

1. The use of the progressive forms of the present tense

The progressive forms consist of the appropriate form of **estar** (see pages 80–81, 197) followed by the present participle of the verb (verbs other than **estar** may also be used, as explained below). The use of the progressive forms in Spanish is by and large similar to their use in English, though they are less common in Spanish.

a) *estar* + *present participle*

The progressive forms present any action essentially as an *activity*. If something cannot be viewed as an activity, the progressive forms are not used in Spanish, for example:

me siento bien
I feel fine/I'm feeling fine

The progressive forms are used for an action which is seen as actually taking place:

no hagas tanto ruido, estoy escuchando la radio
don't make so much noise, I'm listening to the radio
(I'm listening to it right now)

They are also used when an activity was begun in the past and the speaker still feels involved in it, even though it may not actually be happening right now:

estoy escribiendo una tesis sobre la política española
I'm writing a thesis on Spanish politics

I may not be writing it at this very minute (in fact, I may not have worked on it for several weeks), but I've already started and it's one of my current activities.

Compare

no me interrumpas, estoy pensando
don't interrupt me, I'm thinking

and

pienso que tienes razón
I think you're right

In the first sentence, 'thinking' is seen as an activity, in the second it is not.

Unlike English, the progressive forms in Spanish cannot be used to express intentions or to refer to future time. In such cases the standard present must be used:

vamos a España la semana que viene
we are going to Spain next week

They are also rather less widely used in questions and negative statements than their English counterparts:

¿por qué me miras así?
why are you looking at me like that?
no estudio griego
I'm not studying Greek

However, they can be used in such constructions if the idea of activity is to be emphasized:

no está cantando, está gritando
he isn't singing, he's shouting

b) *ir* + *present participle*

ir emphasizes the gradual nature of an action, and also suggests its continuation into the future:

poco a poco nos vamos acostumbrando
we are slowly getting used to it (and will continue to do so)
la tasa de inflación va aumentando
the rate of inflation is rising (and will continue to rise)

c) *venir + present participle*

venir indicates that the action has continued from the past to the present. In fact, it points so clearly towards the past that it is often translated into English not by a present tense, but by a perfect tense:

las medidas que vienen adoptando son inútiles
the measures they have been adopting are pointless

los ejercicios que venimos haciendo no son interesantes
the exercises we've been doing aren't interesting

2. The general present

All other aspects of present time (repeated actions, general truths, and the like) are expressed by the standard forms of the present tense:

vamos a España todos los años
we go to Spain every year

la vida es dura
life is difficult

C. FUTURE TIME IN A MAIN CLAUSE

1. The committed and uncommitted future

Spanish differentiates between a committed future and an uncommitted future, and can also express a completed future. All of these variations on future time can also be expressed as futures in the past.

The committed future is expressed in Spanish by the *present* tense of the verb. The uncommitted future is expressed by the standard future tense. Note however that the present tense can only be used to refer to the future if there is some other word in the sentence which points clearly to future time or if the context clearly relates to the future.

The present tense can also be used to express a committed future in English (e.g. 'I'm leaving tomorrow', 'the ship sails next Tuesday'), but its use is less widespread than it is in Spanish.

a) *present and future tenses*

It must be stressed that the difference between these two futures is in no way related to the action being referred to, or to its distance from the speaker in time. It is quite possible to use both futures in relation to the same action. What determines the speaker's choice is his level of commitment to the action to which he is referring.

Compare the following:

lo hago mañana
lo haré mañana

Both of these mean 'I will do it tomorrow'. However, the first expresses a much more solid intention on the part of the speaker to actually do it.

The committed future is rather more common in the first person singular and plural ('I' and 'we'). However, it is also used with the third persons if the speaker is referring to an event about which he is absolutely certain:

los Reyes visitan Alemania la semana que viene
the King and Queen are visiting (will visit) Germany next week

el primer centenario de la democracia se celebra en 2077
the first centenary of democracy will take place in 2077

Both of these sentences could have been written using the future tense (**irán** and **celebrarán**), but the speaker would in this way have indicated a certain remoteness from the event.

The present tense is also widely used in direct requests for immediate action:

¿me prestas mil pesetas?
will you lend me a thousand pesetas?

A less direct alternative is to use the verbs **poder** or **querer** followed by the infinitive:

¿puedes darme esas tijeras?
will you give me that pair of scissors?

¿quieres pasarme ese bolígrafo?
will you pass me that pen?

The use of the future tense in a request indicates that an immediate response is not being asked for:

¿me terminarás eso?
will you finish that for me? (at some point in the future)

b) *ir a* + *infinitive*

As in the English construction 'I am going to do that later', a committed future can also be expressed in Spanish using **ir a** followed by the infinitive, though it is rather less common than its English equivalent:

voy a estudiar medicina en la universidad
I am going to study medicine at the university

van a ver esa película mañana
they're going to see that movie tomorrow

c) *points to note*

⚠ **An apparent future in English is sometimes not an expression of future time, but of willingness or refusal. Such ideas are expressed by the verbs *querer*, *negarse* or similar in Spanish.**

For example:

se niega a tomar el desayuno por la mañana
he won't eat his breakfast in the morning

no quiere aceptar las reglas
he won't accept the rules

2. The completed future

The completed future is used to relate one action in the future to another action. It indicates that the action in question will have been completed by the time the second action applies. In a main clause, the completed future is expressed by the future perfect tense (for formation see page 179):

ya lo habré hecho cuando vuelvas
I'll already have done it when you come back

si llegamos tarde, ya se habrá marchado
if we arrive late he'll already have gone

It can also be used to indicate that the action will have been completed before a particular moment in time:

lo habré terminado para sábado
I will have finished it by Saturday

ya habrá venido
he will already have arrived

3. Future in the past

The following sentence gives an example of future in the past:

me dijo que iba a España la semana siguiente
he told me he was going to Spain the following week

He said **voy a España**, referring to the future. However, he said this in the past, so this is a case of future in the past.

In a main clause, future in the past is expressed either by the imperfect (committed future) or by the conditional (uncommitted future). However, the conditional is considerably more common in this construction than the imperfect:

me explicó que lo haría después de volver de sus vacaciones
he told me he would do it when he came back from his holidays

The conditional perfect expresses completed future in the past:

me aseguró que habría terminado el trabajo antes de medianoche
he assured me that he would have finished the work by midnight

D. THE FUTURE IN SUBORDINATE CLAUSES OF TIME

A subordinate clause of time is a clause which is introduced by a word or phrase of time such as **cuando, así que, antes de que** and the like.

⚠️ In a subordinate clause of time, future time is expressed by the appropriate tense of the subjunctive of the verb.

1. The future

The future is expressed by the present subjunctive. There is no distinction between a committed and an uncommitted future:

en cuanto llegue, se lo diré
as soon as he arrives, I will tell him

¿qué harás cuando termine tu contrato?
what will you do when your contract runs out?

Note that after the conjunctions **mientras** and **hasta que**, both meaning 'until', the word **no** is sometimes placed before the verb in the subordinate clause. It must be kept in mind that this does *not* make the verb negative. It is simply a quirk of style and does not affect the verb in any way:

no podemos hacerlo mientras no nos autoricen
we can't do it until they authorize us

no podemos mandar las mercancías hasta que no nos manden el pedido
we can't send the goods until they send us the order

2. The completed future

In a subordinate clause of time, the completed future is expressed by the perfect subjunctive:

podrás salir cuando hayas terminado tus deberes
you will be able to go out when you've finished your homework

insisto en que te quedes hasta que lo hayas hecho
I insist that you stay until you have done it

3. Future in the past

In a subordinate clause of time, future in the past is expressed by the imperfect subjunctive:

me aseguró que lo haría en cuanto llegara
he assured me that he would do it as soon as he arrived

nos informaron que los mandarían tan pronto como fuese posible
they informed us they would send them as soon as possible

E. PAST TIME

Spanish distinguishes between four levels of past time. These are:

past related to the present	expressed by	the perfect tense
the past in progress	expressed by	the imperfect tense
the completed past	expressed by	the preterite tense
the more distant past	expressed by	the pluperfect tense

It must be emphasised that the tense you choose is not dependent in any sense on the action to which you are referring. It is not dependent on the nature of the action (i.e. whether it is a single action or a repeated action), nor on the duration of the action (whether it lasted one second or a century), nor on its position in time (whether it happened a minute ago or a thousand years ago).

The tense you choose is determined *entirely* by your subjective perception of the action, particularly as regards its relation to present time and its relation to other actions to which you also refer.

1. Past related to the present

The perfect tense is used to refer to a past action which, though completed, the speaker sees as somehow related to the present. The relationship seen between the past action and present time is often indicated by the presence of related verbs or adverbs referring to present time. There is no limit to how long ago the action or series of actions may have taken place.

By and large, the uses of the perfect tense in Spanish and English coincide (but see 'SPECIAL CASES', page 69):

he visitado a muchos países europeos últimamente
I have visited many European countries recently

**en los últimos diez años he aprendido diez idiomas
extranjeros**
in the last ten years I have learned ten foreign languages

2. The past in progress

The past in progress is expressed by the imperfect tense. An
action will be expressed in the imperfect tense if what is
uppermost in the speaker's mind is the fact that the action
was in progress as opposed to having been completed. There is no
limit to how short or long the action can be.

As a rule, the imperfect is used in Spanish where English would
use the imperfect progressive forms ('I was talking', 'he was
writing' etc.), or forms such as 'I used to talk', and the like:

cuando era pequeño, iba todos los días a la piscina
when I was little, I went (used to go) to the swimming pool
every day

mientras Pepe veía la televisión, Juan hacía sus deberes
while Pepe was watching TV, Juan was doing his homework

**In particular, if one action is presented as occurring while
another is already in progress, the action 'occurring' will
be expressed by the preterite, and the action in progress
⚠ by the imperfect:**

mientras Juan llamaba a la puerta, el teléfono sonó
while Juan was knocking on the door, the telephone rang

Like the present tense, the imperfect also has a progressive form,
formed by the imperfect of **estar** plus the present participle of
the verb. This again presents the action primarily as an activity:

estábamos escuchando la radio cuando María entró
we were listening to the radio when María came in

**Note that an apparent conditional in English is not always
a genuine conditional. In a sentence such as 'he would
always read his paper on the train', the 'would' is used to
highlight the fact that the action is seen extending over
⚠ time. This is translated by the *imperfect* in Spanish:**

siempre leía su periódico en el tren
he would always read his paper on the train

3. The completed past

The completed past indicates that the aspect of the action (or
series of actions) which is most important for the speaker is the
fact that it has been completed. Whether the action was a
repeated one, or whether it lasted a great length of time is

unimportant. If completion is being stressed, the preterite will be used:

hizo esto cada día durante casi diez años
he did this every day for almost ten years

viví en España durante más de veinte años
I lived in Spain for over twenty years

It should be possible from these examples to see that it is perfectly feasible in Spanish to use either the imperfect or the preterite to refer to the same action, depending on how your subjective perception of the action changes. The following small narrative should illustrate the point:

Juan llamó a la puerta. Mientras llamaba a la puerta, el teléfono sonó. Mientras el teléfono sonaba, el bebé empezó a llorar.
Juan knocked at the door. While he was knocking at the door, the telephone rang. While the telephone was ringing, the baby started to cry.

4. Stylistic expressions of past time

a) *Present for preterite*

For reasons of style, past time is often expressed, particularly in written Spanish, by the present tense of the verb (the so-called historic present). This is used to lend a dramatic quality to a narrative. The historic present is also used in English, though to a lesser extent than in Spanish:

en el siglo quince sale Colón para América
in the fifteenth century Columbus set sail for America

It would also have been possible to use present tenses in English here.

b) *Imperfect for preterite*

Again in written Spanish, and once more for reasons of style and dramatic effect, an action is sometimes expressed in the imperfect where a preterite would have been the everyday choice:

en 1975 moría Franco y comenzaba la transición a la democracia
in 1975 Franco died and the transition to democracy began

5. The more distant past

a) *Pluperfect*

The more distant past is expressed by the pluperfect. An action belongs to the more distant past if the speaker wishes to indicate that it was completed *before* another action in the past:

llegué a las tres, pero Juan ya se había marchado
I got there at three, but Juan had already gone

no podía salir porque había perdido su llave
he couldn't go out because he had lost his key

b) *Past anterior*

In very literary Spanish, the more distant past in a subordinate clause of time is sometimes expressed by the past anterior:

cuando hubimos terminado, nos marchamos
when we had finished, we left

The past anterior is never used in spoken Spanish, and is considered distinctly 'unmodern' even in contemporary written Spanish. The pluperfect or the simple preterite are used instead.

F. SPECIAL CASES

1. Actions on the limits of present and past time

a) *The future limit*

Actions which are about to take place are expressed in Spanish by the present tense of **estar a punto de** or less commonly **estar para** followed by the infinitive:

estoy a punto de empezar
I'm just about to start

el tren está para salir
the train is just about to leave

The imperfect is used when this idea is expressed in the past:

estaba a punto de salir cuando Juan llegó
I was just about to go out when Juan arrived

b) *The past limit*

Actions which have just taken place are expressed by the present tense of **acabar de** followed by the infinitive:

acabamos de ver el programa
we have just seen the program

acaban de volver del cine
they've just come back from the movies

Again, the imperfect is used if this idea is expressed in the past:

acabábamos de poner la tele cuando entraron
we had just switched on the TV when they came in

2. Actions continuing from one time to another

An action which starts in the past and continues right up to the present (and may well continue into the future) is considered in Spanish to belong to present time, and is therefore expressed by the present tense.

a) *Present tense + desde (hace)*

The length of time involved is introduced by **desde** if a starting point is indicated, or by **desde hace** if a length of time is stated. This is in complete contrast with English which uses the perfect tense with 'for':

¿desde cuándo esperas aquí?
how long have you been waiting here for?

espero aquí desde hace casi media hora
I've been waiting here for almost half an hour

estudio español desde 1986
I've been studying Spanish since 1986

estudio español desde hace dos años
I've been studying Spanish for two years

b) *hace + present tense + que*

Alternatively, the time span can be introduced by **hace** followed by a subordinate clause introduced by **que**:

hace media hora que espero aquí
I've been waiting here for half an hour

c) *llevar + present participle*

A further possiblity is to use the present tense of the verb **llevar** followed by the present participle of the verb:

llevamos tres meses aprendiendo el ruso
we've been learning Russian for three months

d) *Continuing actions in the past*

When these actions are expressed in the past, all the constructions given above are used in the imperfect (as opposed to the pluperfect in English):

trabajaba desde hacía diez años como profesor
he had been working as a teacher for ten years

hacía veinte años que vivían en España
they'd been living in Spain for twenty years

llevaba quince minutos esperando
I had been waiting for fifteen minutes

6. DESCRIBING AN ACTION

A. THE ADVERB

For the formation of adverbs, see page 165.

⚠ It is essential to remember that adverbs are invariable - they never change their form whatever the circumstances in which they are used:

entraron lenta y silenciosamente
they came in slowly and quietly

tú trabajas mucho más rápidamente que yo
you work much more quickly than me

1. Adverbial phrases

Rather than a simple adverb, Spanish very often uses adverbial phrases formed mostly with the nouns **manera** or **modo**:

esto nos afecta de una manera indirecta
this affects us indirectly

Noun/adjective combinations may also be used:

hablar en alta voz/en voz baja
to speak loudly/quietly

2. The use of adjectives

An attractive feature of Spanish is its ability to use adjectives with almost adverbial force. In this case the adjectives must agree with the *subject* of the verb:

vivieron felices durante muchos años
they lived happily for many years

le miramos atónitos
we looked at him in astonishment

B. VARYING THE FORCE OF AN ADVERB

1. Another adverb

As in English, one adverb may be used to vary the force of another:

lo hizo increíblemente bien
he did it unbelievably well

Adverbs of time and place can be emphasized by adding **mismo** after them. **mismo** is invariable in this usage:

aquí mismo, ahora mismo
right here, right now

2. Comparative and superlative

The comparative and superlative of adverbs are formed in exactly the same way as those of adjectives (see pages 147–148).

tú trabajas más rápidamente que yo
you work more quickly than I do

However, when a phrase of possibility is placed after a superlative, **lo** is always placed before **más** (this construction is rarely translated by a superlative in English):

lo hicimos lo más rápidamente posible
we did it as quickly as possible

7. RELATIONSHIPS BETWEEN ACTIONS

A. THE PRESENT PARTICIPLE

For the formation of the present participle, see page 177–178.

a) *Expressing means*

Only the present participle can be used in Spanish to express the idea of 'by doing', 'by going' and the like. No other construction is available:

gané este dinero trabajando durante las vacaciones
I earned this money by working during the holidays

conseguí hacerlo dejando otras cosas para más tarde
I managed to do it by leaving other things till later

⚠ *por* followed by a present participle is not possible in Spanish. *por* followed by an infinitive does not express means, but *cause*, e.g. *le sirvieron primero por ser cliente regular* (they served him first because he was a regular customer).

b) *Expressing simultaneous action*

The present participle is widely used to express an action taking place simultaneously with another:

entró corriendo
he rushed in (he came in running)

'está bien', dijo sonriendo
'OK', he said smiling

This construction is often the only way of expressing certain phrasal verbs of motion in English (see 'he rushed in' above):

pasó corriendo
he ran past

⚠ The present participle is invariable in Spanish, in other words it *never* changes its form, irrespective of the gender or number of the subject of the verb:

las chicas salieron corriendo
the girls rushed out

After a verb of perception (seeing, hearing etc.), the present participle may be replaced by an infinitive. In fact this construction is, if anything, more common than the use of the present participle:

vi a mi hermano atravesando/atravesar la calle
I saw my brother crossing the street

c) *Cause*

A present participle can also express cause:

estando en Madrid, decidí visitar a mi amigo
since I was in Madrid, I decided to call on my friend

no sabiendo como continuar, decidió pedir ayuda
not knowing how to proceed, he decided to ask for help

d) *Continuation*

The present participle is used with the verbs **seguir** and (less frequently) **continuar** to express the continuation of an action:

siguió trabajando a pesar de todo
he went on working in spite of everything

continuaron repitiendo la misma cosa
they kept on repeating the same thing

B. INFINITIVE OR SUBORDINATE CLAUSE?

When two verbs are linked in Spanish, you must choose whether to put the second verb into the infinitive form (preceded or not by a preposition) or whether to put it into a subordinate clause introduced by **que**.

If the subject of both verbs is the same, in most cases you can use the simple infinitive. If the subjects are different, you must, with very few exceptions, put the second verb into a subordinate clause (and frequently also into the subjunctive). Compare:

1. Same subject

quiero hacerlo
I want to do it

I am not only the person 'wanting', I am also the person who wants 'to do' it. No-one else is involved.

entré sin verle
I came in without seeing him

I came in, and I did not see him.

Spanish goes rather further in the use of this construction than English does:

creyó estar soñando
he thought he was dreaming

creemos poder hacerlo
we think we can do it

2. Different subjects

Compare the sentences given above with:

quiero que tú lo hagas
I want you to do it

There are two people involved here. *I* 'want', but *you* are the person who is 'to do'.

entré sin que él me viera
I came in without him seeing me

I came in, but he did not see me.

3. Verbs where the infinitive may take a different subject

There are a small number of verbs with which the subject of a following infinitive may be different from that of the first verb, see page 207:

me dejaron entrar
they let me come in

4. Infinitives after prepositions

The most obvious exceptions to the general 'rule' are phrases consisting of a preposition followed by an infinitive. In this case the infinitive may have a subject which is different from that of the main verb, but this subject is always placed *after* the infinitive:

quiero hacerlo antes de llegar los otros
I want to do it before the others arrive

However, such expressions are rather literary in style, and even in these cases Spaniards will often prefer to use a subordinate clause:

quiero hacerlo antes de que lleguen los otros
I want to do it before the others arrive

C. THE INFINITIVE

1. verb + preposition + infinitive

A verb used in the infinitive after another verb can either appear on its own, or can be introduced by one of a wide range of prepositions. There are few truly useful rules for predicting which preposition is to be used, and in most cases the preposition required must simply be learned through observation and practice.

For a list of the prepositions required by some common verbs, see pages 207–214.

2. adjective + infinitive

It may be useful at this point to note the following very common construction in Spanish:

(indirect object) + verb + adjective + infinitive

The indirect object may be a pronoun or a noun. The verb may be **ser, parecer, resultar** or similar. A wide range of adjectives is available and any verb can be used in the infinitive after the adjective:

me es difícil creer lo qua está diciendo
it's difficult for me to believe what you're saying

nos parece absurdo proponer tal cosa
it seems absurd to us to suggest such a thing

The same construction can be used with various verbs of 'considering', but in this case there is no indirect object:

encuentro difícil aceptar esto
I find it difficult to accept this

consideramos poco aconsejable continuar así
we consider it inadvisable to continue in this way

3. adjective + *de* + infinitive

If the adjective is not part of an impersonal expression, but relates to an identifiable thing or things already stated in the sentence, it is then followed by **de** + infinitive. The adjective agrees with the thing being described:

estos ejercicios son fáciles de hacer
these exercises are easy to do

encuentro este libro difícil de leer
I find this book difficult to read

4. *que* + infinitive

Note that **que** is placed before the infinitive in expressions such as the following:

tengo una factura que pagar
I've got a bill to pay

nos queda mucho trabajo que hacer
we still have lots of work to do

D. THE SUBORDINATE CLAUSE: INDICATIVE OR SUBJUNCTIVE?

The verb in a subordinate clause will be either in the indicative or in the subjunctive. Since the subjunctive has all but disappeared in English, this can be a difficult concept for the learner of Spanish to grasp.

However, the subjunctive is very widely used in Spanish, and there is really little point in learning 'ways to avoid the subjunctive'. The best approach is to try to understand what the indicative and the subjunctive are used to express.

In general terms the indicative is used to introduce actions which the speaker *believes* to be clear and material statements of fact. The subjunctive, on the other hand, is used if the speaker feels that the statements are untrue, or if he feels unable in some way to guarantee that they will prove to be true, or if, rather than simply stating them, he is expressing an emotional reaction to them. This can be due to a variety of reasons, for example because:

— he doubts, disbelieves or denies the statements;

— the actions have not yet taken place: they belong to the future and therefore cannot be guaranteed;

— the actions are expressed as conditions which are not or cannot be fulfilled;

— the actions are introduced by a statement of emotion.

It is important to realize that there is no single set of rules for the use of the subjunctive in Spanish. For example, different rules apply when referring to future time than when expressing a condition or expressing emotion, and so on. Each case must be dealt with without reference to the others.

In general, however, *any* impersonal expression which does not introduce a straightforward statement of fact will be followed by the subjunctive:

es posible/probable/una pena que esté allí
it's possible/probable/a shame that he'll be there

E. INDIRECT OR REPORTED SPEECH

The indicative is used exclusively for statements and questions in indirect speech in Spanish, since the speaker is simply relating actions which he presents as having actually taken place. The tenses used in Spanish correspond exactly to those used in English.

Contrary to English usage, *all* indirect statements must be introduced by *que* in Spanish. Omission of the *que* would be confusing for your Spanish listener:

dijo que vendría más tarde
he said (that) he would come later

me explicó que ya lo habían hecho
he explained to me that they had already done it

le contesté que no sería posible
I told him in reply that it wouldn't be possible

8. SOME SPECIAL VERBS

A. TO BE

1. *ser* and *estar*

There are two verbs 'to be' in Spanish, **ser** and **estar**. In general terms it can be said that:

ser is used to *define* things.

estar is used to describe characteristics which could change without affecting the essential definition of the thing.

It is not necessarily the case that **ser** describes characteristics which are permanent and **estar** does not. The question of *definition* is much more important in deciding which verb to use.

The uses of these verbs can be divided into three categories:

cases where **ser** is obligatory;
cases where **estar** is obligatory;
cases where either is possible.

These can be summarized as follows:

a) *Cases where **ser** is obligatory*

i) **When the verb 'to be' is followed by a noun, *ser* must be used, since a noun always provides at least a partial definition of the object in question.**

Typical examples would include professions, nationality or origin, names, statements of possession, materials from which something is made, expressions of time and almost all impersonal expressions:

mi padre es minero
my father is a miner

In Spanish, your occupation is considered to be at least part of your 'definition'. The fact that your father may lose his job one day and no longer be a miner (or that it may even be a temporary job) does not alter this in any way.

no somos portugueses, somos españoles
we are not Portuguese, we are Spaniards

España es un país interesante
Spain is an interesting country

Note that **es** goes with the noun **país** and not the adjective **interesante**. Your interest in Spain may diminish later, but it will continue to be a country.

este coche es de mi madre
this car is my mother's

la mesa es de madera
the table is made of wood

¿qué hora es? – son las dos de la tarde
what time is it? – it's two in the afternoon

es necesario hacerlo ahora mismo
it's necessary to do it right now

ii) **ser** + adjectives describing defining characteristics

yo creo que el español es muy fácil de aprender
I think that Spanish is easy to learn

The fact that others might disagree, or that you might later change your mind, is irrelevant. For the time being 'easy' is part of your definition of Spanish.

Note that color and size are usually considered to be defining characteristics in Spanish:

la plaza de toros es muy grande
the bull ring is very large

las paredes eran blancas
the walls were white

They may be painted a different color later, but for the time being 'being white' is part of their definition.

If the color is not seen as a defining characteristic, a different construction (and in some cases a different adjective) is likely to be used:

tenía los ojos enrojecidos
his eyes were red

iii) **ser** is used with the past participle to express the passive in Spanish (for an explanation of the passive, see page 57):

la cosecha fue destruida por las heladas
the crop was destroyed by the frosts

b) *Cases where **estar** is obligatory*

i) **estar** must be used when referring to position, whether of persons or things, whether temporary or permanent. The position of an object, however permanent, is not seen as part of its definition in Spanish:

estuve en la playa ayer
I was at the beach yesterday

**los pirineos están en la frontera entre España y
Francia**
the Pyrenees are on the frontier between Spain and France

They're likely to remain there for some time, but (in theory at
least) the Pyrenees would still be the Pyrenees even if they
turned up somewhere else.

Note that **estar** is used to express not only physical position, but
also mental position and in fact position of any kind:

estamos a favor de las negociaciones
we are in favor of negotiations

estamos en contra de la política del gobierno
we are against the government's policy

el problema está en el precio
the problem is (lies) in the price

ii) **estar** is used with the present participle of the verb to form the
progressive forms in Spanish:

**¿qué estás haciendo? – estoy leyendo una revista
española**
what are you doing? – I'm reading a Spanish magazine

estábamos escuchando la radio cuando Juan entró
we were listening to the radio when Juan came in

iii) **estar** is typically used with adjectives to express moods and
other temporary characteristics:

estoy furioso contigo
I'm furious with you

estoy muy cansado, he trabajado mucho hoy
I'm very tired, I've worked a lot today

'Being tired' is unlikely to be part of your definition. You will still
be the same person when you have recovered your energy.

c) *Cases whether either is possible*

When used with many other adjectives, either **ser** or **estar** may
be possible. Which you choose will depend on the extent to which
you feel that:

— the adjective defines the thing in question, for however short a
time this definition might apply, in which case you will use **ser**:

María es muy guapa
María is very pretty

— the adjective merely describes a characteristic of the thing in
question, in which case you will use **estar**:

María está muy guapa hoy
María is looking very pretty today

mi profesor es muy pesado
my teacher is very boring

estás muy pesado hoy
you're being a real bore today

eres tonto
you're silly

estás tonto
you're being silly

In a negative command with adjectives like **pesado** and **tonto**, however, only **ser** would be used:

no seas tonto
don't be silly

Since silliness is not seen here as a mood in Spanish, **estar** cannot be used. With adjectives of mood, however, **estar** would be used:

no estés furioso
don't be furious

d) *Some special cases*

A few adjectives actually change their meaning when used with **ser** and **estar**:

	ser	*estar*
bueno	good	well (in good health)
cansado	tiring (person)	tired
consciente	aware	conscious (awake, not unconscious)
grave	serious	seriously ill
listo	clever	ready
malo	bad	ill (in poor health)
moreno	dark-haired	suntanned
pesado	heavy (thing)	boring (person)
rico	rich	cute (child), nice (food)
seguro	sure (thing) safe (thing)	sure, certain (person)
verde	green	unripe

Other changes are more subtle. Compare **ser viejo** (to be old) with **estar viejo** (to look older than you are), **ser pequeño** (to be small) with **estar pequeño** (to be small for your age).

Note that, when referring to happiness, Spaniards invariably say **estar contento**, but both **ser feliz** and **estar feliz** are possible, depending on whether it refers to a defining characteristic or a mood.

2. encontrarse, hallarse, verse, quedar

encontrarse and **hallarse** can sometimes replace **estar**:

el lago se encuentra detrás de la casa
the lake is behind the house

no me encuentro bien hoy
I don't feel well today

Both **verse** and **quedar** can replace **ser** when used with a past participle. **verse** is almost always used in preference to **ser** with **obligado**:

el gobierno se vio obligado a retirar su propuesta
the government was forced to withdraw its proposal

la casa quedó completamente destruida
the house was completely destroyed

3. haber

'there is' and 'there are' are expressed in Spanish by **hay**. **hay** is in fact the third person singular of the present tense of **haber** - **ha** with the obsolete word **y** (there) tagged on at the end:

hay mucha gente en la playa
there are lots of people on the beach

It is important to realize that this is in fact part of the verb **haber** since it is the standard parts of **haber** which are used in all other tenses and constructions:

había por lo menos cincuenta personas en la habitación
there were at least fifty people in the room

Note that the singular form is always used, even when referring to a plural noun (**personas**). Note also the following infinitive construction:

debe haber otra manera de abordar el problema
there must be another way of approaching the problem

'there must be' is *never* **debe ser** or **debe estar**, which mean 'it must be'. However, in the following construction the appropriate forms of **ser** and **estar** are indeed used:

¿cuántos sois? – somos siete
how many of you are there? – there are seven of us

estábamos cinco en la cocina
there were five of us in the kitchen

4. deber

'is to', 'was to' and the like, indicating that something is due to happen or was supposed to happen, are translated by the present or imperfect of **deber**:

el trabajo debía empezar el día cinco
work was to begin on the fifth

la factura debe pagarse a la entrega de las mercancías
the invoice is to be paid on delivery of the goods

5. General weather conditions

Most descriptions of general weather conditions are made using the verbs **hacer** and **haber**:

¿qué tiempo hace?	what's the weather like?
hace frío/calor	it's cold/warm
hace buen/mal tiempo	the weather is fine/bad
hace mucho sol	it's very sunny
hace/hay mucho viento	it's very windy
hay neblina	it's misty
había luna	the moon was shining

Since Spanish uses nouns here as opposed to the English adjectives, the idea of 'very' is expressed by the appropriate form of **mucho** (or any other appropriate adjective or adjectival clause):

hace mucho calor
it's very hot

está haciendo un frío que pela
it's bitingly cold

Some weather conditions are expressed simply by a verb:

llueve, está lloviendo	it's raining
nieva, está nevando	it's snowing
hiela, está helando	it's freezing
truena, está tronando mucho	there's a lot of thunder

6. Personal descriptions

Many personal descriptions are made using the verb **tener**:

tengo hambre/sed	I'm hungry/thirsty
tiene sueño/miedo	he's sleepy/afraid
tenemos frío/calor	we're cold/hot
tengo ganas de ir	I'm anxious to go
hemos tenido suerte	we were lucky

Again, since Spanish uses nouns here, 'very' is expressed by **mucho** or a similar adjective:

tenemos mucho frío
we are very cold

B. TO BECOME

There is no verb 'to become' in Spanish. How you translate this idea will depend on its context:

1. 'become' with an adjective

With an adjective, 'become' is usually expressed by **hacerse, ponerse** or **volverse. ponerse** indicates a temporary change, **volverse** indicates a longer-lasting one:

se puso furioso cuando oyó esta noticia
he became furious when he heard this piece of news

se hacía oscuro fuera
it was becoming dark outside

se volvió muy antipático
he became very unfriendly

2. 'become' with a noun

With a noun, 'become' is usually expressed by **hacerse** or **convertirse en**:

esta empresa se ha convertido en la más importante de España
this firm has become Spain's leading company

se hizo diputado a los 30 años de edad
he became a congressman at the age of 30

If there is an idea of achievement, **llegar a ser** can also be used:

llegó a ser presidente a pesar de todas las dificultades
he became president despite all the difficulties

3. Other Verbs

In many cases where the verb 'become' would be used in English, Spanish would choose a different approach altogether:

España ingresó en el Mercado Común en 1986
Spain became a member of the Common Market in 1986

C. TO HAVE

1. *tener* and *haber*

a) *tener*

tener expresses 'to have' in the sense of 'to possess':

¿tienes coche?
do you have a car?

¿cuánto dinero tienes?
how much money do you have?

contar con and **disponer de** are also often used to express 'to have', less in the sense of 'to own' but 'to have at one's disposal':

España cuenta con nueve centrales nucleares
Spain has nine nuclear power stations

See also the following section.

b) *haber*

haber is used with the participle to form the compound tenses of verbs (see pages 179–183).

⚠ Note that in these constructions the past participle *never* changes its form, irrespective of the number and gender of either the subject or the object of the verb:

¿habéis visto la última película de Carlos Saura?
have you seen Carlos Saura's latest film?

visto is unaffected by the fact that **habéis** is plural (**vosotros**) or that **película** is feminine.

tener is sometimes used with the participle to express an idea similar to those of the compound tenses. This construction cannot be used unless the verb has an object, and the past participle agrees with the object of the verb:

ya tengo escritas las cartas
I have written the letters

The following two usages are particularly common:

tenemos pensado ir a jugar al tenis
we intend to go and play tennis

tengo entendido que ha sido un éxito
I understand it was a success

2. hacer

Note that phrases of the type 'to have a house built', 'to have the room painted' etc. are expressed in Spanish using the verb **hacer**. The second verb goes into the infinitive, unlike English where the past participle is used:

se hicieron construir una casa en el campo
they had a house built in the country

haremos ejecutar su pedido cuanto antes
we will have your order carried out as soon as possible

D. TO KNOW

There are two verbs 'to know' in Spanish, **conocer** and **saber**. **conocer** means to know in the sense of 'to be familiar with', 'to be acquainted with'. **saber** is to know in a mental or intellectual sense, to have learned or understood, to know something to be a fact. Compare the following:

> **¿conoces el alfabeto griego?**
> do you know the Greek alphabet?

Are you familiar with the Greek alphabet? Can you use the Greek alphabet? Do you know which letter represents which sound, which letter you would use in a particular context etc?

> **¿tu sabes el alfabeto griego?**
> do you know the Greek alphabet?

Can you recite the Greek alphabet? Do you know it by heart? You may be able to answer sí to this question without having any idea how to actually use the Greek alphabet.

conocer is invariably used with people, countries and the like:

> **conozco muy bien a Pedro**
> I know Pedro very well

> **no conozco España**
> I don't know Spain (I've never been there)

saber is invariably used with noun clauses:

> **sé lo que estás pensando**
> I know what you're thinking

> **no sé como ocurrió esto**
> I don't know how this happened

E. ACTIONS CONSIDERED IMPERSONAL IN SPANISH

A number of commonly expressed actions take a personal subject in English, but are used impersonally in Spanish. As a result, what is considered to be the object of the verb in English becomes the subject of the Spanish verb, and it is with this subject that the verb agrees. The subject of the English verb is then expressed by an indirect object in Spanish.

The commonest of these verbs are:

verb	meaning	used to translate
faltar	to be absent	not to have enough of, to need, to be left
gustar	to please	to like
parecer	to seem	to think

quedar	to remain	to have . . . left
sobrar	to exist in greater	to have too much of,
	amounts than required	to have . . . left

1. faltar

me faltan mil pesetas
I'm a thousand pesetas short

faltan dos horas

there are two hours left

hacer falta is also used with the same meaning:

me hace falta más tiempo
I need more time

2. gustar

It must be borne clearly in mind that *gustar* does not
actually mean 'to like', it means 'to please'. Consequently
the English object becomes the Spanish subject, and the
English subject becomes the Spanish indirect object.
⚠ *gustar* agrees in number with the thing 'liked':

a Juan no le gustan estos caramelos
Juan does not like these sweets (literally, the sweets are not
  pleasing to Juan)

nos gusta mucho la tortilla española
we like Spanish tortilla very much

The chances of a form such as **gusto** or **gustamos** appearing in
Spanish are extremely slim. If you are tempted to use one of
these form, you are almost certainly misunderstanding how to
use **gustar**.

If 'like' does not include the idea of 'please', **gustar** is not used:

quisiera más información sobre este hotel
I would like more information about this hotel

It is not that this information would be pleasing to you (it might
in fact be unpleasant). You are simply asking for information.

3. parecer

¿qué te parece mi nuevo coche? - me parece estupendo
what do you think of my new car? - I think it's great

esa idea me parece ridícula
I find that idea ridiculous

4. quedar

¿cuánto dinero te queda?
how much money do you have left?

nos quedaban dos horas
we had two hours left

5. sobrar

aquí sobran jefes y faltan guerreros
there are too many chiefs here and not enough Indians

me sobran diez mil pesetas
I have ten thousand pesetas left

nos sobra tiempo
we've got loads of time

Note also the phrase:

basta y sobra
there's enough and more than enough

9. COMMUNICATING IN SPANISH

A. BELIEF/DISBELIEF/ DOUBT/DENIAL

Statements of belief in the positive, however vague, are followed by the verb in the indicative *irrespective of whether the statement is actually true in fact*. The fact that the statement is presented as being true is sufficient to require the indicative to be used:

> **tenía la impresión de que ya te habías marchado**
> I was under the impression you'd already left

The fact that you're still here is irrelevant.

> **supongo que vendrá**
> I suppose he'll come
>
> **creo que tienes razón**
> I think you're right

Note that Spanish uses **que** in expressions such as the following:

> **creo que sí**   **creo que no**
> I think so   I don't think so

1. Direct questions

In the case of a direct question, either the indicative or the subjunctive may be used. The subjunctive expresses actual doubt on the part of the speaker. If the speaker is simply unsure, the indicative is used. In usage the indicative is more common in this construction than the the the subjunctive:

> **¿crees que Juan vendrá mañana?**
> do you think that Juan will come tomorrow?
>
> **¿crees que Juan venga?**
> do you think that Juan will come? (I suspect he won't)

2. Verbs of belief in the negative, or verbs of doubting or denying in the positive

If a verb of belief is used in the negative, or if a verb of doubting or denying is used, the verb in the subordinate clause is in the subjunctive:

> **no creo que sea justo decir eso**
> I don't think it's fair to say that

> **dudo que consiga hacerlo**
> I doubt that he'll manage to do it

> **niego absolutamente que sea así**
> I absolutely deny that this is the case

It is important to differentiate between statements of opinion and indirect speech. In the latter the indicative is *always* used whether the introductory verb is positive or negative:

> **yo no digo que el Gobierno tenga razón**
> I'm not saying that the Government is right

> **yo no dije que Juan había llegado**
> I didn't say that Juan had arrived

The first of these is a statement of opinion. The second is a narrative of events which happened (or did not happen) in the past.

3. Verbs of doubting or denying in the negative

If a verb of doubting or denying is used in the negative, either the subjunctive or the indicative may be used. The indicative is used if the speaker is very positive about what is being said:

> **no dudo que tengas/tienes razón**

The use of **tengas** implies something like 'I don't doubt that you might be right', whereas the use of **tienes** means 'I am quite sure that you are right':

> **no niego que sea/es posible hacerlo**
> I don't deny that it might be/is possible to do it

B. CONDITIONS

Conditions in Spanish can be divided into two large groups, each of which requires a different use of the verb:

Type	*Definition*	*Verb*
open-ended conditions	those which may or may not be fulfilled, those whose outcome has not yet been decided	indicative
unfulfilled conditions	those which are presented as unfulfilled, those which the speaker believes not to be the case or not to have been carried out	subjunctive

You must be clear which kind of condition you are dealing with, since the rules for expressing the different kinds of conditions are markedly different from each other.

— If the condition is perceived as open-ended in the sense that it may or may not be fulfilled, the indicative is used (with one exception—see open-ended conditions of future time below):

si llueve mañana, iré al cine
if it rains tomorrow, I'll go to the movies

— If the condition is perceived as genuinely unreal in the sense that it has not been or cannot be fulfilled, the subjunctive is used in the **si** clause:

si fuera rico, no trabajaría
if I was rich, I wouldn't work

Do not confuse conditions with the conditional tenses. The *tenses* used in Spanish are in all cases identical to English. The differences between the two languages relate to the uses of the indicative and the subjunctive.

1. Open-ended conditions

Open-ended conditions in Spanish can relate to present, future or past time. They are expressed as follows:

a) *Present time*

Open-ended conditions relating to present time are expressed in Spanish by the present indicative. The verb in the main clause is usually in the present indicative or sometimes in the imperative:

si quieres evitar más problemas, cállate
if you want to avoid further problems, keep quiet

i.e. if you want to avoid problems *now*. You may choose either to avoid the problems or not.

si no te gusta éste, puedes tomar otro
if you don't like this one, you can take another

You may in fact like this one, in which case you won't take another.

b) *Future time*

Conditions relating to future time are by definition open-ended since their outcome cannot yet be known. Future conditions are expressed in Spanish by the present indicative. The verb in the main clause is usually future (committed or uncommitted):

si no lo termino a tiempo, no podré salir
if I don't finish in time, I won't be able to go out

si lo haces, te doy mil pesetas
if you do it, I'll give you a thousand pesetas

However, an open-ended condition or future time *may* take the imperfect subjunctive if the speaker wishes to present it as a more remote possibility. The conditional is then used in the main clause:

si hicieras eso, los otros se enfadarían
if you were to do that, the others would be annoyed

This is a more remote condition than:

si haces eso, los otros se enfadarán
if you do that the others will be annoyed

but both refer to future time.

c) *Past time*

Open-ended conditions relating to past time take the same tense of the verb as in English:

si no ha hecho sus deberes, no podrá salir
if he hasn't done his homework, he won't be able to go out

He may indeed have done it. You are expressing this condition precisely because you are unsure. The condition may indeed have been fulfilled.

si lo utilizó, sabrá como funciona
if he used it, he'll know how it works

You are unable to say for certain whether he used it or not.

si no llovía, ¿por qué estás mojado?
if it wasn't raining, why are you wet?

2. Unfulfilled conditions

Unfulfilled conditions relate only to present time and past time.

a) *Present time*

Unfulfilled conditions relating to present time are expressed in Spanish by the imperfect subjunctive. Either form of the imperfect subjunctive may be used. The verb in the main clause is usually, though not always, in the conditional:

si Juan estuviera aquí, hablaría con él
if Juan was here I'd speak to him

i.e. if he was here *now*. You would not be saying this unless you believed that he was *not* there. The fact that he might be there is irrelevant. In your opinion this is an unfulfilled condition.

si tuviera dinero, iría a España
if I had money, I'd go to Spain

si fuera más barato, lo compraríamos
if it was cheaper, we'd buy it

Again, you are only saying this because you do not believe you have enough money.

b) *The completed past*

Unfulfilled conditions relating to the completed past are expressed in Spanish by the pluperfect subjunctive (either the **hubiera** or the **hubiese** forms). They are unfulfilled in that they refer to events which did not in fact take place. The verb in the main clause is usually in the conditional perfect or less commonly in the pluperfect subjunctive (**hubiera** forms):

si lo hubiéramos sabido, habríamos venido
if we had known, we would have come

We didn't know, so we didn't come.

si hubieras llegado a tiempo, le habrías visto
if you'd arrived on time, you'd have seen him

3. *como* + present subjunctive

In colloquial Spanish, **como** + present subjunctive is frequently used to express a condition of future time. The subjunctive is *always* used in this construction even though the condition is open-ended:

como llegues tarde me enfado
if you arrive late I'll be angry

como is not interchangeable with **si** in all cases. If you are unsure, it is always safer to use **si**.

4. *de* + infinitive

In formal written Spanish, a condition is sometimes expressed by the preposition **de** followed by the infinitive:

de continuar así, suspenderá el examen
if he goes on like this, he'll fail the exam

For past time the perfect infinitive is used:

de haberlo sabido, no habría venido
if I had known I wouldn't have come

5. Negative conditions

Any condition can be made negative by simply placing **no** before the verb in the conditional clause or by using some other negative:

si no haces tus deberes, no podrás salir
if you don't do your homework, you won't be able to go out

However, negative conditions can also be expressed either by **a menos que** or more formally by **a no ser que**. Both mean 'unless', and are always followed by the appropriate tense of the subjunctive:

saldremos mañana a menos que llueva/a no ser que llueva
we'll go out tomorrow unless it rains

6. Conditions introduced by conditional conjunctions

Conditional clauses introduced by conditional conjunctions always have their verb in the subjunctive. The most common of these conjunctions are:

en caso de que	if
a condición de que	on condition that, provided that
con tal que	so long as
siempre que	so long as

en caso de que venga, se lo diré
if he comes, I'll tell him

puedes salir con tal que prometas volver antes de medianoche
you can go out so long as you promise to be home by midnight

los compraremos a condición de que sean baratos
we'll buy them provided they're cheap

7. Points to note

Not all conditions are introduced in English by 'if'. Other forms are sometimes used. This choice is not available in Spanish. If you are translating, you must use **si** (or the **de** + infinitive construction) no matter what the form of the English condition:

had I known, I would have told you
si lo hubiera sabido/de haberlo sabido, te lo habría dicho

were this the case, I would agree with you
si fuera así/de ser así, estaría de acuerdo contigo

If **si** means 'whenever', it introduces a clause of time and only
  the indicatives are used:

si tenía mucho que hacer, nunca salía antes de las nueve
if I had a lot to do, I never went out before nine

If **si** means 'whether', it introduces an indirect question and again
the indicative is used:

me preguntó si lo haría
he asked me if (i.e. whether) I would do it

no sé si vendrá
I don't know if he'll come

C. CONTRADICTING A PREVIOUS STATEMENT

1. *pero* and *sino*

The idea of 'but' is expressed by two words in Spanish, **pero** and
sino. **sino** is used to introduce a statement which contradicts a
previous one. **pero** *cannot* be used in such situations:

el coche es grande pero no cuesta mucho
the car is big but it doesn't cost a lot

el coche no es verde, sino rojo
the car isn't green, but red

mi padre no es médico, sino profesor
my father isn't a doctor, but a teacher

If the contradiction is contained in a clause, **sino que** is used:

no se come, sino que se bebe
you don't eat it, you drink it

If the intention is not to contradict, but to emphasise a following
affirmation, **pero sí** is used:

no conozco a España, pero sí conozco a Portugal
I don't know Spain, but I do know Portugal

no es moderno, pero sí interesante
it isn't modern, but it is interesting

2. no es que, no porque

Both of these expressions are followed by a verb in the
subjunctive:

no es que no tenga confianza en ti
it's not that I don't trust you

lo hace no porque quiera hacerlo, sino porque no tiene más remedio
he does it not because he wants to, but because he has no choice

D. DISCOUNTING A DIFFICULTY

1. despite

The simplest way of discounting a difficulty is to use the compound preposition **a pesar de** followed by the noun. In written Spanish, **pese a** is sometimes used instead of **a pesar de**:

decidió continuar a pesar de las dificultades
he decided to continue in spite of the difficulties

2. although

The idea of 'although' can be expressed either by **aunque** or **a pesar de que**. In written Spanish **si bien** is a fairly frequent alternative to **aunque**, though it is little used in the spoken language.

aunque may be followed by either the indicative or the subjunctive, depending on the speaker's perception of the difficulty. The indicative suggests a real difficulty, whereas the subjunctive implies a potential difficulty:

no se ha puesto el abrigo aunque hace mucho frío
he hasn't put on his coat even though it's very cold

continuaremos aunque haya problemas
we'll continue even though there may be problems

a pesar de que is used mostly with reference to present and past time and is therefore usually followed by the indicative:

lo hizo a pesar de que nadie estaba de acuerdo con él
he did it even though nobody agreed with him

si bien is always followed by the indicative:

se cambiará la ley, si bien hay mucha oposición
the law will be changed although there is a lot of opposition

In written Spanish, **con** + infinitive is sometimes used to express the idea of 'although', though this is not a common usage:

con ser pobres, viven bien
although they're poor, they live well

3. 'however'/'no matter how' + adjective or adverb + verb

This idea is expressed as follows in Spanish: **por** + adjective/adverb + **que** + verb in the subjunctive:

las compraremos, por caras que sean
we'll buy them, however expensive they are (might be)

no dejaré de hacerlo, por difícil que parezca
I won't fail to do it, no matter how difficult it might seem

por bien que lo haga, no lo aceptaré
however well she does it, I won't accept it

4. 'whatever', 'however', 'wherever' etc + verb

There are two ways of expressing this idea in Spanish:

a) verb in the subjunctive + relative + verb in the subjunctive. The same verb is repeated in this construction:

lo compraremos, cueste lo que cueste
we'll buy it, whatever it costs

no quiero verle, sea quien sea
I don't want to see him, whoever he is (might be)

le encontraremos, esté donde esté
we'll find him, wherever he is (might be)

b) indefinite pronoun or adjective + **que** + verb in the subjunctive. The indefinite pronouns and adjectives are formed by adding **–quiera** to the end of the corresponding relative (there is no equivalent form for **lo que**):

no quiero verle, quienquiera que sea
I don't want to see him, whoever he is (might be)

le encontraremos, dondequiera que esté
we'll find him, wherever he is (might be)

If the pronoun or adjective is to be made plural, it is the part before the **– quiera** which becomes plural **-quiera** itself remains unchanged:

no quiero verlos, quienesquiera que sean
I don't want to see them, whoever they are

E. EMOTION/FEAR/HOPE/REGRET

1. Emotion

a) *One subject*

An expression of emotion where there is only one subject is followed by the verb in the infinitive:

estamos muy contentos de veros
we are very pleased to see you

We are pleased, and we see you—there is only one subject.

espero poder hablar con él mañana
I hope to be able to speak to him tomorrow

b) *More than one subject*

However, if more than one subject is involved, the expression of emotion is followed by a verb in the subjunctive. The range of emotions goes from approval to disapproval, pleasure to anger and the like:

me alegra que pienses así
I'm glad you feel that way

le molestó que no estuviéramos de acuerdo con él
it annoyed him that we did not agree with him

The expression of emotion may be implicit in an impersonal construction:

es triste/lógico/natural/una pena que sea así
it's sad/logical/natural/a shame that it should be like this

All of these expressions imply an emotional reaction (however implicit) on the speaker's part rather than a straightforward statement of fact.

Note that the verb is in the subjunctive only if it belongs to a clause introduced by **que** which is *directly* dependent on the expression of emotion. If the clause is introduced by **porque** or if it is dependent on some other verb, the subjunctive is not used.

estaba triste porque todos le habían abandonado
he was sad because everyone had left him

se puso furioso al ver que nadie le escuchaba
he became furious when he saw that no-one was listening to him

In this case the clause is dependent on the verb *ver*, not on the expression of emotion.

99

2. Fear

a) *to fear something / be afraid of something*

The simplest expression of fear is to use a phrase such as **tener miedo a**, or less commonly the verb **temer**. Note that the preposition used with **tener miedo** can be either **a** or **de** (as opposed to only 'of' in 'to be afraid of' in English):

tengo miedo a los perros
I'm afraid of dogs

In colloquial Spanish, the phrase **dar miedo** may also be used. However, the object of the English verb becomes the subject of the Spanish verb, and the subject of the English verb becomes the indirect object of the Spanish verb (see **gustar**, page 87):

me dan miedo las arañas
I'm afraid of spiders

b) *'to fear' + verb*

The rules for one or more subjects mentioned earlier (see section E.1) also apply here:

me da miedo salir por la noche
I am afraid of going out at night

temo que surjan problemas imprevistos
I'm afraid that unforeseen problems might crop up

Note that the expression 'I'm afraid' is often used in English to introduce statements of fact or possibility where there is no real suggestion of any fear. **Temer** may also be used in this way in Spanish (it is frequently used reflexively in this context).

In this case **temerse** may be followed by either the indicative or the subjunctive. The indicative is used for a statement of fact. The subjunctive suggests the possibility that something may have happened:

me temo que lo ha/haya perdido
I'm afraid he's lost it/he may have lost it

c) *Other expressions*

Other expressions indicating genuine fear are also followed by the subjunctive:

se escondió por miedo a que se burlasen de él
he hid for fear that they would laugh at him

3. Hope

a) *to hope for something*

This is expressed simply by **esperar**. The idea of 'for' is included in the verb, so that no preposition is used:

esperábamos una respuesta más positiva
we were hoping for a more positive reply

b) *'to hope' + verb*

'to hope' is again usually expressed in this context by the verb **esperar**. With this meaning **esperar** may take either the indicative or the subjunctive (**esperar** meaning 'to wait' is *always* followed by the subjunctive).

When followed by the indicative **esperar** expresses a wish. When followed by the subjunctive it expresses genuine hope. Compare the following:

espero que vendrá (indicative)
I hope he'll come

I'm counting on him coming. I'll be disappointed/annoyed if he doesn't come.

espero que tengas éxito (subjunctive)
I hope you succeed

This is genuine hope, and does not have the connotations of 'counting on' mentioned above.

c) *Impersonal expressions*

Impersonal expressions of hope are followed by the subjunctive:

hay pocas esperanzas de que venga
there's little hope that he'll come

mi ilusión es que un día se resuelva el problema
my hope is that one day the problem will be solved

d) *ojalá*

In spoken Spanish **ojalá** is frequently used to introduce an expression of hope. **ojalá** is invariable and never changes its form. It is always followed by the subjunctive:

ojalá no llueva mañana
I hope it doesn't rain tomorrow

ojalá venga
I hope he comes

4. Regret

a) *Apologizing for something*

The simplest statements of apology are of course **perdón,
perdone** (an imperative) and **lo siento**. They are different in
that **perdón** and **perdone** are both requests for forgiveness,
whereas **lo siento** is a direct expression of regret:

¡ay, perdona! no te vi
oh, sorry! I didn't see you

In this case the **tú** form of the imperative (**perdona**) is used.

lo siento, pero no será posible terminarlo hoy
sorry, but it won't be possible to finish it today

When the thing or action regretted is explicitly stated, the **lo** of
lo siento is no longer used. The idea of 'for' is included in the
verb and is not explicitly stated in Spanish:

sentimos la molestia
we are sorry/apologize for the inconvenience

In more formal Spanish, **lamentar** is often used in preference to
sentir:

lamentamos la molestia que les hemos causado
we regret the inconvenience we have caused

b) *'to regret' + verb*

If there is only one subject, the infinitive is used, otherwise a
clause with the verb in the subjunctive is required:

sentimos tener que molestarle
we are sorry to have to bother you

sentimos mucho que no hayas podido hacerlo
we are very sorry that you were not able to do it

Again, the clause must be directly dependent on the verb
expressing regret. If it is dependent on any other verb, the
indicative will be used:

lamentamos informarles que ya no están disponibles
we are sorry to inform you that they are no longer available

The clause here is dependent on **informar** and not on
lamentamos.

F. INTENTIONS AND OBJECTIVES

1. Statements of intention

Simple statements of intention are expressed using the verb **pensar** or the phrase **tener la intención de**, both followed by the infinitive. In spoken Spanish, the construction **tener pensado** + infinitive is also widely used:

pensamos ir en coche/tenemos la intención de ir en coche
we intend to go by car

tengo pensado salir esta noche
I intend to go out this evening

2. Statement of objectives

a) *One subject*

If only one person is involved, objectives are usually expressed by the preposition **para** followed by the infinitive. More formal alternatives are **a fin de, con el fin de, con la intención de, con el objetivo de** or **con la finalidad de**, all followed by the infinitive:

lo hice para ganar un poco de dinero
I did it to earn a little money

me dirijo a Vds. con el objetivo de pedir información
I am writing to you to ask for information

After verbs of motion, intention is usually expressed by the preposition **a** followed by the infinitive, though **para** is also possible:

vine aquí a hablar contigo
I came here to speak to you

Other verbs are followed by different prepositions (see pages 209–214):

luchaban por mejorar sus condiciones de vida
they were fighting to improve their living conditions

b) *Two different subjects*

If more than one subject is involved, **para que** followed by the subjunctive is necessary. A straightforward infinitive will be wrong in Spanish:

les ayudamos para que pudieran acabarlo pronto
we helped them so that they could get it done sooner

The more formal alternatives given earlier can also be used followed by **que** and the subjunctive:

me voy, a fin de que puedan empezar inmediatamente
I'm going, so that they can start immediately

G. OBLIGATION

1. General obligation

A number of constructions exist in Spanish to express obligation on a very general level. The commonest of these are:

hay que + infinitive
es preciso + infinitive
es necesario + infinitive

The degree of obligation can be heightened as follows:

es esencial + infinitive
es imprescindible + infinitive

These expressions are not addressed to any one person in particular. They simply express a general obligation.

hay que tener cuidado
you (i.e. one) must be careful

¿hay que ser miembro para poder jugar aquí?
do I/you have to be a member to play here?

hay que verificarlo
it'll have to be checked

será necesario verificarlo con él
it will be necessary to check it with him

2. Personal obligation

More personal kinds of obligation (i.e. those affecting particular people or groups of people) are expressed using the verb **deber** + infinitive or the verb **tener** followed by **que** + infinitive:

tendrás que trabajar mucho
you'll have to work hard

tengo que terminarlo cuanto antes
I have to finish it as soon as possible

debemos salir a las ocho en punto
we must leave at eight on the dot

The sense of obligation can be heightened by using one of the phrases given earlier under 1 (with the exception of **hay que**) followed by **que** and a verb in the subjunctive:

es imprescindible que lo hagas ahora mismo
you absolutely must do it right now

Note that 'have to' in English does not always denote an
obligation. For example, in the phrase 'I had to laugh', you were
not, of course, obliged to laugh. This simply means that you could
not stop yourself from laughing. This idea is expressed in Spanish
as follows:

no pudimos por menos de reír
we had to laugh/could not help laughing

3. Moral obligation

Moral obligation is expressed in Spanish by the conditional (or
less frequently the imperfect) of **deber** followed by the
infinitive. This is usually expressed in English by 'should' or
'ought to':

deberíamos ir a verle
we should go and see him

This is not an obligation in the sense that we are being *forced* to
go and see him, but we feel that it is our 'duty'.

**The use of 'should' in English to express moral
obligation can *never* be translated into Spanish by the
conditional. For example, *haría* can never express the
idea of 'I ought to do'. Only *debería hacer* will convey
⚠ this idea successfully.**

To put this idea into the past, use the perfect infinitive after the
conditional of **deber**:

deberíamos haberlo hecho antes
we should have done it sooner

no deberías haber bebido tanto
you shouldn't have drunk so much

4. Obliging someone to do something

This idea is usually expressed by **obligar** or **forzar** + **a** +
infinitive. Alternatively, **hacer** + infinitive can be used. The
subject of the infinitive will be different from that of **obligar**:

me obligaron a salir   **me hizo levantarme temprano**
they forced me to leave   he made me get up early

When used passively, **verse** is almost always used in preference
to **ser**:

me vi obligado a devolverlo
I was obliged to give it back

H. PROBABILITY/IMPROBABILITY

The adverb **probablemente** (like all adverbs) has no effect on whether the verb is in the indicative or the subjunctive:

probablemente vendrá mañana
he'll probably come tomorrow

However, any impersonal expression of either probability or improbability is followed by a subordinate clause with its verb in the subjunctive:

es probable que salga por la tarde
I'll probably go out this evening (it's probable that
  I'll go out . . .)

es improbable que vuelva
he's unlikely to come back (it's improbable that he'll come back)

me parece increíble que consiga hacerlo
I find it unlikely that he'll manage to do it

tenemos que aceptar la probabilidad de que esto ocurra
we must accept the likelihood that this will happen

I. PERMISSION/PREVENTION/ PROHIBITION

1. General permission and prohibition

The most general forms of permission and prohibition are expressed using the verb **poder**:

¿puedo pasar?
may I come in?

¿se puede aparcar por aquí?
can you (i.e. one) park around here?

no puedes pasar ahora
you may not come in just now

The prohibition corresponding to **se puede** is **se prohíbe, está prohibido** or simply **prohibido**. These are found mostly in official signs:

prohibido/se prohíbe pisar el césped
please do not walk on the grass

This can be emphasized as follows:

queda terminantemente prohibido cruzar la vía
crossing the line is strictly forbidden

2. Personal permission, prevention and prohibition

The commonest verbs of permitting, preventing and prohibiting belong to that group which may be followed by an infinitive with a different subject (see page 207). This usually avoids the need for a subordinate clause:

me dejaron entrar pero me impidieron verle
they let me go in but they prevented me from seeing him

nos prohibieron fumar
they did not allow us to smoke

Note the very common phrase:

¿me permite?
may I?

In many cases a straightforward imperative may be used:

no digas tacos
don't use bad words

J. POSSIBILITY/IMPOSSIBILITY

1. In a personal sense

a) *poder* and related verbs

The simplest way of expressing possibility is to use the verb **poder**:

no podré venir mañana
I won't be able to come tomorrow

no habríamos podido hacerlo sin ti
we wouldn't have been able to do it without you

The verbs **conseguir** and **lograr** are used with the same meaning (of these **conseguir** is the more common):

no conseguimos llegar a tiempo
we didn't manage to arrive on time

logramos evitar un conflicto
we managed to avoid a conflict

A further alternative is to use the impersonal expression **ser (im)posible**. The person for whom the action is (im)possible becomes the indirect object:

no me será posible venir
I won't be able (it won't be possible for me) to come

nos fue imposible resolver el problema
we couldn't solve the problem

resultar is sometimes used instead of **ser**:

me resultó imposible hacer lo que quería
I could not do what he wanted

b) *saber*

Note that 'to be able' in the sense of 'to know how to' rather than 'to be capable of' is expressed in Spanish by **saber** rather than **poder**:

¿sabes tocar la guitarra?
can you play the guitar?

sí, pero no sé tocar el piano
yes, but I can't play the piano

This is a skill rather than a physical ability.

c) *Verbs of perception*

'to be able' with verbs of perception (seeing, hearing and the like) is not usually expressed in Spanish unless you wish to suggest that there is some kind of obstacle involved:

¿me oyes?
can you hear me?

no podía verle por la niebla
I couldn't see him because of the fog

2. In a general sense

a) *quizá, quizás, tal vez*

Possibility in a more general sense (i.e. not 'being able to do something', but the possibility that something might happen or not) can be expressed by one of the adverbs **quizás, quizá** or **tal vez. quizás** and **quizá** are more widely used.

These may be followed by either the indicative or the subjunctive, depending on your view of how likely it is that the thing will in fact happen. The indicative expresses a greater degree of confidence than the subjunctive:

quizás venga mañana, no sé (subjunctive)
he may come tomorrow, I don't know

tal vez tienes razón (indicative)
you may be right

b) *Verbal forms*

poder can also be used to express a general possibility:

puede haber cambios importantes dentro de poco
there may be important changes soon

This idea can also be expressed by the impersonal expressions **es posible que** and **puede que** followed by the appropiate form of the subjunctive:

> **es posible que venga mañana**
> he may come tomorrow

> **puede que no sea verdad**
> it may not be true

In fact, any impersonal expression of possibility or chance is followed by the subjunctive:

> **existe la posibilidad de que surjan problemas**
> there is the possibility that problems will crop up

Note the following expression:

> **parece mentira que esto haya ocurrido**
> it seems impossible that this should have happened

K. REQUESTS AND COMMANDS

1. Direct requests

a) *Informal requests*

Spaniards are rather more direct in their requests than the average English speaker, who tends to introduce most requests with 'would you' and the like. A straightforward question is more likely in Spanish:

> **¿me pasas esa revista?**
> would you pass me that magazine?

> **¿me prestas mil pesetas?**
> would you lend me a thousand pesetas?

Alternatively, for a slightly less direct request ('could you' in English), the appropriate form of **poder** + infinitive can be used:

> **¿puedes abrir la ventana?**
> could you open the window?

> **¿podría decirme qué hora es?**
> could you tell me the time, please?

The expression **hacer el favor de** + infinitive is also used if a little more formality is required:

> **¿me hace el favor de cerrar la ventana?**
> would you be so kind as to close the window, please

b) *Formal requests*

There are much more formal ways of introducing a request, particularly in written Spanish. The most common of these are the expressions **tenga(n) la bondad de** + infinitive and **le(s) ruego que** followed by the verb in the subjunctive:

tenga la bondad de cerrar la puerta
be so kind as to close the door

In the very formal Spanish of a business letter, the **que** is sometimes omitted after **le(s) ruego**. This usage should not be imitated in contexts others than commercial correspondence:

les rogamos nos manden dos cajas
please send us two boxes

c) *Ultra-formal requests*

In very formal Spanish, the old-fashioned form **sírvase** can still be found. This is in fact an imperative. If a addressed to more than one person, **sírvanse** is used instead. This construction is restricted to commercial correspondence and official signs:

sírvanse mandarnos más información
please send us more information

2. Indirect requests

Since there are always at least two subjects involved in an indirect request, the verb is always followed by a subordinate clause with its verb in the subjunctive.

The most common verb used to introduce an indirect request is **pedir**. In more formal Spanish, **rogar** is again sometimes used in preference to **pedir**:

le pedí que se callara
I asked him to be quiet

nos rogaron que les ayudáramos
they asked us to help them

⚠ **It is essential not to confuse *pedir* and *preguntar*. *preguntar* means 'to ask a *question*', and is used to introduce an indirect question. It does not involve the idea of a request.**

More intense requests can be expressed by verbs such as **suplicar**:

me suplicó que no revelara su secreto
he pleaded with me not to reveal his secret

3. Indirect commands

For direct commands (the imperative) see pages 56, 109, 182.

There are always at least two subjects involved in an indirect command. Normally, this means a subordinate clause with the verb in the subjunctive:

me dijo que lo hiciera inmediatamente
he told me to do it immediately

insistimos en que nos lo devuelvan ahora mismo
we insist that you give us it back right now

However, the verbs **mandar** and **ordenar** belong to that small group of verbs which can be used with a direct infinitive (see page 207):

me mandó salir del edificio
he ordered me to leave the building

L. SUPPOSITION

1. Future tense

Apart from the usual verbs of supposition (for example **suponer**), the simplest way of expressing supposition in Spanish is to use the future tense for a supposition in the present, and a conditional for a supposition in the past. A similar construction exists in English, though it is less used than its Spanish equivalent:

supongo que vendrá
I imagine he'll come

¿qué hora es? – serán las once
what time is it – it must be about eleven (it'll be about eleven)

la casa estará por aquí
the house must be around here somewhere (will be around here somewhere)

serían las cinco más o menos cuando llegó
it must have been about five (it would be about five) when he arrived

2. *deber de* + infinitive

Supposition can also be expressed by the verb **deber** followed by **de** and the infinitive. Do not confuse this with **deber** followed by a direct infinitive, which expresses an obligation.

debes de estar cansado después de tanto trabajo
you must be tired after so much work

Note that the Spanish verb *asumir* does *not* mean 'to assume' in the sense of 'to suppose', but in the sense of 'to take on' as in 'to assume power'. If you need to translate

111

'assume' in the sense of 'suppose', either use *suponer* or one of the constructions explained above.

M. THANKS

1. Simple expressions of thanks

a) *gracias* and related terms

The simplest expression of thanks is, of course, **gracias**. Since thanking someone always involves the idea of an exchange (you thank someone in exchange for what they have given you, or done for you), the preposition used with **gracias** is always **por**:

muchas gracias por el regalo
thanks a lot for the present

me dio las gracias por el regalo
he thanked me for the present

A verb used after **gracias** may put into either the present or the perfect infinitive:

gracias por ayudarme/haberme ayudado
thanks for helping me

Likewise, any noun or adjective expressing thanks or gratitude is followed by **por**:

queremos expresar nuestro reconocimiento por todo
we want to express our gratitude for everything

b) *agradecer*

In more formal Spanish, **gracias** is almost always replaced by the appropriate form of the verb **agradecer. agradecer** is an exception to what has been said above in that the idea of 'for' is contained within the verb:

⚠ *agradecer* is not followed by any kind of preposition in Spanish:

les agradecemos su cooperación en este asunto
we thank you for your cooperation in this matter

nos agradecieron nuestra ayuda
they thanked us for our help

2. Subordinate clauses

The verb in a subordinate clause following an expression of gratitude goes into the subjunctive. The commonest occurrences of such expressions are the following:

agradeceremos mucho que nos ayuden

agradeceríamos mucho que nos ayudasen

Both of these are Spanish equivalents of 'we would be grateful if you could help us'. Either my be used on any occasion, despite the difference in tenses. Note the idea of 'could' is not expressed in Spanish.

⚠ **Note that, unlike English, Spanish does not consider this kind of expression to be a condition, so no *si* clause is used.**

In the very formal Spanish of commercial correspondence, the **que** may be omitted from this expression. This should not be imitated in contexts other than commercial correspondence:

agradeceremos nos manden diez cajas
we would be grateful if you could send us ten boxes

N. WISHES/DESIRES/PREFERENCES

1. One subject

If only one subject is involved, a straightforward infinitive is used:

quiero hablar contigo
I want to speak to you

preferiría salir ahora
I would prefer to leave now

valdría más empezar enseguida
it would be better to start right away

The expression of a wish can always be 'softened' in Spanish by using the imperfect subjunctive of **querer**:

quisiéramos comer ahora
we'd like to eat now

2. Two subjects

In this case the verb of wishing must be followed by a subordinate clause with its verb in the subjunctive:

quiero que lo hagan ellos mismos
I want them to do it themselves

me gustaría que Vds. empezaran enseguida
I would like you to start right away

hubiera preferido que escogieras otra cosa
I would have preferred you to choose something else

10. NUMBERS AND NUMBER-RELATED FUNCTIONS

A. NUMBERS

1. The cardinal numbers

For the forms of the cardinal numbers, see page 218.

Note that, though most numbers are invariable (i.e. they never change their form), there are feminine forms of **uno** and of all the hundreds between 200 and 900 inclusive. It is a very common error not to make the hundreds agree:

> **me costó quinientas pesetas**
> it cost me five hundred pesetas

uno also agrees in compound numbers:

> **veintiuna pesetas**
> twenty-one pesetas

(It is possible to hear **veintiuna peseta** in colloquial Spanish, but this should not be imitated).

Note that 'one' is not expressed in expressions such as the following:

> **¿qué coche prefieres? – el rojo**
> which car do you prefer? – the red one

> **preferiría uno más grande**
> I'd like a bigger one

No article is used with **cien** or **mil**, or with the adjective **medio**:

> **cien mil soldados**
> one hundred thousand soldiers

> **esperamos media hora**
> we waited for half an hour

Note that both **millón** and **billón** are nouns and *must* be followed by **de**:

el gobierno invertirá cien millones de pesetas
the government will invest one hundred million pesetas

un billón in Spanish still means one million million (in most other countries the term 'billion' has come to mean one thousand million). In the Spanish press, the word **billón** is frequently written in italics to highlight this difference.

2. The ordinal numbers

For the formation of the ordinal numbers, see page 220.

These are seldom used beyond **décimo**, being usually replaced by the cardinal numbers:

vivo en el tercer piso
I live on the third floor

but: **en el siglo veinte**
in the twentieth century

en la página treinta y dos
on page thirty-two

3. Approximate numbers

An approximate number can be made from any multiple of ten by dropping the final vowel and adding the ending **– ena**, though such numbers are in fact very rare beyond forty:

una veintena de muchachos
about twenty boys

Some other numbers also formed with this ending have become words in their own right:

una docena   a dozen
una quincena   two weeks

The approximate numbers corresponding to **ciento** and **mil** are **centenar** and **millar**, though **cientos** and **miles** may also be used:

vinieron millares de hinchas
thousands of fans turned up

Approximate numbers can also be expressed by a variety of terms such as **en torno a, alrededor de, aproximadamente, más o menos,** or the plural article **unos** (**a eso de** is limited to expressions of time):

había aproximadamente cincuenta personas en la sala
there were about fifty people in the room

llegaron unos diez hombres
about ten men arrived

cuesta unas dos mil pesetas
it costs about two thousand pesetas

Note also the following:

se lo dije hasta veinte veces
I told him as many as twenty times

por lo menos doscientos
at least two hundred

cuarenta y tantos
forty odd

unos pocos, unos cuantos
a few

4. Fractions and decimals

a) *Fractions*

Note that, when used with another number, the phrase **y medio** comes after the *noun* and not after the number as in English:

dos horas y media
two and a half hours

This also applies in the case of the nouns **millón** and **billón**:

seis millones y medio de turistas británicos
six and a half million British tourists

b) *Decimals*

Spaniards use a comma to indicate a decimal fraction, and not a point as in English:

dos coma siete por ciento (2,7 por 100)
two point seven per cent

In colloquial Spanish, the word **coma** is often replaced by **con**:

cinco con cuatro millones (5,4 millones)
five point four million

B. TIME

1. There are several words in Spanish for 'time'. They all have different meanings and must not be confused:

la hora	time on the clock
la época	a period of time of unspecified duration but not measured by the clock
el tiempo	time in general
la vez	an occasion

quizás podríamos vernos a una hora conveniente
perhaps we could meet at a convenient time

siempre hay muchos turistas en esta época del año
there are always lots of tourists at this time of year

pasó mucho tiempo en España
he spent a long time in Spain

una vez/dos veces al año
once/twice a year

ya te lo he dicho por lo menos diez veces
I've already told you at least ten times

Note also the following:

de una vez por todas
once and for all

a la tercera va la vencida (Spanish proverb)
third time lucky

2. Time on the clock

Time on the clock is expressed as follows:

¿qué hora es?	**son las tres**
what time is it?	it's three o'clock
es la una	**son las diez**
it's one o'clock	it's ten o'clock

The feminine definite articles are used became the word understood but not expressed is **hora** or **horas**:

Time after the hour is expressed as follows:

son las tres y cinco	it's five past three
son las siete y cuarto	it's a quarter past seven
son las ocho y veinticinco	its twenty-five past eight
son las once y media	it's half past eleven

Time to the hour:

es la una menos diez	it's ten to one
son las cuatro menos cuarto	it's a quarter to four

'at' is expressed by **a**:

a mediodía, a medianoche	at midday, at midnight
a las seis y diez	at ten past six

Note also:

a las diez en punto	at ten o'clock on the dot
a eso de las ocho	at around eight o'clock
a las tres y pico	just after three
¿qué hora tienes?	what time do you have?
tengo las ocho	I have eight o'clock
daban las diez	it was striking ten o'clock

For the purposes of specifying time, the Spanish day is divided into more sections than its English equivalent:

la madrugada	from midnight till dawn
la mañana	from dawn till noon
el mediodía	from noon till early afternoon
la tarde	from early afternoon till dark
la noche	from nightfall till midnight

madrugada can be replaced by **mañana**. The use of **madrugada** emphasizes the fact that the speaker considers the time in question to be very early (or very late) from his point of view:

me levanté/me acosté a las dos de la madrugada
I got up/went to bed at two in the morning

a las tres de la madrugada	at three in the morning
a las diez de la mañana	at ten in the morning
a la una del mediodía	at one in the afternoon
a las cinco de la tarde	at five in the evening
a las diez de la noche	at ten in the evening

The twenty-four hour clock is also used in timetables and official announcements, though it is not used conversationally:

a las quince treinta y cinco   at fifteen thirty-five

If no specific time of day is mentioned, broad time of day is expressed using the preposition **por**:

salieron por la mañana
they went out in the morning

volveremos por la tarde
we'll come back in the afternoon

Note also the following:

anoche	last night
ayer	yesterday
antes de ayer/anteayer	the day before yesterday
mañana	tomorrow
pasado mañana	the day after tomorrow
ayer por la mañana	yesterday morning
mañana por la noche	tomorrow evening
dos veces por hora	twice an hour
ochenta kilómetros por hora	eighty kilometres an hour

3. Days of the week

For a list of days, months and seasons, see page 221.

Days of the week are written with a small letter. 'on' is expressed simply by the definite article. No preposition is used:

fuimos al cinema el sábado
we went to the movies on Saturday

vamos a la playa los domingos
we go to the beach on Sundays

el lunes por la mañana
on Monday morning

los lunes por la mañana
on Monday mornings

Note also:

el miércoles pasado
last Wednesday

el sábado que viene
next Saturday

dos veces al día
twice a day

cinco veces a la semana
five times a week

diez mil pesetas por semana
ten thousand pesetas per week

4. The date

The months are written with a small letter. 'the first' may be expressed as **el primero** or **el uno**. All other dates are expressed only by the appropriate cardinal number (i.e. three, four etc. not third, fourth etc.)

'on' is expressed simply by the definite article, or by placing **el día** in front of the number. The only exception is in the heading to a letter, where no article is used:

¿a cuántos estamos hoy?/¿a qué día del mes estamos?/¿qué día es hoy?
what date is it today?

hoy estamos a dos
today is the second

llegaremos el 12 de febrero
we will arrive on February 12

salieron el día 9
they left on the 9th

In a full date, both the month and the year are introduced by **de**:

el quince de octubre de mil ochocientos ochenta y ocho
the fifteenth of October nineteen eighty-eight

Note also:

el siglo veinte the twentieth century	**el siglo dieciocho** the eighteenth century
en los años treinta in the thirties	**la España de los años ochenta** the Spain of the eighties
a principios/primeros de enero	at the beginning of January
a mediados de marzo	in the middle of March
a finales/fines de octubre	at the end of October
en lo que va de año this year so far	**a lo largo del año** throughout the year
dos veces al mes twice a month	**cuatro veces al año** four times a year

5. The seasons

The names of the seasons are preceded by a definite article unless used with **en**:

la primavera es muy agradable en España
spring is very pleasant in Spain

iremos a España en otoño
we're going to Spain in the autumn

6. Age

Age is expressed as follows:

¿cuántos años tienes?
how old are you?

¿qué edad tiene tu hermano?
what age is your brother?

tengo diecisiete años
I'm seventeen

The word **años** cannot be omitted in Spanish.

Note also the following:

ronda los cuarenta	**hoy cumplo veinte años**
he's going on forty	I'm twenty today
la juventud	**la tercera edad**
youth, young people	senior citizens

7. Some useful expressions of time

hoy en día, hoy día	nowadays
hoy por hoy	nowadays
en la actualidad	nowadays
a corto/medio/largo plazo	in the short/medium/long term
hace diez años	ten years ago
diez años antes	ten years earlier
a partir de ahora	from now on
de aquí/hoy en adelante	from now on
en el futuro	in future
en el porvenir	in future
en lo sucesivo (*formal*)	in future
en lo venidero (*formal*)	in future
en los años venideros	in the years to come
al día siguiente	the following day
la próxima semana	next week
la semana siguiente	the next week
la semana anterior	the previous week

C. PRICES/MEASUREMENTS/PERCENTAGES

1. Prices

Rate in prices is expressed by the definite article:

este vino cuesta doscientas pesetas el litro
this wine costs two hundred pesetas a liter

lo vendían a mil pesetas el kilo
they were selling it at one thousand pesetas a kilo

Note also:

¿cuánto cuestan/valen las manzanas?/¿a cómo se venden las manzanas?
how much are the apples?

2. Measurements

Measurements may be expressed using either the adjective or the noun relating to the measurement in question (length, height, breadth etc.:

¿cuál es la altura del muro?
how high is the wall?

el muro tiene dos metros de alto/altura
the wall is two meters high

la calle tiene cien metros de largo/longitud
the street is one hundred meters long

Note that in the following construction the adjective agrees:

la calle es cien metros de larga
the street is one hundred meters long

Note also:

¿cuánto pesas?	**¿cuánto mides?**
what do you weigh?	how tall are you?

mide casi dos metros
he's almost two meters tall

tiene una superficie de cien metros cuadrados
it has a surface area of one hundred square meters

tiene una capacidad de dos metros cúbicos
it has a capacity of two cubic meters

Distance is always indicated by the preposition **a**:

¿a qué distancia está la playa?—a unos cinco kilómetros
how far away is the beach?—about five kilometers

3. Percentages

Percentages in Spanish are invariably preceded by either a definite or an indefinite article. There is no difference in meaning:

la inflación ha aumentado en un diez por ciento
inflation has gone up ten percent

el treinta por ciento de las personas entrevistadas no contestó
thirty percent of those interviewed did not give an answer

Percentages are usually written in Spanish as **5 por 100** and the like. **100 por 100** is almost invariably pronounced **cien por cien**.

The amount by which a percentage increases or decreases is indicated in Spanish by the preposition **en**. The commonest verbs used in this connection are:

Increase:

aumentar, incrementar, crecer, subir

Decrease:

caer, bajar, reducir(se)
hemos reducido nuestros precios en un 15 por 100
we have reduced our prices by 15 per cent

If a percentage is not involved, normally no preposition is used:

los precious han bajado treinta pesetas
prices have come down by thirty pesetas

11. SENTENCE STRUCTURE

Sentence structure is not the same as word order. Sentence structure concerns the place occupied by the different *component parts* of the sentence, and not the place of individual words. Any of these component parts can consist of a number of words. For example, in a sentence such as the following:

> **el padre del amigo de mi hermano trabaja en Santander**
> my brother's friend's father works in Santander

the words **el padre del amigo de mi hermano** all go together to form the subject of the verb **trabaja**. The verb itself occupies the second *place* in the sentence, although it is the eighth *word*.

The most important elements of any sentence are the verb, the subject of the verb (i.e. who or what is carrying out the action of the verb), and the object or complement. A transitive verb takes an object, an intransitive verb is followed by a complement. There are other elements—adverbs, prepositional phrases etc.—but these are less essential and are not dealt with here.

1. English sentence structure

Sentence structure is very predictable in English. Most English sentences follow the order subject – verb – object/complement, e.g.:

subject	*verb*	*object / complement*
the boys	watch	the television (object)
Spanish	is	easy (complement)

The only consistent exception to this order in English is questions, where the order verb—subject—object/complement is more common:

verb	*subject*	*object / complement*
is	Spanish	easy

2. Spanish sentence structure

Sentence structure is *very* much more flexible in Spanish than it is in English. This is not to suggest that the order subject – verb – object/complement is in any sense uncommon in Spanish. On the contrary, it is probably the commonest pattern in spoken Spanish, and is also commonly used in questions. Nonetheless, it is nowhere near as dominant in Spanish as it is in English, and a Spanish speaker will happily place the verb before the subject, and on occasions will even place the object before the verb.

There are few rules governing sentence structure in Spanish, but in general it could be said that:

— the closer any element of the sentence is to the beginning of the sentence, the more emphasis it receives, the first position in the sentence being obviously the most emphatic.

— it is unusual for the verb not to occupy the first or second *position* in the sentence (see the difference between position and word order given above).

The choice made by a Spanish speaker may be based on reasons of emphasis, but more often it will have to do with the rhythm of the sentence. Rhythms are not something which can be taught. A feeling for such rhythms can be obtained only through exposure to large amounts of genuine spoken Spanish.

3. Examples of different sentence structures

a) *subject – verb*

mi hermano está estudiando inglés
my brother is studying English

¿el coche está en el garaje?
is the car in the garage?

b) *verb – subject*

llegaron dos tíos y se pusieron a trabajar
two fellows came along and started to work

me lo dijo una vez mi padre
my father told me so once

c) *object – verb – subject*

el cuadro lo pintó un amigo mío
one of my friends painted the picture

la moto la compramos Juan y yo
Juan and I bought the motorcycle

Note that when the object is placed before the verb, the corresponding object pronoun *must* also be placed before the verb.

d) *use of first position for emphasis*

a mí no me gusta nada
I don't like it at all

125

tal decisión no la apoyaremos nunca
we shall never support such a decision

a ella no la puede ver
he can't stand her

4. Punctuation

Punctuation in Spanish is by and large identical to English. Remember, however, that the upside-down question marks and exclamation marks are written at the beginnng of the question and of the exclamation respectively. This is not necessarily at the beginning of the sentence:

¿qué quieres tomar?
what will you have?

y éste, ¿cuánto cuesta?
and how much does this one cost?

estuviste anoche en la discoteca, ¿verdad?
you were at the dance club last night, weren't you?

el público gritó '¡olé!'
the crowd shouted 'olé!

Forms

1. ACCENTUATION

Written accents in Spanish relate primarily to *spoken* stress. If you know how a word is pronounced, you can tell by applying a few simple rules if it requires a written accent, and, if so, where the accent should be written.

1. Syllables

In order to know when and where to write an accent, it is important to understand what is meant by a 'syllable'. A syllable is a group of letters within a word at least one of which *must* be a vowel. If there is no vowel, there is no syllable. In many cases, the number of syllables in a word is the same as the number of vowels:

ca-sa (two syllables) **con-cen-tra-da** (four syllables)

If there is one or more consonants between each vowel, as in the examples just given, the division into syllables is quite straightforward. However, the situation is slightly more complex if two or more vowels are written together.

Vowels in Spanish are divided into strong and weak vowels.

the strong vowels are: A, E and O
the weak vowels are: I and U

The rules regarding whether or not two or more vowels written together form one or more syllables are as follows:

a) When two strong vowels appear together they belong to two distinct syllables:

pa-se-ar (three syllables)

pe-or (two syllables)

b) When a strong and weak vowel appear together and there is no written accent on any of the weak vowels, they form only one syllable, and the strong vowel takes the stress:

fuer-te (two syllables)

vie-jo (two syllables)

an-cia-no (three syllables)

If one of the weak vowels is accentuated, it forms a separate syllable.

ha-cí-a (three syllables)

pú-a (two syllables)

c) When two or more weak vowels appear together they form only one syllable and the stress falls on the second vowel:

viu-da (two syllables)
fui (one syllable)

These rules apply to *pronunciation* only, and are unaffected by the way a word is written. For example, the **o** and **i** of **prohibir** belong to the same syllable, despite the fact that there is a written (but completely unpronounced) **h** between them. The **e** and **u** of **rehusar** belong to the same syllable for the same reason.

2. Spoken stress

All words in Spanish have one main stressed vowel, and it is the position of this stressed vowel in the word which determines whether or not there is a written accent. The rules for spoken stress are as follows:

a) The stress falls naturally on the next to last syllable of the word when:

— the word ends in a vowel

li*a*-mo, re-b*a*-ño, v*e*-o, v*a*-rio, re-ci-bie-ra

— the word ends in -**n** or -**s**

c*a*n-tan, l*i*-bros, j*o*-ven

b) The stress falls naturally on the last syllable when the word ends in a consonant other than -**n** and -**s**:

can-t*a*r, ciu-d*a*d, no-mi-n*a*l

3. Primary use of the written accent

The written accent is used mainly in Spanish to show deviations from the rules for natural spoken stress given above. The pronunciation of the vowel on which the accent is written is not otherwise affected.

If the stress falls where the rules say it should fall, there is no written accent. If it does not, a written accent is placed over the vowel actually carrying the stress. This accounts for the overwhelming majority of cases of written accents in Spanish.

The general rules are, therefore:

— If a word ending in a vowel, -**n** or -**s** is *not* stressed on the next to last syllable, a written accent is placed on the vowel which is in fact stressed:

men*ú*, regi*ó*n, ingl*é*s

129

— If a word ending in a consonant other than **-n** or **-s** is not stressed on the last syllable, a written accent is placed on the vowel which is in fact stressed:

césped, fácil

More specifically, it can be seen that:

— Any word stressed on the third from last syllable carries an accent on the stressed vowel irrespective of its ending:

música, régimen

— Any word ending in a stressed vowel carries an accent on that vowel:

café, rubí

— In any combination of a weak vowel and a strong vowel where it is the weak vowel which carries the stress, this weak vowel will have a written accent:

quería, vacío

Further examples:

stress in 'natural' position (no accent)		*stress out of position (written accent)*	
varias	several	**varías**	you vary
continuo	continuous	**continúo**	I continue
amar	to love	**ámbar**	amber
fabrica	he manufactures	**fábrica**	factory

Remember again that what counts is pronunciation and not spelling. The written accent on **prohíbo** or **rehúso** is explained by the fact that the weak vowel in the spoken syllables **oi** and **eu** is stressed.

Note also that written accents may have to be omitted from or added to plural forms:

región   regiones   joven   jóvenes

4. Secondary uses of the written accent

Other uses of the written accent are:

— to differentiate between two words which have the same spelling:

el (the) — **él** (he)	**si** (if) — **sí** (yes)
tu (your) — **tú** (you)	**de** (of) — **dé** (give)
mi (my) — **mí** (me)	

— to identify the interrogative and exclamatory forms of certain pronouns and adverbs:

donde — **¿dónde?**	**quien** — **¿quién?**
where — where?	who — who?

— to differentiate the pronoun forms from the adjectival forms of the demonstratives (the pronouns are written with an accent):

este — éste	**aquella — aquélla**
this — this one	that — that one

Since the neuter pronouns cannot be confused with any other forms, no accent is required:

esto	**eso**	**aquello**
this	that	that

5. The dieresis

A dieresis is only ever written over the letter **u** in Spanish, in which case it appears as **ü**. The dieresis occurs only in the combinations **güe** and **güi**, and indicates that the **ü** is to be pronounced as a separate vowel. If no dieresis is present, the **u** is not pronounced:

la cigüeña	the stork
la vergüenza	shame
la lingüística	linguistics
el piragüismo	canoeing

Compare these with words such as **la guerra, la guirnalda** and the like, where the **u** is not pronounced.

Note that a dieresis must sometimes be added or indeed omitted in certain forms of certain verbs, to ensure that the pronunciation of the verb is correctly reflected in the spelling, eg:

averiguo (*indicative*: I find out)
averigüe (*subjunctive*)

avergonzarse (*infinitive*: to be ashamed)
me avergüenzo (*first person singular*)

arguyo (*first personal singular*)
argüir (*infinitive*: to argue)

2. GENDER

In Spanish all nouns are either *masculine* or *feminine*. There is no equivalent of the English neuter gender for nouns.

All words used with any noun (adjectives, articles, etc.) take the same gender as the noun.

1. Gender by ending

The gender of a noun can often be deduced from its ending:

a) Most nouns ending in **-o** are masculine:

el libro	**el dinero**	**el piano**
the book	the money	the piano

There are a few common exceptions:

la radio	**la mano**
the radio	the hand

b) Most nouns ending in **-a** are feminine:

la aduana	**la casa**	**la mañana**
the Customs	the house	the morning

Some common exceptions to this:

el día	**el mapa**	**el idioma**	**el clima**
the day	the map	the language	the climate

Also, most nouns ending in **-ema** and a few ending in **-ama** are masculine:

el problema, el sistema, el lema, el programa, el drama, el telegrama
the problem, the system, the slogan, the program, the drama, the telegram

c) Almost all nouns ending in **-d** are feminine:

la ciudad, la vid, la juventud, la pared, la difficultad
the city, the vine, youth, the wall, the difficulty

d) **Almost all nouns ending in *-ión* are feminine:**

⚠

la nación	**la región**
the nation	the region

There are a few common exceptions:

el camión	**el avión**
the truck	the plane

2. Gender by meaning

a) People and animals

When referring to people and animals, often, though not always, the meaning of the noun decides its gender, e.g.:

el hombre	**la mujer**	**la vaca**
the man	the woman	the cow

However, there are some exceptions to the above, for example **la víctima** is the Spanish for a victim of whatever sex.

b) Some nouns are going through a period of transition:

el diputado is the Spanish for congressperson in general, but, with the growing number of women congresspersons in Spain, you will now hear and read **la diputada**.

Some combinations can seem very unusual at first. For example, Mrs. Thatcher has been referred to in the Spanish press as **la Primer Ministro** and **la Primera Ministra**.

c) Words with both genders

There are many words ending in **-ista**, which can be either masculine or feminine, according to the gender of the person referred to:

el socialista, la socialista
the socialist

el periodista, la periodista
the journalist

⚠ **There is no separate 'masculine' form of these nouns—all the masculine forms end in *-ista*, like the feminine ones.**

d) Nouns with corresponding forms for both genders

Some nouns may have both genders, depending on the gender of the person described:

el camarero	**la camarera**
the waiter	the waitress
el niño	**la niña**
the boy	the girl

Sometimes, a more substantial change of spelling is required:

el director	**la directriz**
the male manager	the female manager
el actor	**la actriz**
the actor	the actress

e) Nouns with different meanings for different genders

Some nouns may appear with either gender, but their meanings change:

el policía the policeman	**la policía** the police force
el guía the guide (*person*)	**la guía** the guidebook
el capital capital (*money*)	**la capital** the capital city
el cura the parish priest	**la cura** the cure
el pendiente the earring	**la pendiente** the slope
el moral the mulberry bush	**la moral** ethics

3. THE NOUN—PLURAL OF NOUNS

1. Formation

The plural of Spanish nouns is formed as follows:

a) Adding **-s** to nouns ending in an unstressed vowel:

los libros
the books

las reglas
the rulers

b) Most nouns ending in a stressed vowel add **-es**:

el rubí
the ruby

los rubíes
the rubies

but some common nouns only add **-s**:

los cafés, las mamás, los papás
the cafes, the moms, the dads

c) Adding **-es** to nouns ending in a consonant other than **-s**:

los señores
the men

las tempestades
the storms

d) Nouns already ending in **-s**

If the last syllable is stressed, add **-es**:

el inglés
the Englishman

los ingleses
(the) Englishmen

However, if the last syllable is not stressed, the word does not change:

el lunes
Monday

los lunes
Mondays

e) Some nouns require a spelling change in the plural

Where nouns end in **-z**, this changes to **-ces**:

la actriz
the actress

las actrices
the actresses

f) Changes in written accent

Most singular nouns having a written accent on the last syllable lose this accent in the plural as it is no longer necessary:

la nación	**las naciones**
the nation	the nations

The few nouns ending in **-n** and which are stressed on the second to last syllable in the singular need a written accent in the plural:

el joven	**los jóvenes**
the young man	the young men
el crimen	**los crímenes**
the crime	the crimes

g) There are two plurals in Spanish which actually change their accentuation from the singular to the plural form:

el carácter	**los caracteres**
the character	the characters
el régimen	**los regímenes**
the regime	the regimes

h) In the case of acronyms, plural forms are indicated by doubling the initials:

EE.UU.	**Estados Unidos** (USA)
CC.OO.	**Comisiones Obreras** (Trade Union)
FF.AA	**Fuerzas Armadas** (Armed Forces)

i) Most English words used in Spanish keep the form of the English plural:

el camping	**los campings**
el poster	**los posters**
el comic	**los comics**

However, some English words which have been used in Spanish for a long time have also adopted a Spanish plural:

el club	**los clubes**
el bar	**los bares**
el superman	**los supermanes**

2. Special use of the masculine plural

The masculine plural form is frequently used to indicate both genders:

mis padres	**los Reyes**	**mis tíos**
my parents	the King and Queen	my aunt and uncle

4. THE ARTICLES

1. The definite article

a) The standard form

The definite article (the) has both a masculine and a feminine form, each of which can also be put into the plural:

	masculine	*feminine*
singular	**el**	**la**
plural	**los**	**las**

el señor	**la chica**
the man	the girl
los señores	**las chicas**
the men	the girls

b) A special feminine form

Note that the form of the feminine definite article used immediately before nouns which begin with a stressed **a-** or **ha-** is **el** and not **la**:

el agua	**el hambre**
the water	hunger

This change does not affect the *gender* of the noun. Other words accompanying the noun continue to take the feminine form:

el agua está fría
the water is cold

c) Contraction of the definite article

The masculine definite article joins together with the prepositions **a** and **de** to give the following forms:

a + el = al   **de + el = del**

fui al cine
I went to the movies

la casa del profesor
the teacher's house

This does not happen if the **el** is part of a title in capital letters:

escribí a El Diario
I wrote to El Diario

However, feminines and plurals *never* contract.

d) Countries whose names are preceded by the definite article

The names of the following countries are preceded by the appropriate form of the definite article:

el Brasil	Brazil
el Ecuador	Ecuador
la India	India
el Japón	Japan
el Perú	Peru
el Uruguay	Uruguay

2. The indefinite article

a) The standard form

The indefinite article has both a masculine and a feminine form. Unlike English, both of these can also be put into the plural.

	masculine	*feminine*
singular	**un**	**una**
plural	**unos**	**unas**

un hombre	**una cantidad**
a man	a quantity

b) A special feminine form

Note that the form of the feminine indefinite article used immediately before nouns which begin with a stressed **a-** or **ha-** is **un**:

un hacha	**un ala**
an axe	a wing

This change does not affect the *gender* of the noun. Other words accompanying the noun continue to take the feminine form:

construyeron un ala nueva
they built a new wing

c) The plural forms are used:

– with nouns which exist only in the plural or are normally used in the plural

– to express the idea of 'some', 'a few'

Otherwise, they are not required:

compré unos pantalones
I bought a pair of pants

tengo un libro	**tengo unos libros**	**tengo libros**
I have a book	I have some books	I have books

5. THE DEMONSTRATIVES

1. The demonstrative adjectives

The demonstrative adjectives in Spanish are **este** (this) and **ese** and **aquel** (both meaning 'that'). Their forms are as follows:

	masculine	*feminine*
singular	**este**	**esta**
plural	**estos**	**estas**
singular	**ese**	**esa**
plural	**esos**	**esas**
singular	**aquel**	**aquella**
plural	**aquellos**	**aquellas**

The demonstrative adjectives are placed *before* the noun:

este mes	**ese sillón**	**aquella bicicleta**
this month	that armchair	that bike

See page 20 for their uses.

2. The demonstrative pronouns

The demonstrative pronouns are identical to the demonstrative adjectives with the single exception that they carry a written accent on the stressed vowel:

éste, éstos, ésta, éstas
ése, ésos, ésa, ésas
aquél, aquéllos, aquélla, aquéllas

There is also a neuter form which is *not* written with an accent (see page 21).

esto, eso, aquello

See pages 20–21 for their uses.

6. THE POSSESSIVE ADJECTIVES AND PRONOUNS

1. The weak possessive adjectives

The weak possessive adjectives are placed before the noun. Their forms are as follows:

	masc. sing.	*fem. sing.*	*masc. plural*	*fem. plural*
my	**mi**	**mi**	**mis**	**mis**
your	**tu**	**tu**	**tus**	**tus**
his/her its/your	**su**	**su**	**sus**	**sus**
our	**nuestro**	**nuestra**	**nuestros**	**nuestras**
your	**vuestro**	**vuestra**	**vuestros**	**vuestras**
their your	**su**	**su**	**sus**	**sus**

mi cuchillo
my knife

mi cuchara
my spoon

mis cuchillos
my knives

mis cucharas
my spoons

tu pañuelo
your handkerchief

tu chaqueta
your jacket

tus pañuelos
your handkerchiefs

tus chaquetas
your jackets

su saco
his/her/your bag

su maleta
his/her/your suitcase

sus sacos
his/her/your bags

sus maletas
his/her/your suitcases

nuestro piso
our apartment

nuestra casa
our house

nuestros pisos our apartments	**nuestras casas** our houses
vuestro sombrero your hat	**vuestra camisa** your shirt
vuestros sombreros your hats	**vuestras camisas** your shirts
su saco your/their bag	**su maleta** your/their suitcase
sus sacos your/their bags	**sus maletas** your/their suitcases

For a fuller treatment of **su** and **sus**, see page 26.

2. The strong possessive adjectives and pronouns

The strong possessive adjectives and the possessive pronouns are identical in form. They are as follows:

masc. sing.	*fem. sing.*	*masc. plural*	*fem. plural*
mío	mía	míos	mías
tuyo	tuya	tuyos	tuyas
suyo	suya	suyos	suyas
nuestro	nuestra	nuestros	nuestras
vuestro	vuestra	vuestros	vuestras
suyo	suya	suyos	suyas

See pages 25–27 for an explanation of the use of these forms.

7. AUGMENTATIVES AND DIMINUTIVES

1. The augmentatives

a) The following suffixes are added to nouns, adjectives, participles and adverbs as augmentatives (see pages 29–30):

masculine	**-ón**	**-azo**	**-acho**	**-ote**
feminine	**-ona**	**-aza**	**-acha**	**-ota**

b) Any vowel at the end of the original word is dropped,

un muchachazo
a big boy

un hombrote
a big man

2. The diminutives

a) The following suffixes are added to nouns, adjectives, participles and adverbs as diminutives (see pages 29–30):

-ito	longer forms: **-cito, -ecito**
-illo	longer forms: **-cillo, -ecillo**
-uelo	longer forms: **-zuelo, -ezuelo**
-ín	(no longer forms)
-ucho	(no longer forms)

All of these endings can be made feminine by changing the **-o** to **-a** (**-ín** becomes **-ina**).

b) When the word ends in a vowel, this is dropped:

Ana, Anita   **señora, señorita**

c) Of the longer forms, **-cito**, **-cillo** and **-zuelo** are used with words of more than one syllable which end in **-n** or **-r**:

salón	>	**saloncito**
calor	>	**calorcito**

d) The forms **-ecito**, **-ecillo** and **-ezuelo** are used with words of one syllable:

flor	>	**florecita, florecilla**
pez	>	**pececito, pececillo**

Note that spelling changes (**z** to **c**) may be necessary.

They are also used with words of two syllables when the first syllable is **-ie** or **-ue**. The final vowel is dropped:

pueblo	>	**pueblecito**
nieto	>	**nietecito**

e) Written accents are dropped from the ending of the original word when a suffix is added:

salón	>	**saloncito**

a written accent is added to the weak vowel of the suffix when the original word ends in an accentuated vowel:

mamá	>	**mamaíta**

8. THE ADJECTIVE

1. Shortened form of adjectives

a) Certain adjectives drop the **-o** from the masculine singular immediately before the noun:

alguno	**¿hay *algún* autobús por aquí?** are there any buses around here?
ninguno	**no veo *ningún* tren** I don't see any trains
bueno	**un *buen* vino** a good wine
malo	**el *mal* tiempo** the bad weather
primero	**el *primer* día del año** the first day of the year
tercero	**el *tercer* edificio** the third building

Note that **ninguno** and **alguno** require a written accent when shortened in this way.

b) **grande** is shortened to **gran** before both masculine and feminine singular nouns:

un gran señor   **una gran señora**
a great man   a great lady

When **grande** refers to physical size, it usually comes after the noun, in which case it is not shortened:

un coche grande   **una cocina grande**
a large car   a large kitchen

c) **cualquiera** becomes **cualquier** before both masculine and feminine singular nouns:

cualquier libro   **cualquier casa**
any book   any house

The plural of this adjective is **cualesquiera**. It is seldom used.

d) **santo** becomes **san** before saints' names, except those beginning with either **Do-** or **To-**:

San Pablo	**San Pedro**
Santo Domingo	**Santo Tomás**

2. Forming the feminine of adjectives

a) Adjectives ending in **-o** change to **-a**:

un vuelo corto	**una estancia corta**
a short flight	a short stay

b) Adjectives ending in other vowels or consonants (other than those in sections c) and d) have the same form for both masculine and feminine:

un coche verde	**una hoja verde**
a green car	a green leaf
un problema fundamental	**una dificultad fundamental**
a fundamental problem	a fundamental difficulty

c) Those ending in **-án**, **-ón**, and **-or** add **-a**:

un niño hablador	**una mujer habladora**
a talkative boy	a talkative woman

The exceptions are the comparative adjectives ending in **-or**, see page 147:

una idea mejor
a better idea

Note also that those ending in **-án** and **-ón** lose their accent in the feminine:

una muchacha muy holgazana
a very lazy girl

d) Adjectives indicating nationality or where someone or something comes from add **-a** if they end in a consonant. Any written accent is also lost:

un hotel inglés	**una pensión inglesa**
an English hotel	an English boarding house
un vino andaluz	**una sopa andaluza**
an Andalusian wine	an Andalusian soup

e) Adjectives ending in **-ícola** and **-ista** have the same form for both masculine and feminine:

un país agrícola	**una región vinícola**
an agricultural country	a wine-growing region
el partido comunista	**la ideología socialista**
the communist party	socialist ideology

⚠ Note that there is no separate 'masculine' form for these adjectives. The masculine forms end in *-ista* and *-ícola* like the feminines.

3. The plural of adjectives

Adjectives follow the same rules as nouns for the formation of the plural (see page 135):

estos libros son viejos y sucios
these books are old and dirty

unas personas amables
some friendly people

The same spelling and accentuation changes also occur:

feliz — felices   **holgazán — holgazanes**

9. THE COMPARATIVE

See pages 34–36 for uses of the comparative.

1. The standard forms

To form the comparative in Spanish, simply place the word **más** (more), or **menos** (less) before the adjective:

más barato
cheaper

más caro
more expensive

menos guapo
less handsome

menos feo
less ugly

2. Irregular comparatives

There are six irregular comparatives:

bueno	(good)	>	**mejor**	(better)
grande	(big)	>	**mayor**	(bigger)*
malo	(bad)	>	**peor**	(worse)
mucho	(a lot)	>	**más**	(more)
pequeño	(small)	>	**menor**	(smaller)*
poco	(a little)	>	**menos**	(less)

A number of other adjectives are considered to belong to this group, although their comparative meaning has to some extent been lost:

superior   (superior)
inferior   (inferior)
anterior   (previous)
posterior   (rear, subsequent)

When referring to age, **mayor** is often treated in spoken Spanish as a simple adjective meaning 'old', 'grown up' and is sometimes itself put into the comparative:

mi hermano más mayor
my older brother

* **más grande** and **más pequeño** exist, but refer rather to physical size. **mayor** and **menor** refer more to the relative importance of the object or person, or to age.

Although fairly widespread, this usage is ungrammatical and should certainly not be imitated in formal written Spanish.

superior and **inferior** are widely used with numbers, amounts, quantities etc:

el paro es superior a tres millones
unemployment is in excess of three million

los beneficios son inferiores a los del año pasado
profits are down on last year's

10. THE SUPERLATIVE

1. The relative superlative

The relative superlative is identical in form to the comparative:

Juan es el estudiante más insolente de la clase
Juan is the most insolent student in class

este coche es el más caro
this car is the most expensive

es la peor película que jamás he visto
it's the worst film I've ever seen

2. The absolute superlative

The absolute superlative is formed by adding the ending **-ísimo** to the adjective. If the adjective already ends in a vowel, this is dropped:

alto	**altísimo**
importante	**importantísimo**
fácil	**facilísimo**

When a vowel is dropped from the adjective, spelling changes may be necessary to ensure that the pronunciation of the absolute superlative is properly reflected in the spelling of the word:

rico	**riquísimo**
feliz	**felicísimo**
largo	**larguísimo**

Like any other adjective, the relative superlative agrees with the noun described:

estás guapísima hoy, María
you're looking extremely pretty today, María

estos libros son carísimos
these books are very expensive

11. PREPOSITIONS

A

to	destination	**voy a la escuela/a casa** I am going to school/home
		¿adónde fuiste? where did you go?
at / in	place	**llega a Madrid mañana** he arrives in Madrid tomorrow
at / on	time	**comemos a la una** we eat at one o'clock
		se fue a los quince años he left at the age of fifteen
		al día siguiente murió he died (on) the next day
at / on	place where	**torcieron a la izquierda** they turned to the left
		sentarse a la mesa to sit down at the table
on	means of transport	**a pie, a caballo** on foot, on horseback
at	cost	**los vendían a cien pesetas cada uno** they were selling them at a hundred pesetas each
away from	place/time	**a los dos días volvió** he came back two days later
		la casa se sitúa a cien metros de aquí the house is a hundred meters from here
a	frequency	**dos veces al día** twice a day
in	opinion	**a mi ver, a mi juicio, a mis ojos** in my opinion, in my view
purpose	verbs of motion	**fui a comprar pan** I went to buy bread
personal *a*	see page 58	**he visto a Juan** I saw Juan

ANTE

before	in the presence of	**le llevaron ante el rey** they brought him before the king
before	in the face of	**ante tanto trabajo huyó** in the face of so much work he fled

BAJO

under(neath)	place	**construyeron un túnel bajo el mar** they built a tunnel under the sea
	figuratively	**bajo el reinado de Felipe II** under the reign of Philip II

CON

with	association	**se fueron con su primo** they left with their cousin
	means	**lo cortó con las tijeras** she cut it with the scissors
to		**hablaba con su amigo** he was talking to his friend
towards	figuratively	**ne seas cruel conmigo** don't be cruel to me

In this last meaning, **con** is sometimes preceded by **para**:

> **era muy amable para con todos**
> he was very kind to everyone

CONTRA

against	position	**se apoyaba contra la pared** he was leaning against the wall
	opposition	**los rebeldes luchaban contra el gobierno** the rebels were fighting against the government

In this last meaning, the compound preposition **en contra de** is often preferred:

> **votaron en contra de la ley**
> they voted against the bill

DE

of	possession	**es el coche de mi hermana** it's my sister's car

	material	**el vestido es de lana** the dress is made of wool
	contents	**un paquete de cigarrillos** a pack of cigarettes
(*for*)	purpose	**una cuchara de café** a coffee spoon
from	place	**es de Londres** he comes from London
		va de Madrid a Salamanca he goes from Madrid to Salamanca
	time	**de año en año vienen aquí** they come here year after year
		cenamos de diez a once we had dinner from ten to eleven
		se fueron de pequeños they left as little children
	number	**el peso es de cien kilos** the weight is one hundred kilos
		el total era de mil pesetas the total was a thousand pesetas
	cost	**un coche de diez mil dólores** a car costing ten thousand dollars
with	descriptions	**la muchacha de los ojos azules** the girl with the blue eyes
		el señor de la barba the man with the beard
		¡el bobo del niño! the silly boy!
to form adjectival phrases		**la comida de siempre** the usual food
		la parte de fuera the outside part
to form compound prepositions		**además de, alrededor de** etc. See page 157.

DESDE

from	place	**le vi llegar desde mi ventana** I saw him arrive from my window
from / since	time	**toca la guitarra desde niño** he has been playing the guitar since he was a boy

with **hasta** *from ... to/till*	time	**desde las dos hasta las cuatro** from two o'clock till four
from ... to	place	**desde Madrid hasta Barcelona** from Madrid to Barcelona

EN

in/at/on	position	**paró en la puerta** he stopped in the doorway
		quedarse en casa to stay at home
		el ordenador está en la mesa the computer is on the table
		lo vimos en la Feria de Muestras we saw it at the Exhibition
	opinion	**en mi opinión sería imprudente** in my opinion it would be unwise
into	numbers	**lo dividió en tres partes** he divided it into three
within	time	**no le he visto en quince días** I haven't seen him in fifteen days

by	increase/
	decrease
		**los precios han aumentado en
		    un diez por ciento**
		the prices have gone up by
		    ten percent

phrases		**en balde, en vano** in vain **en seguida** immediately **en absoluto** absolutely not

ENTRE

between		**entre la puerta y la pared** between the door and the wall
		entre tú y yo between you and me
among		**lo encontré entre tus papeles** I found it among your papers
together		**lo hicimos entre todos** we did it together

HACIA

towards	place	**fue corriendo hacia su padre** he ran towards his father

	figuratively	**muestra hostilidad hacia el jefe**
		he shows hostility to the boss
about	time	**llegaron hacia las tres**
		they arrived about three o'clock

HASTA

until	time	**esto continuó hasta el siglo veinte**
		this continued until the 20th century
up to	number	**vinieron hasta cien personas**
		as many as a hundred people turned up
as far as	place	**te acompaño hasta tu casa**
		I'll walk you home
even	figuratively	**hasta los niños quieren acompañarnos**
		even the children want to come with us

INCLUSO

even		**incluso mi padre está de acuerdo**
		even my father agrees

MEDIANTE

by means of		**lo consiguió mediante mucho trabajo**
		he achieved it by hard work

PARA

in order to	purpose	**salió para lavar el coche**
		he went out to wash the car
		compró una navaja para cortar la cuerda
		she bought a penknife to cut the rope
		estudió para cura
		he studied to become a priest
for	in the direction of	**se fueron para Estados Unidos**
		they left for the USA
by	time by which	**quiero ese trabajo para mañana**
		I want that work by tomorrow
		para entonces ya me habré marchado
		I'll have gone away by then

for	as concerns	**el cálculo no es difícil para ella** the calculation isn't difficult for her
for	concession	**para ser español, habla muy bien inglés** for a Spaniard, he speaks very good English
to		**siempre murmuraba para sí** she was always muttering to herself
with **estar**	on the point of	**estábamos todos para salir** we were all ready to go out
idioms		**bastante ... para** enough ... to/for
		demasiado ... para too much ... to/for
		suficiente ... para enough ... to/for
		cuesta demasiado para mí it's too expensive for me

POR

by	agent	**el reparo fue terminado por el jefe** the repair was finished by the boss
for	time during	**habló por dos minutos** he spoke for two minutes
		ocurrió el robo el domingo por la noche the robbery took place on Sunday night
out of		**lo echó por la ventana** she threw it out of the window
through		**pasaron por Valencia** they went through Valencia
about	place	**rodaron por las cercanías** they roamed about the neighborhood
		vive por aquí he lives around here
by / through	means	**por mí se informaron sobre el desastre** they found out about the disaster through me

		por avión, por teléfono by air, by telephone
in exchange for		**vendió el coche por dos cientos dólares** he sold the car for two hundred dollars
per / by	rate/sequence	**cincuenta kilómetros por hora** fifty kilometers per hour
out of / by	cause	**por no estudiar no aprobó el examen** he failed the exam through not having studied
for the sake of / through		**por amor le siguió a España** she followed him to Spain out of love
times	multiplication	**dos por dos son cuatro** two times two are four
for	to get	**voy por hielo** I am going to get some ice
idioms	tomar ... por	**¿me tomas por idiota?** do you take me for a fool?
	pasar por	**pasa por buen conductor** he is considered a good driver
	estar por	**los platos están por lavar** the dishes still have to be washed
		estoy por salir I feel like going out

SEGÚN

according to	**según él, es peligroso** according to him, it's dangerous
	los precios varían según la época del año the prices vary according to the time of year

SIN

without	**continuaremos sin su ayuda** we will go on without your help
	sin saber without knowing

SOBRE

on / over	place	**las tazas están sobre la mesa** the cups are on the table
		el avión voló sobre las montañas the plane flew over the mountains
around	time	**vendrá sobre las siete** he will come around seven o'clock
on / about	concerning	**he leído un artículo sobre la guerra** I read an article about the war

TRAS

after	time	**tras una reunión de tres horas** after a three hour meeting
	succession	**uno tras otro** one after the other

COMPOUND PREPOSITIONS

acerca de	about/ concerning	**me habló el jefe acerca del empleado** the boss spoke to me about the employee
a causa de	because of	**no salimos a causa de la tormenta** we are not going out because of the storm
a favor de	in favour of/ for	**¿estás a favor de la energía nuclear?** are you in favor of nuclear energy?
a fuerza de	by dint of	**consiguió terminar a fuerza de trabajar noche y día** he managed to get finished by working both night and day
a pesar de	in spite of	**salieron a pesar de la lluvia** they went out in spite of the rain
a lo largo de	along	**hay flores a lo largo del río** there are flowers all along the riverside
	throughout	**a lo largo del mes de agosto** throughout the month of August

a través de	across/through	**la luz entra a través de la ventana** the light comes in through the window
además de	besides/ as well as	**compré pan además de mantequilla** I bought bread as well as butter
alrededor de	about/around	**gana alrededor de veinte dólares al día** he earns around twenty dollars a day
		las casas están situadas alrededor de la iglesia the houses are situated around the church
antes de	before (time)	**antes de entrar dejen salir** let people off before getting on
cerca de	near	**la casa está cerca del colegio** the house is near the school
	around	**tiene cerca de mil ovejas** he has nearly a thousand sheep
debajo de	under	**se pararon debajo del árbol** they stopped under the tree
delante de	in front of	**el coche se detuvo delante del hotel** the car stopped in front of the hotel
dentro de	inside	**encontró un regalo dentro del paquete** she found a gift inside the parcel
después de	after	**salió después de terminar su trabajo** he went out after finishing his work
		después de las dos after two o'clock
		después de todo after all
detrás de	behind	**el bar se encuentra detrás del mercado** the bar is behind the market
en lugar de / *en vez de*	instead of	**en lugar de telefonear, les escribió** instead of phoning, he wrote to them

en medio de	in the midst of	**paró en medio de tocar la sonata** he stopped in the midst of playing the sonata
encima de	on (top of)	**colocó el vaso encima de la mesa** she put the glass on the table
enfrente de	opposite	**la iglesia está enfrente del Ayuntamiento** the church is opposite the Town Hall
fuera de	apart from	**fuera de los de al lado, no concozco a nadie** apart from the next-door neighbors, I don't know anyone
	outside	**la granja está situada fuera de la aldea** the farm is outside the village
lejos de	far from	**la iglesia no está lejos de la escuela** the church is not far from the school
		lejos de acatar la ley far from respecting the law
por medio de	by (means of)	**consiguio obtener el dinero por medio de un embuste** he managed to get the money by means of trickery

12. RELATIVE PRONOUNS

For a detailed explanation of the use of relative pronouns, see pages 38–40.

1. Simple relative pronouns

a) **que** (who, whom, which, that)

que relates to either persons or things, singular or plural. Note that it is invariable.

b) **quien/quienes** (who, whom, that)

quien (singular), **quienes** (plural) relate exclusively to people and are normally used after prepositions.

2. Compound relative pronouns

The compound relative pronouns have separate forms for masculine singular and plural, and feminine singular and plural. They also have a neuter form.

a) **el que** (who, whom, which, that)

	masculine	*feminine*	*neuter*
singular	**el que**	**la que**	**lo que**
plural	**los que**	**las que**	

b) **el cual** (who, whom, which, that)

	masculine	*feminine*	*neuter*
singular	**el cual**	**la cual**	**lo cual**
plural	**los cuales**	**las cuales**	

13. PRONOUNS

1. Subject pronouns

	singular	*plural*
1st person	**yo** (I)	**nosotros, nosotras** (we)
2nd person	**tú** (you)	**vosotros, vosotras** (you)
3rd person	**él** (he, it)	**ellos** (they)
	ella (she, it)	**ellas** (they)
	ello (it)	
	usted (you)	**ustedes** (you)

usted and **ustedes** are commonly abbreviated to **Vd.** and **Vds.**
(or occasionally to **Ud.** and **Uds.**). They are followed by the *third*
person forms of the verb. For the difference between **Vd.** and **tú**,
see pages 43–44. For the use of **ello** see page 42.

2. Weak object pronouns

For the use of the weak object pronouns, see pages 47–49.

a) Direct object pronouns

	singular	*plural*
1st person	**me** (me)	**nos** (us)
2nd person	**te** (you)	**os** (you)
3rd person	**le** (him, you)	**les** (them, you)
	la (her, it, you)	**las** (them, you)
	lo (it)	**los** (them)

le and **les** are the masculine pronouns used for people
lo and **los** are the masculine pronouns used for things
la and **las** are the feminine pronouns for either people or things

b) Indirect object pronouns

	singular	*plural*
1st person	**me** (to me)	**nos** (to us)
2nd person	**te** (to you)	**os** (to you)
3rd person	**le** (to him/her/it/you)	**les** (to them/you)

c) Reflexive pronouns (myself etc.)

	singular	*plural*
1st person	**me**	**nos**
2nd person	**te**	**os**
3rd person	**se**	**se**

161

3. Strong object pronouns

For the use of the strong object pronouns, see page 49.

	singular	*plural*
1st person	**mí**	**nosotros, nosotras**
2nd person	**ti**	**vosotros, vosotras**
3rd person	**él, ella, ello**	**ellos, ellas**
	Vd.	**Vds.**
(reflexive)	**sí**	**sí**

mí, ti and **sí** combine with **con** to give the following forms:

conmigo	with me
contigo	with you
consigo	with himself/herself/yourself/ themselves/yourselves

4. Position of the pronouns

The weak object pronouns normally come before the verb. In the compound tenses they are placed before the auxiliary verb:

él lo hizo	**yo le he visto**
he did it	I saw him
nos hemos levantado	**Vd. se despierta**
we got up	you wake up

In the following three cases the pronouns come after the verb and are joined to it:

a) when the verb is in the infinitive:

quiero verla	**salió después de hacerlo**
I want to see her	he went out after doing it

However, if the infinitive immediately follows another verb, the pronoun may precede the first verb:

	querían encontrarnos	they wanted to meet us
OR	**nos querían encontrar**	

b) when the verb is in the present participle:

estoy pintándolo	**estaba cantándola**
I am painting it	he was singing it

Again, in the case of a progressive form of the verb, the pronoun may precede the first verb:

	están llevándolo	they are carrying it
OR	**lo están llevando**	

c) when giving a positive command:

¡déjalo!	**¡date prisa!**
leave it!	hurry up!
¡quédese aquí!	**¡espéreme!**
stay here!	wait for me!

However, the pronoun precedes the verb in a negative command:

¡no lo hagas!	**¡no te muevas!**
don't do it!	don't move!

5. Changes in accentuation and spelling

a) Accents

Note that when more than one pronoun is added to an infinitive, a present participle or an imperative, a written accent is usually required on the original verb to indicate spoken stress if this has moved to the third from last syllable (see pages 129–130):

¿quieres pasarme el vino?	**¿quieres pasármelo?**
will you pass me the wine?	will you pass me it?
está explicándome la lección	
he is explaining the lesson to me	
está explicándomela	
he is explaining it to me	
dame el libro	**dámelo**
give me the book	give me it
ponga el libro en la mesa	**póngalo en la mesa**
put the book on the table	put it on the table
dígame	
hello (on the phone)	

b) Changes in spelling

When **-se** is joined to the verb, any final s of the verb ending is dropped:

vendámoselo
let's sell it to him

The final **s** of the first person plural is dropped before the reflexive pronoun **nos**:

sentémonos
let's sit down

The **d** of the second person plural imperative is dropped before the reflexive pronoun **os**:

sentaos, por favor
have a seat, please

With third conjugation verbs, an accent is then required on the **i**:

vestíos
get dressed

The only exception is the verb **ir**, where the **d** of the imperative is in fact retained:

idos
go away

6. Order of pronouns

When two or more pronouns are being used together they come in the following order:

a) The reflexive **se** must always come first:

se me ha ocurrido	**se le olvidó**
it occurred to me	he forgot

b) When a direct and an indirect object pronoun are both being used, the indirect comes first:

me lo dio	**nos la mostraron**
he gave me it	they showed it to us

c) If there are both a third person direct object pronoun (**la, lo, le, los, las, les**) and a third person indirect object pronoun (**le, les**), the indirect **le** and **les** are both replaced by **se** before the direct object pronoun:

se la vendieron (a ella)	**se los mandó (a Vd.)**
they sold it to her	he sent them to you

The addition of **a él, a ella, a Vd.** or **a Vds.** and the like can clarify to whom the **se** refers.

d) In those cases where the direct object pronouns **me, te, nos** or **os** are used with another indirect object pronoun, the direct object pronoun stands before the verb, and the indirect pronoun is replaced by **a** + the corresponding strong pronoun after the verb:

me mandaron a ti
they sent me to you

nos acercamos a ellos
we approached them

14. ADVERBS

Adverbs are used with verbs, adjectives and other adverbs. When used with a verb, they describe:

how an action is done	adverbs of manner
when an action is done	adverbs of time
where an action is done	adverbs of place
to what degree an action is done	adverbs of degree

1. Adverbs of manner

a) Most of these adverbs can be formed by adding **-mente** to the feminine singular form of the adjective:

lenta (slow)	**lentamente** (slowly)
extensa (wide)	**extensamente** (widely)

Accents appearing on the adjective are retained on the adverb:

lógica (logical)	**lógicamente** (logically)
rápida (quick)	**rápidamente** (quickly)

b) When two or more adverbs are used to describe the same verb, only the last one takes **-mente**, but the initial ones retain the feminine form of the adjective:

caminaron nerviosa y rápidamente
they traveled anxiously and fast

c) The following adverbs of manner do not have a form in **-mente**:

bien (well)	**mal** (badly)
adrede (on purpose)	**así** (in this way)
despacio (slowly)	**deprisa** (quickly)

caminaban despacio por el calor que hacía
they traveled slowly because of the heat

tú has trabajado bien, Juanito
you've done a good job, Juanito

2. Adverbs of time

Most of these adverbs are not formed from adjectives. The commonest are:

ahora	(now)
anoche	(last night)
anteanoche	(the night before last)
anteayer/antes de ayer	(the day before yesterday)

antes	(before)
ayer	(yesterday)
después	(after)
entonces	(then)
hoy	(today)
luego	(presently)
mañana	(tomorrow)
nunca	(never)
pasado mañana	(the day after tomorrow)
primero	(firstly)
pronto	(soon)
prontísimo	(very soon)
siempre	(always)
tarde	(late)
tardísimo	(very late)
temprano	(early)
tempranísimo	(very early)
todavía	(still/yet)
ya	(already/now/presently)

Some common adverbial phrases of time:

a continuación	(next)
acto seguido	(immediately after)
algunas veces	(sometimes)
a menudo	(often)
a veces	(sometimes)
dentro de poco	(soon)
de vez en cuando	(from time to time)
en breve	(soon)
muchas veces	(often)
nunca más	(never again)
otra vez	(again)
pocas veces	(rarely)
rara vez	(seldom)
repetidas veces	(again and again)
una y otra vez	(again and again)

quiero empezar ahora, no espero hasta mañana
I want to start now, I'm not waiting until tomorrow

siempre va en tren hasta el centro, luego coge el autobús
she always takes the train into the center and then catches a bus

quedamos en vernos pasado mañana, no mañana
we agreed to meet the day after tomorrow, not tomorrow

Points to note

a) As well as meaning 'already', **ya** is used in everyday speech to mean 'right away':

¡**ya voy**!
I'm coming right away!

There are times when **ya** has no clear translation into English as it is often used as a filler:

ya me lo decía yo
I thought so

In the negative **ya no** means 'no longer':

siempre iba a ver a su tía el sábado, pero ya no va
he always used to visit his aunt on Saturdays, but he no longer goes

(!) **It should not be confused with** *todavía no*, **which means** 'not yet':

todavía no han llegado
they haven't arrived yet

b) **luego** can also mean 'therefore':

pienso luego existo
I think, therefore I am

c) **recientemente** is shortened to **recién** before past participles. **recién** is invariable and does not change its form whatever the gender or number of the past participle:

una niña recién nacida
a new-born baby girl

los recién casados
the newly-weds

3. Adverbs of place

The commonest of these are:

abajo	(down/below)
ahí/allí	(there)
allá	(over there)
aquí	(here)
arriba	(up/above)
cerca	(near)
debajo	(below/beneath)
delante	(forward/in front)
dentro	(inside)
detrás	(behind/back)
donde	(where)
encima	(over/above/on)
enfrente	(opposite)
fuera	(outside)
lejos	(far)

Some adverbial phrases:

en alguna parte	(somewhere)
en otra parte	(somewhere else)
en/por todas partes	(everywhere)

la aldea donde nací
the village where I was born

¿dónde está Juan?—está dentro
where's Juan?—he's inside

¿hay alguna tienda por aquí cerca?
is there a shop nearby?

se me cayeron encima
they fell on me

Points to note

a) **aquí, allí** and **allá** express the same relationships as the demonstrative adjectives **este, ese** and **aquel** (see page 20):

   aquí means here, near me
   allí means there, near you
   allá means there, far from both of us

b) The forms **arriba, abajo, adelante** and **atrás** can be used immediately after a noun in adverbial phrases such as:

   andábamos calle abajo
   we walked down the street

   aquello sucedió años atrás
   that event took place years later

   adentro and **a través** also appear in set phrases:

   mar adentro
   out at sea

   campo a través
   cross country

4. Adverbs of degree

The commonest of these are:

algo	(somewhat)
apenas	(hardly)
bastante	(fairly/rather/enough)
casi	(almost)
como	(about)
cuánto	(how/how much)
demasiado	(too much)
más	(more)
menos	(less)

mitad/medio	(half)
mucho	(very much)
muy	(very much)
nada	(not at all)
poco	(little)
qué	(how)
suficientemente	(enough)
tan	(so/as)
tanto	(so much/as much)
todo	(entirely)
un poco	(a little)

la casa es muy vieja pero es bastante grande
the house is very old but it is fairly big

me gusta mucho la tortilla, pero no me gustan nada los calamares
I like tortilla very much, but I don't like squid at all

tiene casi tres años, todavía es demasiado pequeño para ir solo
he is almost three, still too little to go by himself

hoy se siente un poco mejor
he is feeling a little better today

Points to note

a) This use of **qué** is restricted to exclamations:

¡qué inteligente eres!
how clever you are!

b) **muy** is used with adjectives and adjectival phrases, and adverbs:

estoy muy cansado
I am very tired

me parece muy temprano
it seems very early to me

In a few exceptional cases, it can be used with a noun:

es muy amigo mío
he's a very good friend of mine

When used as an adverb, **mucho** goes with verbs, comparative adverbs, and comparative adjectives:

me gustó mucho
I liked it a lot

está mucho mejor
he's much better

169

c) When used as an adverb, **medio** never changes its form:

> **María estaba medio dormida**
> María was half asleep

d) Note the common construction with **suficientemente**:

> **no es lo suficientemente inteligente como para entender esto**
> he isn't smart enough to understand this

15. THE VERB

DIFFERENT CATEGORIES OF VERBS: THE CONJUGATIONS

There are three conjugations of verbs in Spanish. The infinitive of a verb indicates which conjugation it belongs to.

> all verbs ending in **-ar** belong to the first conjugation
> all verbs ending in **-er** belong to the second conjugation
> all verbs ending in **-ir** belong to the third conjugation

Some verbs are irregular, and others have minor deviations from the rules. These will be treated separately.

Spanish has many 'radical changing verbs' where changes are made to the stressed vowel of the stem, although the endings of these verbs are perfectly normal. These verbs will be dealt with in a separate section.

All newly coined verbs automatically go into the first conjugation and adopt its endings and forms, e.g. **informatizar** (to computerize).

A. THE TENSES OF THE INDICATIVE— THE SIMPLE TENSES

Tenses may be either simple—consisting of one word only—or compound, where an auxiliary verb is used with a participle of the main verb.

1. The present tense

The stem for the present tense of the verb is found by removing the endings **-ar**, **-er** or **-ir** from the infinitive. The present tense itself is then formed by adding the following endings to the stem:

1st conjugation	**-o, -as, -a, -amos, -áis, -an**
2nd conjugation	**-o, -es, -e, -emos, -éis, -en**
3rd conjugation	**-o, -es, -e, -imos, -ís, -en**

cant-ar	beb-er	recib-ir
canto	bebo	recibo
cantas	bebes	recibes
canta	bebe	recibe
cantamos	bebemos	recibimos
cantáis	bebéis	recibís
cantan	beben	reciben

a) Irregularities in the present tense

For **ser** and **estar**, and the irregular verbs **dar** and **ir**, see pages 196–197. For radical changing verbs see pages 199–200.

b) First conjugation verbs ending in **-iar** and **-uar**

Most of these verbs have the spoken accent and also a written accent on the final **i** and **u** of the stem in all but the first and second persons plural:

enviar	continuar
envío	continúo
envías	continúas
envía	continúa
enviamos	continuamos
enviáis	continuáis
envían	continúan

The commonest exceptions are the verbs **cambiar** (to change) and **averiguar** (to ascertain).

c) Second conjugation verbs ending in **-ecer**

The ending of the first person singular is **-ezco**. All other forms are regular:

parecer	parezco, pareces ...
crecer	crezco, creces ...

d) Third conjugation verbs ending in **-uir**, and the verb **oír**

These verbs add **y** to the stem *unless* the stem is followed by a stressed **i**, i.e. in all but the first and second persons plural. Note that **oír** also has an irregular first person singular (see below):

construir	oír
construyo	oigo
construyes	oyes
construye	oye
construimos	oímos
construís	oís
construyen	oyen

e) Third conjugation verbs ending in **-ucir**

The ending of the first person singular is **-uzco**. All other forms are regular:

conducir	conduzco, conduces ...
producir	produzco, produces ...

f) Second and third conjugation verbs whose stem ends in **c** or **g**

Such verbs change the **c** to **z** and the **g** to **j** in the first person singular. All other forms are regular:

vencer	venzo, vences ...
esparcir	esparzo, esparces ...

| escoger | escojo, escoges ... |
| rugir | rujo, ruges ... |

g) Third conjugation verbs whose stem ends in **qu** or **gu**

Such verbs change the **qu** to **c** and the **gu** to **g** in the first person singular. All other forms are regular:

| delinquir | delinco, delinques ... |
| distinguir | distingo, distingues ... |

h) Third conjugation verbs whose infinitive ends in **-güir**

These verbs drop the dieresis except in the first and second persons plural:

| argüir | arguyo, arguyes, arguye, |
| | argüimos, argüís, arguyen |

i) Verbs with an irregular first person singular

The following verbs have largely unpredictable irregularities in the first person singular:

caber	(to fit)	quepo
caer	(to fall)	caigo
conocer	(to know)	conozco
decir	(to say)	digo
estar	(to be)	estoy
hacer	(to do/make)	hago
ir	(to go)	voy
oír	(to hear)	oigo
saber	(to know)	sé
salir	(to go out/leave)	salgo
ser	(to be)	soy
tener	(to have)	tengo
traer	(to bring)	traigo
valer	(to be worth)	valgo
venir	(to come)	vengo

Any compound form of these verbs shares the same irregularities.

| contradecir | (to contradict) | contradigo |
| obtener | (to obtain) | obtengo |

Note that **satisfacer** behaves as a compound of **hacer**:

| satisfacer | (to satisfy) | satisfago |

2. The future tense

The future tense of all conjugations is formed by adding the following endings to the infinitive of the verb, irrespective of its conjugation:

-é, -ás, -á, -emos, -éis, -án

cantaré	beberé	recibiré
cantarás	beberás	recibirás
cantará	beberá	recibirá
cantaremos	beberemos	recibiremos
cantaréis	beberéis	recibiréis
cantarán	beberán	recibirán

Irregularities in the future tense

A number of verbs add these endings to an irregular stem:

caber	(to fit)	cabré
decir	(to say)	diré
haber	(to have)	habré
hacer	(to do/make)	haré
poder	(to be able)	podré
poner	(to put)	pondré
querer	(to want)	querré
saber	(to know)	sabré
salir	(to go out/leave)	saldré
tener	(to have)	tendré
valer	(to be worth)	valdrá
venir	(to come)	vendré

Again, any compounds share the same irregularities:

deshacer	(to undo)	desharé
convenir	(to agree/suit)	convendré

3. The imperfect tense

The imperfect tense is formed by adding the following endings to the stem of the infinitive:

1st conjugation	-aba, -abas, -aba, -ábamos, -abais, -aban
2nd & 3rd conjugations	-ía, -ías, -ía, -íamos, -íais, -ían

cantaba	bebía	recibía
cantabas	bebías	recibías
cantaba	bebía	recibía
cantábamos	bebíamos	recibíamos
cantabais	bebíais	recibíais
cantaban	bebían	recibían

Irregularities in the imperfect tense

There are only three irregular imperfects in Spanish:

ser	ir	ver
era	iba	veía
eras	ibas	veías
era	iba	veía

éramos	íbamos	veíamos
erais	ibais	veíais
eran	iban	veían

4. The preterite tense

The preterite is formed by adding the following endings to the stem of the infinitive:

1st conjugation	**-é, -aste, -ó, amos, -asteis, -aron**
2nd & 3rd conjugations	**-í, -iste, -ió, -imos, -isteis, -ieron**

canté	bebí	recibí
cantaste	bebiste	recibiste
cantó	bebió	recibió
cantamos	bebimos	recibimos
cantasteis	bebisteis	recibisteis
cantaron	bebieron	recibieron

Irregularities in the preterite tense

a) The so-called **pretérito grave**

This group comprises a sizeable number of mostly second and third conjugation verbs which all add the following endings to irregular stems:

-e, -iste, -o, -imos, -isteis, -ieron

Note in particular that the first and third person singular endings are not stressed (the term **grave** in **pretérito grave** means 'stressed on the *next to last* syllable').

If the stem itself ends in **j**, the third person plural ending is shortened to **-eron**.

andar	anduve, anduviste, anduvo, anduvimos, anduvisteis, anduvieron
caber	cupe, cupiste, cupo, cupimos, cupisteis, cupieron
decir	dije, dijiste, dijo, dijimos, dijisteis, dijeron
estar	estuve, estuviste, estuvo, estuvimos, estuvisteis, estuvieron
haber	hube, hubiste, hubo, hubimos, hubisteis, hubieron
hacer	hice, hiziste, hizo, hicimos, hicisteis, hicieron
poder	pude, pudiste, pudo, pudimos, pudisteis, pudieron
poner	puse, pusiste, puso, pusimos, pusisteis, pusieron
querer	quise, quisiste, quiso, quisimos, quisisteis, quisieron
tener	tuve, tuviste, tuvo, tuvimos, tuvisteis, tuvieron
traer	traje, trajiste, trajo, trajimos, trajisteis, trajeron
saber	supe, supiste, supo, supimos, supisteis, supieron
venir	vine, viniste, vino, vinimos, vinisteis, vinieron

All compounds of these verbs share the same irregularities:

contraer	contraje . . .
componer	compuse . . .

This group also comprises all verbs ending in **-ucir**, with the exception of **lucir**, which is regular. Their stem for the preterite ends in **uj**:

producir	produje, produjiste, produjo, produjimos, produjisteis, produjeron

b) Other verbs

The following verbs are also irregular:

dar	di, diste, dio, dimos, disteis, dieron
ir	fui, fuiste, fue, fuimos, fuisteis, fueron
ser	fui, fuiste, fue, fuimos, fuisteis, fueron
ver	vi, viste, vio, vimos, visteis, vieron

As can be seen, the preterites of **ir** and **ser** are identical. However, the context always indicates clearly which one is involved.

c) Spelling changes

First conjugation verbs whose stems end in **c** or **g** change these to **qu** and **gu** in the first person singular of the preterite. All other forms are regular:

explicar	expliqué, explicaste . . .
llegar	llegué, llegaste . . .

Verbs ending in **-aer**, **-eer**, **-oer** and **-uir**

In these verbs, the **i** of the third person singular and plural ending change to **y**. All other forms are regular:

caer	cayó	cayeron
construir	construyó	construyeron
leer	leyó	leyeron
roer	royó	royeron

oír also belongs to this group:

oír	oyó	oyeron

Third conjugation verbs ending in **-güir** drop the dieresis in the third persons singular and plural:

argüir	argüí, argüiste, arguyó, argüimos, argüisteis, arguyeron

Second and third conjugation verbs whose stem ends in **ñ** drop the **i** from the third person singular and plural endings:

gruñir	gruñó	gruñeron
tañer	tañó	tañeron

5. The conditional

The conditional is formed for all conjugations by adding the
following endings to the infinitive of the verb:

-ía, -ías, -ía, -íamos, -íais, -ían

cantaría	bebería	recibiría
cantarías	beberías	recibirías
cantaría	bebería	recibiría
cantaríamos	beberíamos	recibiríamos
cantaríais	beberíais	recibiríais
cantarían	beberían	recibirían

Irregularities in the conditional

Any verb with an irregular stem in the future uses the same
stem for the formation of the conditional (see page 174):

hacer	haría
venir	vendría

and so on.

B. COMPOUND TENSES

Compound tenses are formed by using an auxiliary verb with
either the present or the past participle.

1. The present participle

a) The regular forms

The present participle is formed by adding the following endings
to the stem of the infinitive:

1st conjugation	**-ando**
2nd & 3rd conjugations	**-iendo**

b) Irregular present participles

Verbs ending in **-aer**, **-eer**, **-oer** and **-uir**, and the verb **oír**.

In these verbs the **i** of the ending is changed to **y**:

caer	cayendo
construir	construyendo
creer	creyendo
oír	oyendo
roer	royendo

Verbs ending in **-güir** drop the dieresis in the present participle:

argüir	arguyendo

Second and third conjugation verbs whose stem ends in **ñ** drop the **i** from the ending:

gruñir	**gruñendo**
tañer	**tañendo**

Third conjugation radical changing verbs of groups 3, 4 and 5 also have irregular present participles (see pages 188–190):

dormir	**durmiendo**
pedir	**pidiendo**
sentir	**sintiendo**

2. The past participle

a) The regular forms

To form the past participle of a regular verb remove the infinitive ending and add:

1st conjugation	**-ado**	**cantado**
2nd & 3rd conjugations	**-ido**	**bebido, recibido**

b) Irregular past participles

Some verbs have irregular past participles. The most common are:

abrir (to open)	**abierto** (opened)
cubrir (to cover)	**cubierto** (covered)
decir (to say)	**dicho** (said)
escribir (to write)	**escrito** (written)
hacer (to make/to do)	**hecho** (made/done)
morir (to die)	**muerto** (dead)
poner (to put)	**puesto** (put)
resolver (to solve)	**resuelto** (solved)
ver (to see)	**visto** (seen)
volver(to return)	**vuelto** (returned)

Compounds of these verbs have the same irregularities in their past participles, e.g.:

descubrir (to discover)	**descubierto** (discovered)
describir (to describe)	**descrito** (described)

The verb **satisfacer** behaves as a compound of **hacer**:

satisfacer (to satisfy)	**satisfecho** (satisfied)

3. The progressive forms of the tenses

A progressive form of any tense can be formed by using **estar** (or one of an associated group of verbs) with the present participle. For the full conjugation of **estar**, see page 197:

estamos trabajando
we are working

yo estaba estudiando cuando Juan entró
I was studying when Juan came in

For a full discussion of the progressive tenses, see pages 60–62.

4. The perfect tense

The compound past tenses are formed with the appropriate tense of the verb **haber** together with the past participle of the verb. For the full conjugation of **haber**, see page 198.

The perfect tense is formed by using the present tense of **haber** with the past participle of the main verb:

he cantado	he bebido	he recibido
has cantado	has bebido	has recibido
ha cantado	ha bebido	ha recibido
hemos cantado	hemos bebido	hemos recibido
habéis cantado	habéis bebido	habéis recibido
han cantado	han bebido	han recibido

5. The pluperfect tense

The pluperfect tense is formed by using the imperfect of **haber** with the past participle of the main verb:

había cantado	había lebido	había recibido
habías cantado	habías bebido	habías recibido
había cantado	había bebido	había recibido
habíamos cantado	habíamos bebido	habíamos recibido
habíais cantado	habíais bebido	habíais recibido
habían cantado	habían bebido	habían recibido

6. The future perfect tense

The future perfect tense is formed by using the future of **haber** with the past participle of the main verb:

habré cantado	habré bebido	habré recibido
habrás cantado	habrás bebido	habrás recibido
habrá cantado	habrá bebido	habrá recibido
habremos cantado	habremos bebido	habremos recibido
habréis cantado	habréis bebido	habréis recibido
habrán cantado	habrán bebido	habrán recibido

7. The past anterior tense

The past anterior tense is formed by using the preterite of **haber** with the past participle of the main verb:

hube cantado	hube bebido	hube recibido
hubiste cantado	hubiste bebido	hubiste recibido

hubo cantado	hubo bebido	hubo recibido
hubimos cantado	hubimos bebido	hubimos recibido
hubisteis cantado	hubisteis bebido	hubisteis recibido
hubieron cantado	hubieron bebido	hubieron recibido

8. The conditional perfect

The conditional perfect is formed by using the conditional of **haber** with the past participle of the main verb:

habría cantado	habría bebido	habría recibido
habrías cantado	habrías bebido	habrías recibido
habría cantado	habría bebido	habría recibido
habríamos cantado	habríamos bebido	habríamos recibido
habríais cantado	habríais bebido	habríais recibido
habrían cantado	habrían bebido	habrían recibido

C. THE TENSES OF THE SUBJUNCTIVE MOOD

1. The present subjunctive

With the exception of a few irregular verbs (**estar, ser, ir, dar**) the stem for the present subjunctive of a verb is found by removing the **-o** from the ending of the first personal singular of the present tense. The subjunctive is then formed by adding the following endings to that stem.

1st conjugation	-e, -es, -e, -emos, -éis, -en
2nd & 3rd conjugations	-a, -as, -a, -amos, -áis, -an

cant-o	beb-o	recib-o
cante	beba	reciba
cantes	bebas	recibas
cante	beba	reciba
cantemos	bebamos	recibamos
cantéis	bebáis	recibáis
canten	beban	reciban

Irregularities in the present subjunctive

For radical changing verbs see pages 184–191.

a) Verbs in **-iar** and **-uar**

Such verbs have the same pattern of accentuation in the subjunctive as they do in the indicative, i.e. a written accent on the **i** or **u** of the stem in all but the first and second persons plural:

enviar	envíe, envíes, envíe, enviemos, enviéis, envíen
continuar	continúe, continúes, continúe, continuemos, continuéis, continúen

b) *Irregular stems*

Since the stem of the subjunctive is based on the first person singular of the indicative, any irregularities there appear throughout the present subjunctive, for example:

infinitive	*1st pers pres*	*subjunctive*
decir	**digo**	**diga, digas, diga, digamos, digáis, digan**
coger	**cojo**	**coja, cojas, coja, cojamos, cojáis, cojan**
parecer	**parezco**	**parezca, parezcas, parezca, parezcamos, parezcáis, parezcan**
poner	**pongo**	**ponga, pongas, ponga, pongamos, pongáis, pongan**
vencer	**venzo**	**venza, venzas, venza, venzamos, venzáis, venzan**

c) *Spelling changes*

First conjugation verbs whose stems end in **c** or **g** change these to **qu** and **gu** throughout the present subjunctive.

buscar	**busque, busques, busque, busquemos, busquéis, busquen**
llegar	**llegue, llegues, llegue, lleguemos, lleguemos, lleguen**

First conjugation verbs ending in **-guar** require a dieresis throughout the present subjunctive.

averiguar	**averigüe, averigües, averigüe, averigüemos, averigüéis, averigüen**

2. The imperfect subjunctive

The stem for the imperfect subjunctive is found by removing the ending **-ron** from the third person plural of the preterite of the verb. The imperfect subjunctive has two possible forms, formed by adding the following endings to that stem:

1st conjugation	-ara, -aras, -ara, -áramos, -arais -aran -ase, -ases, -ase, -ásemos, -aseis, -asen
2nd & 3rd conjugations	-iera, -ieras, -iera, -iéramos, -ierais, -ieran -iese, -ieses, -iese, -iésemos, -ieseis, -iesen

cantara/cantase	bebiera/bebiese
cantaras/cantases	bebieras/bebieses
cantara/cantase	bebiera/bebiese
cantáramos/cantásemos	bebiéramos/bebiésemos
cantárais/cantaseis	bebiéramos/bebiésemos
cantaran/cantasen	bebieran/bebiesen

recibiera/recibiese
recibieras/recibieses
recibiera/recibiese
recibiéramos/recibiésemos
recibierais/recibieseis
recibieran/recibiesen

In general, the first form of each pair is more common in spoken Spanish.

Verbs whose preterites are irregular display the same irregularity in the imperfect subjunctive:

infinitive	*preterite*	*imperfect subjunctive*
decir	dijeron	dijera/dijese
tener	tuvieron	tuviera/tuviese
venir	vinieron	viniera/viniese

Compounds of these verbs display the same irregularities:

convenir	conviniera/conviniese
obtener	obtuviera/obtuviese

3. The perfect subjunctive

The perfect tense of the subjunctive is formed by using the present subjunctive of **haber** with the past participle of the main verb:

haya cantado	haya bebido	haya recibido
hayas cantado	hayas bebido	hayas recibido
haya cantado	haya bebido	haya recibido
hayamos cantado	hayamos bebido	hayamos recibido
hayáis cantado	hayáis bebido	hayáis recibido
hayan cantado	hayan bebido	hayan recibido

4. The pluperfect subjunctive

The pluperfect of the subjunctive is formed by using the imperfect subjunctive of **haber** with the past participle of the main verb:

hubiera cantado	hubiera bebido	hubiera recibido
hubieras cantado	hubieras bebido	hubieras recibido
hubiera cantado	hubiera bebido	hubiera recibido

hubiéramos cantado	hubiéramos bebido	hubiéramos recibido
hubierais cantado	hubierais bebido	hubierais recibido
hubieran cantado	hubieran bebido	hubieran recibido
hubiese cantado	hubiese bebido	hubiese recibido
hubieses cantado	hubieses bebido	hubieses recibido
hubiese cantado	hubiese bebido	hubiese recibido
hubiésemos cantado	hubiésemos bebido	hubiésemos recibido
hubieseis cantado	hubieseis bebido	hubieseis recibido
hubiesen cantado	hubiesen bebido	hubiesen recibido

5. The imperative

The imperative proper exists only for the **tú** and **vosotros** forms of the verb, and is used *only* in positive commands. It is formed as follows:

tú	Remove the **s** from the second person singular of the verb. This applies for all conjugations.
vosotros	First and second conjugations: remove the **is** from the second person plural of the verb and replace it by **d**. Third conjugation: remove the **s** from the second person plural of the verb and replace it by **d**.

hablar	habla	hablad
comer	come	comed
escribir	escribe	escribid

Note that, since the **tú** form is based on the second person singular of the verb, any radical changes will also be present in the singular, but not in the plural from of the imperative:

cerrar	cierra	cerrad
torcer	tuerce	torced
pedir	pide	pedid

There are a number of irregular imperatives in the **tú** form:

decir	di	decid
hacer	haz	haced
ir	ve	id
poner	pon	poned
salir	sal	salid
ser	sé	**sed** (also irregular in plural)
tener	ten	tened
valer	val	valed
venir	ven	venid

Commands addressed to all other persons—**Vd., Vds.**, third and first person commands—and *all* negative commands are formed using the subjunctive. See pages 56–57 for details.

D. THE RADICAL CHANGING VERBS

Some verbs have spelling changes to their stem when the latter is stressed. The endings are not affected unless the verb itself is irregular.

1. e changes to **ie** (first and second conjugations only)

The commonest of these verbs are:

acertar	to guess correctly
alentar	to encourage
apretar	to squeeze
ascender	to go up, come to
atender	to attend to
aterrar	to terrify
atravesar	to cross
calentar	to heat
cerrar	to close
comenzar	to begin
concertar	to agree to
condescender	to condescend
confesar	to confess
defender	to defend
desalentar	to discourage
desatender	to disregard
descender	to come down
desconcertar	to disconcert
despertar	to waken
desplegar	to unfold
discernir	to discern
empezar	to begin
encender	to light, switch on
encerrar	to enclose
encomendar	to entrust
entender	to understand
enterrar	to bury
extender	to extend
fregar	to scrub
gobernar	to govern
helar	to freeze
manifestar	to show
merendar	to have a snack
negar	to deny
nevar	to snow
pensar	to think
perder	to lose
quebrar	to break
recomendar	to recommend

regar	to irrigate
reventar	to burst
sembrar	to sow
sentarse	to sit
sosegar	to calm
temblar	to tremble
*tener	to have
tender	to stretch out
tentar	to attempt
tropezar	to stumble
verter	to pour

The change occurs in the present indicative and the present subjunctive only, wherever the **e** is stressed, i.e. the three persons of the singular and the third person plural:

PRESENT INDICATIVE	PRESENT SUBJUNCTIVE
atravieso	**atraviese**
atraviesas	**atravieses**
atraviesa	**atraviese**
atravesamos	**atravesemos**
atravesáis	**atraveséis**
atraviesan	**atraviesen**

Note that if the **e** is the first letter in the word, it changes to **ye** and not **ie**:

errar	to wander	**yerro, yerras, yerra, erramos, erráis, yerran**

*tener has an irregular first person singular: **tengo**

The subjunctive of **tener** is based on this irregular first person singular:

tenga, tengas, tenga, tengamos, tengáis, tengan

2. **o** changes to **ue** (first and second conjugations only)

The commonest verbs in this group are:

absolver	to absolve
acordarse	to remember
acostarse	to go to bed
almorzar	to have lunch
apostar	to bet
aprobar	to approve
avergonzarse	to be ashamed
cocer	to cook
colarse	to slip in
colgar	to hang
comprobar	to check

concordar	to agree
conmover	to move
consolar	to console
contar	to count, tell
costar	to cost
demostrar	to demonstrate
desaprobar	to disapprove
descolgar	to take down
descontar	to deduct
desenvolverse	to get by
despoblar	to depopulate
devolver	to give back
disolver	to dissolve
doler	to hurt
encontrar	to meet, find
envolver	to wrap
esforzarse	to endeavor
forzar	to force
holgar	to be idle
*jugar	to play
llover	to rain
moler	to grind
morder	to bite
mostrar	to show
mover	to move
**oler	to smell
probar	to try, taste
promover	to promote
recordar	to remember
renovar	to renew
resolver	to resolve
resollar	to wheeze
resonar	to resound
revolver	to revolve
rodar	to prowl
rogar	to ask
soldar	to weld
soler	to be in the habit of
soltar	to let go
sonar	to ring, sound
soñar	to dream
torcer	to twist, turn
tostar	to toast
trocar	to exchange
tronar	to thunder
volar	to fly
volcar	to tip over
volver	to return

The pattern of change is identical to that of group 1:

PRESENT INDICATIVE	PRESENT SUBJUNCTIVE
vuelvo	**vuelva**
vuelves	**vuelvas**
vuelve	**vuelva**
volvemos	**volvamos**
volvéis	**volváis**
vuelven	**vuelvan**

***jugar**: the **u** changes to **ue** when stressed: **juego**.

****oler**: **h** is added to all forms where the change occurs: **huele** etc.

3. **e** changes to **ie** and **i** (third conjugation only)

The commonest verbs in this group are:

adherir	to join
***adquirir**	to acquire
advertir	to notice
arrepentirse	to repent
asentir	to agree
conferir	to confer
consentir	to agree
convertir	to convert
digerir	to digest
divertir	to amuse
****erguir**	to raise
herir	to wound
hervir	to boil
inferir	to infer
***inquirir**	to inquire into
invertir	to invest
mentir	to tell lies
pervertir	to pervert
preferir	to prefer
presentir	to foresee
proferir	to utter
referir	to refer
requerir	to require
resentirse	to resent
sentir	to feel
subvertir	to subvert
sugerir	to suggest
transferir	to transfer
*****venir**	to come

The tenses affected are:

When stressed, **e** changes to **ie** in the present indicative, present subjunctive, and imperative singular.

Also, unstressed **e** changes to **i** in:

- the 1st and 2nd persons plural of the present subjunctive
- the present participle
- the 3rd persons singular and plural of the preterite
- all of the imperfect subjunctive:

PRESENT	PRETERITE
siento	**sentí**
sientes	**sentiste**
siente	**sintió**
sentimos	**sentimos**
sentís	**sentisteis**
sienten	**sintieron**

PRESENT SUBJUNCTIVE	IMPERFECT SUBJUNCTIVE
sienta	**sintiera/sintiese**
sientas	**sintieras/sintieses**
sienta	**sintiera/sintiese**
sintamos	**sintiéramos/sintiéseis**
sintáis	**sintierais/sintieseis**
sientan	**sintieran/sintieses**

IMPERATIVE	PRESENT PARTICIPLE
siente	**sintiendo**

*In the case of **adquirir** and **inquirir** it is the **i** of the stem which changes to **ie**.

When stressed, the **e of **erguir** changes to **ye** and not **ie**:

yergo, yergues, yergue, erguimos, erguís, yerguen

***venir** has an irregular first person singular: **vengo**

The subjunctive of **venir** is based on this irregular first person singular:

venga, vengas, venga, vengamos, vengáis, vengan

4. **e** changes to **i** (third conjugation only)

The commonest verbs in this group are:

colegir	to collect
competir	to compete
concebir	to design
conseguir	to manage
corregir	to correct
derretir	to melt
despedir	to say goodbye
elegir	to elect
expedir	to dispatch

gemir	to groan
impedir	to prevent
invertir	to invest
medir	to measure
pedir	to ask for
perseguir	to persecute
proseguir	to continue
regir	to govern
rendir	to yield
repetir	to repeat
seguir	to follow
servir	to serve
vestir	to dress

When stressed, **e** changes to **i** in the present indicative, present subjunctive, and imperative singular.

Also, unstressed **e** changes to **i** in:

– the 1st and 2nd persons plural of the present subjunctive
– the present participle
– the 3rd persons singular and plural of the preterite
– all of the imperfect subjunctive:

PRESENT	PRETERITE
pido	**pedí**
pides	**pediste**
pide	**pidió**
pedimos	**pedimos**
pedís	**pedisteis**
piden	**pidieron**

PRESENT SUBJUNCTIVE	IMPERFECT SUBJUNCTIVE
pida	**pidiera/pidiese**
pidas	**pidieras/pidieses**
pida	**pidiera/pidiese**
pidamos	**pidiéramos/pidiésemos**
pidáis	**pidiéramos/pidiésemos**
pidan	**pidieran/pidiesen**

IMPERATIVE	PRESENT PARTICIPLE
pide	**pidiendo**

Verbs in this group which end in **-eír** and **-eñir** make an additional change: if the ending begins with an unstressed **i**, this **i** is dropped if it comes immediately after the **ñ** or **i** of the stem. This occurs only in the present participle, the third persons singular and plural of the preterite, and in the imperfect subjunctive.

The commonest verbs in this group are:

ceñir	to fit closely
desteñir	to fade
freír	to fry
reír	to laugh
reñir	to scold
sonreír	to smile
teñir	to dye

reír	ceñir
riendo	ciñendo
rio	ciñó
rieron	ciñeron

5. **o changes to ue and u (third conjugation only)**

The pattern of changes is identical to that of group 3 above. In other words:

When stressed, **o** changes to **ue** in the present indicative, present subjunctive, and imperative singular.

Unstressed **o** changes to **u** in:

- the 1st and 2nd persons plural of the present subjunctive
- the present participle
- the 3rd persons singular and plural of the preterite
- all of the imperfect subjunctive.

The commonest verbs in this group are

| **dormir** | to sleep | **morir** | to die |

and their compounds.

PRESENT	PRETERITE
duermo	dormí
duermes	dormiste
duerme	durmió
dormimos	dormimos
dormís	dormisteis
duermen	durmieron

PRESENT SUBJUNCTIVE	IMPERFECT SUBJUNCTIVE
duerma	durmiera/durmiese
duermas	durmieras/durmieses
duerma	durmiera/durmiese
durmamos	durmiéramos/durmiésemos
durmáis	durmierais/durmieseis
duerman	durmieran/durmiesen

IMPERATIVE	PRESENT PARTICIPLE
duerme	durmiendo

E. CONJUGATION TABLES

The following verbs provide the main patterns of conjugation, including the conjugation of the most common irregular verbs:

-ar verb	*(see rest of section 15)*	HABLAR
-er verb	*(see rest of section 15)*	COMER
-ir verb	*(see rest of section 15)*	VIVIR
Reflexive verbs	*(see page 54)*	BAÑARSE
Auxiliaries:	*(see pages 79–82)*	SER
	(see pages 79–82)	ESTAR
	(see pages 85–86)	HABER
Common irregular verbs:		DAR
		IR
		TENER
		VENIR

'Harrap's Spanish Verbs', a fully comprehensive list of Spanish verbs and their conjugations, is also available in this series.

HABLAR
to speak

PRESENT	IMPERFECT	FUTURE
1. hablo	hablaba	hablaré
2. hablas	hablabas	hablarás
3. habla	hablaba	hablará
1. hablamos	hablábamos	hablaremos
2. habláis	hablabais	hablaréis
3. hablan	hablaban	hablarán

PRETERITE	PERFECT	PLUPERFECT
1. hablé	he hablado	había hablado
2. hablaste	has hablado	habías hablado
3. habló	ha hablado	había hablado
1. hablamos	hemos hablado	habíamos hablado
2. hablasteis	habéis hablado	habíais hablado
3. hablaron	han hablado	habían hablado

PAST ANTERIOR	FUTURE PERFECT
hube hablado etc.	habré hablado etc.

CONDITIONAL		*IMPERATIVE*
PRESENT	**PAST**	
1. hablaría	habría hablado	
2. hablarías	habrías hablado	(tú) habla
3. hablaría	habría hablado	(Vd) hable
1. hablaríamos	habríamos hablado	(nosotros) hablemos
2. hablaríais	habríais hablado	(vosotros) hablad
3. hablarían	habrían hablado	(Vds) hablen

SUBJUNCTIVE

PRESENT	IMPERFECT	PLUPERFECT
1. hable	habl-ara/ase	hubiera hablado
2. hables	habl-aras/ases	hubieras hablado
3. hable	habl-ara/ase	hubiera hablado
1. hablemos	habl-áramos/ásemos	hubiéramos hablado
2. habléis	habl-arais/aseis	hubierais hablado
3. hablen	habl-aran/asen	hubieran hablado

PERFECT   haya hablado etc.

INFINITIVE	*PARTICIPLE*
PRESENT	**PRESENT**
hablar	hablando
PAST	**PAST**
haber hablado	hablado

COMER
to eat

PRESENT	IMPERFECT	FUTURE
1. como	comía	comeré
2. comes	comías	comerás
3. come	comía	comerá
1. comemos	comíamos	comeremos
2. coméis	comíais	comeréis
3. comen	comían	comerán

PRETERITE	PERFECT	PLUPERFECT
1. comí	he comido	había comido
2. comiste	has comido	habías comido
3. comió	ha comido	había comido
1. comimos	hemos comido	habíamos comido
2. comisteis	habéis comido	habíais comido
3. comieron	han comido	habían comido

PAST ANTERIOR	FUTURE PERFECT
hube comido etc.	habré comido etc.

CONDITIONAL		IMPERATIVE
PRESENT	PAST	
1. comería	habría comido	
2. comerías	habrías comido	(tú) come
3. comería	habría comido	(Vd) coma
1. comeríamos	habríamos comido	(nosotros) comamos
2. comeríais	habríais comido	(vosotros) comed
3. comerían	habrían comido	(Vds) coman

SUBJUNCTIVE

PRESENT	IMPERFECT	PLUPERFECT
1. coma	com-iera/iese	hubiera comido
2. comas	com-ieras/ieses	hubieras comido
3. coma	com-iera/iese	hubiera comido
1. comamos	com-iéramos/iésemos	hubiéramos comido
2. comáis	com-ierais/ieseis	hubierais comido
3. coman	com-ieran/iesen	hubieran comido

PERFECT   haya comido etc.

INFINITIVE	PARTICIPLE
PRESENT	PRESENT
comer	comiendo
PAST	PAST
haber comido	comido

VIVIR
to live

PRESENT	IMPERFECT	FUTURE
1. vivo	vivía	viviré
2. vives	vivías	vivirás
3. vive	vivía	vivirá
1. vivimos	vivíamos	viviremos
2. vivís	vivíais	viviréis
3. viven	vivían	vivirán

PRETERITE	PERFECT	PLUPERFECT
1. viví	he vivido	había vivido
2. viviste	has vivido	habías vivido
3. vivió	ha vivido	había vivido
1. vivimos	hemos vivido	habíamos vivido
2. vivisteis	habéis vivido	habíais vivido
3. vivieron	han vivido	habían vivido

PAST ANTERIOR	FUTURE PERFECT
hube vivido etc.	habré vivido etc.

CONDITIONAL		IMPERATIVE
PRESENT	PAST	
1. viviría	habría vivido	
2. vivirías	habrías vivido	(tú) vive
3. viviría	habría vivido	(Vd) viva
1. viviríamos	habríamos vivido	(nosotros) vivamos
2. viviríais	habríais vivido	(vosotros) vivid
3. vivirían	habrían vivido	(Vds) vivan

SUBJUNCTIVE

PRESENT	IMPERFECT	PLUPERFECT
1. viva	viv-iera/iese	hubiera vivido
2. vivas	viv-ieras/ieses	hubieras vivido
3. viva	viv-iera/iese	hubiera vivido
1. vivamos	viv-iéramos/iésemos	hubiéramos vivido
2. viváis	viv-ierais/ieseis	hubierais vivido
3. vivan	viv-ieran/iesen	hubieran vivido

PERFECT	haya vivido etc.

INFINITIVE	PARTICIPLE
PRESENT	PRESENT
vivir	viviendo
PAST	PAST
haber vivido	vivido

BAÑARSE
to take a bath

PRESENT	IMPERFECT	FUTURE
1. me baño	me bañaba	me bañaré
2. te bañas	te bañabas	te bañarás
3. se bana	se bañaba	se bañará
1. nos bañamos	nos bañábamos	nos bañaremos
2. os bañáis	os bañabais	os bañaréis
3. se bañan	se bañaban	se bañarán

PRETERITE	PERFECT	PLUPERFECT
1. me bañé	me he bañado	me había bañado
2. te bañaste	te has bañado	te habías bañado
3. se bañó	se ha bañado	se había bañado
1. nos bañamos	nos hemos bañado	nos habíamos bañado
2. os bañasteis	os habéis bañado	os habíais bañado
3. se bañaron	se han bañado	se habían bañado

PAST ANTERIOR	FUTURE PERFECT
me hube bañado etc.	me habré bañado etc.

CONDITIONAL		*IMPERATIVE*
PRESENT	**PAST**	
1. me bañaría	me habría bañado	
2. te bañarías	te habrías bañado	(tú) báñate
3. se bañaría	se habría bañado	(Vd) báñense
1. nos bañaríamos	nos habríamos bañado	(nosotros) bañémonos
2. os bañaríais	os habríais bañado	(vosotros) bañaos
3. se bañarían	se habrían bañado	(Vds) báñense

SUBJUNCTIVE		
PRESENT	**IMPERFECT**	**PLUPERFECT**
1. me bañe	me bañ-ara/ase	me hubiera bañado
2. te bañes	te bañ-aras/ases	te hubieras bañado
3. se bañe	se bañ-ara/ase	se hubiera bañado
1. nos bañemos	nos bañ-áramos/ásemos	nos hubiéramos bañado
2. os bañéis	os bañ-arais/aseis	os hubierais bañado
3. se bañen	se bañ-aran/asen	se hubieran bañado

PERFECT   me haya bañado etc.

INFINITIVE	*PARTICIPLE*
PRESENT	**PRESENT**
bañarse	bañándose
PAST	**PAST**
haberse bañado	bañado

SER
to be

PRESENT	IMPERFECT	FUTURE
1. soy	era	seré
2. eres	eras	serás
3. es	era	será
1. somos	éramos	seremos
2. sois	erais	seréis
3. son	eran	serán

PRETERITE	PERFECT	PLUPERFECT
1. fui	he sido	había sido
2. fuiste	has sido	habías sido
3. fue	ha sido	había sido
1. fuimos	hemos sido	habíamos sido
2. fuisteis	habéis sido	habíais sido
3. fueron	han sido	habían sido

PAST ANTERIOR	FUTURE PERFECT
hube sido etc.	habré sido etc.

CONDITIONAL		IMPERATIVE
PRESENT	PAST	
1. sería	habría sido	
2. serías	habrías sido	(tú) sé
3. sería	habría sido	(Vd) sea
1. seríamos	habríamos sido	(nosotros) seamos
2. seríais	habríais sido	(vosotros) sed
3. serían	habrían sido	(Vds) sean

SUBJUNCTIVE

PRESENT	IMPERFECT	PLUPERFECT
1. sea	fu-era/ese	hubiera sido
2. seas	fu-eras/eses	hubieras sido
3. sea	fu-era/ese	hubiera sido
1. seamos	fu-éramos/ésemos	hubiéramos sido
2. seáis	fu-erais/eseis	hubierais sido
3. sean	fu-eran/esen	hubieran sido

PERFECT   haya sido etc.

INFINITIVE	PARTICIPLE
PRESENT	PRESENT
ser	siendo
PAST	PAST
haber sido	sido

ESTAR
to be

PRESENT	IMPERFECT	FUTURE
1. estoy	estaba	estaré
2. estás	estabas	estarás
3. está	estaba	estará
1. estamos	estábamos	estaremos
2. estáis	estabais	estaréis
3. están	estaban	estarán

PRETERITE	PERFECT	PLUPERFECT
1. estuve	he estado	había estado
2. estuviste	has estado	habías estado
3. estuvo	ha estado	había estado
1. estuvimos	hemos estado	habíamos estado
2. estuvisteis	habéis estado	habíais estado
3. estuvieron	han estado	habían estado

PAST ANTERIOR	FUTURE PERFECT
hube estado etc.	habré estado etc.

CONDITIONAL		*IMPERATIVE*
PRESENT	**PAST**	
1. estaría	habría estado	
2. estarías	habrías estado	(tú) está
3. estaría	habría estado	(Vd) esté
1. estaríamos	habríamos estado	(nosotros) estemos
2. estaríais	habríais estado	(vosotros) estad
3. estarían	habrían estado	(Vds) estén

SUBJUNCTIVE

PRESENT	IMPERFECT	PLUPERFECT
1. esté	estuv-iera/iese	hubiera estado
2. estés	estuv-ieras/ieses	hubieras estado
3. esté	estuv-iera/iese	hubiera estado
1. estemos	estuv-iéramos/iésemos	hubiéramos estado
2. estéis	estuv-ierais/ieseis	hubierais estado
3. estén	estuv-ieran/iesen	hubieran estado

PERFECT   haya estado etc.

INFINITIVE	*PARTICIPLE*
PRESENT	**PRESENT**
estar	estando
PAST	**PAST**
haber estado	estado

HABER
to have (auxiliary)

PRESENT	IMPERFECT	FUTURE
1. he	había	habré
2. has	habías	habrás
3. ha/hay*	había	habrá
1. hemos	habíamos	habremos
2. habéis	habíais	habréis
3. han	habían	habrán

PRETERITE	PERFECT	PLUPERFECT
1. hube		
2. hubiste		
3. hubo	ha habido	había habido
1. hubimos		
2. hubisteis		
3. hubieron		

PAST ANTERIOR	FUTURE PERFECT
hubo habido etc.	habrá habido etc.

CONDITIONAL		IMPERATIVE
PRESENT	**PAST**	
1. habría		
2. habrías		
3. habría	habría habido	
1. habríamos		
2. habríais		
3. habrían		

SUBJUNCTIVE

PRESENT	IMPERFECT	PLUPERFECT
1. haya	hub-iera/iese	
2. hayas	hub-ieras/ieses	
3. haya	hub-iera/iese	hubiera habido
1. hayamos	hub-iéramos/iésemos	
2. hayáis	hub-ierais/ieseis	
3. hayan	hub-ieran/iesen	

PERFECT haya habido etc.

INFINITIVE	PARTICIPLE	NOTE
PRESENT	**PRESENT**	This verb is an auxiliary
haber	habiendo	used for compound tenses
		(e.g. he bebido - I have
		drunk) - see also TENER.
		*'hay' means 'there is/are'.
PAST	**PAST**	
haber habido	habido	

DAR
to give

PRESENT	IMPERFECT	FUTURE
1. doy	daba	daré
2. das	dabas	darás
3. da	daba	dará
1. damos	dábamos	daremos
2. dais	dabais	daréis
3. dan	daban	darán

PRETERITE	PERFECT	PLUPERFECT
1. di	he dado	había dado
2. diste	has dado	habías dado
3. dio	ha dado	había dado
1. dimos	hemos dado	habíamos dado
2. disteis	habéis dado	habíais dado
3. dieron	han dado	habían dado

PAST ANTERIOR	FUTURE PERFECT
hube dado etc.	habré dado etc.

CONDITIONAL		*IMPERATIVE*
PRESENT	**PAST**	
1. daría	habría dado	
2. darías	habrías dado	(tú) da
3. daría	habría dado	(Vd) dé
1. daríamos	habríamos dado	(nosotros) demos
2. daríais	habríais dado	(vosotros) dad
3. darían	habrían dado	(Vds) den

SUBJUNCTIVE

PRESENT	IMPERFECT	PLUPERFECT
1. dé	di-era/ese	hubiera dado
2. des	di-eras/eses	hubieras dado
3. dé	di-era/ese	hubiera dado
1. demos	di-éramos/ésemos	hubiéramos dado
2. deis	di-erais/eseis	hubierais dado
3. den	di-eran/esen	hubieran dado

PERFECT   haya dado etc.

INFINITIVE	*PARTICIPLE*
PRESENT	**PRESENT**
dar	dando
PAST	**PAST**
haber dado	dado

IR
to go

PRESENT	IMPERFECT	FUTURE
1. voy	iba	iré
2. vas	ibas	irás
3. va	iba	irá
1. vamos	íbamos	iremos
2. vais	ibais	iréis
3. van	iban	irán

PRETERITE	PERFECT	PLUPERFECT
1. fui	he ido	había ido
2. fuiste	has ido	habías ido
3. fue	ha ido	había ido
1. fuimos	hemos ido	habíamos ido
2. fuisteis	habéis ido	habíais ido
3. fueron	han ido	habían ido

PAST ANTERIOR	FUTURE PERFECT
hube ido etc.	habré ido etc.

CONDITIONAL		*IMPERATIVE*
PRESENT	**PAST**	
1. iría	habría ido	
2. irías	habrías ido	(tú) ve
3. iría	habría ido	(Vd) vaya
1. iríamos	habríamos ido	(nosotros) vamos
2. iríais	habríais ido	(vosotros) id
3. irían	habrían ido	(Vds) vayan

SUBJUNCTIVE

PRESENT	IMPERFECT	PLUPERFECT
1. vaya	fu-era/ese	hubiera ido
2. vayas	fu-eras/eses	hubieras ido
3. vaya	fu-era/ese	hubiera ido
1. vayamos	fu-éramos/ésemos	hubiéramos ido
2. vayáis	fu-erais/eseis	hubierais ido
3. vayan	fu-eran/esen	hubieran ido

PERFECT haya ido etc.

INFINITIVE	*PARTICIPLE*
PRESENT	**PRESENT**
ir	yendo
PAST	**PAST**
haber ido	ido

TENER
to have

PRESENT	IMPERFECT	FUTURE
1. tengo	tenía	tendré
2. tienes	tenías	tendrás
3. tiene	tenía	tendrá
1. tenemos	teníamos	tendremos
2. tenéis	teníais	tendréis
3. tienen	tenían	tendrán

PRETERITE	PERFECT	PLUPERFECT
1. tuve	he tenido	había tenido
2. tuviste	has tenido	habías tenido
3. tuvo	ha tenido	había tenido
1. tuvimos	hemos tenido	habíamos tenido
2. tuvisteis	habéis tenido	habíais tenido
3. tuvieron	han tenido	habían tenido

PAST ANTERIOR	FUTURE PERFECT
hube tenido etc.	habré tenido etc.

CONDITIONAL		IMPERATIVE
PRESENT	PAST	
1. tendría	habría tenido	
2. tendrías	habrías tenido	(tú) ten
3. tendría	habría tenido	(Vd) tenga
1. tendríamos	habríamos tenido	(nosotros) tengamos
2. tendríais	habríais tenido	(vosotros) tened
3. tendrían	habrían tenido	(Vds) tengan

SUBJUNCTIVE		
PRESENT	IMPERFECT	PLUPERFECT
1. tenga	tuv-iera/iese	hubiera tenido
2. tengas	tuv-ieras/ieses	hubieras tenido
3. tenga	tuv-iera/iese	hubiera tenido
1. tengamos	tuv-iéramos/iésemos	hubiéramos tenido
2. tengáis	tuv-ierais/ieseis	hubierais tenido
3. tengan	tuv-ieran/iesen	hubieran tenido

PERFECT	haya tenido etc.

INFINITIVE	PARTICIPLE
PRESENT	PRESENT
tener	teniendo
PAST	PAST
haber tenido	tenido

VENIR
to come

PRESENT	**IMPERFECT**	**FUTURE**
1. vengo	venía	vendré
2. vienes	venías	vendrás
3. viene	venía	vendrá
1. venimos	veníamos	vendremos
2. venís	veníais	vendréis
3. vienen	venían	vendrán

PRETERITE	**PERFECT**	**PLUPERFECT**
1. vine	he venido	había venido
2. viniste	has venido	habías venido
3. vino	ha venido	había venido
1. vinimos	hemos venido	habíamos venido
2. vinisteis	habéis venido	habíais venido
3. vinieron	han venido	habían venido

PAST ANTERIOR	**FUTURE PERFECT**
hube venido etc.	habré venido etc.

CONDITIONAL		*IMPERATIVE*
PRESENT	**PAST**	
1. vendría	habría venido	
2. vendrías	habrías venido	(tú) ven
3. vendría	habría venido	(Vd) venga
1. vendríamos	habríamos venido	(nosotros) vengamos
2. vendríais	habríais venido	(vosotros) venid
3. vendrían	habrían venido	(Vds) vengan

SUBJUNCTIVE

PRESENT	**IMPERFECT**	**PLUPERFECT**
1. venga	vin-iera/iese	hubiera venido
2. vengas	vin-ieras/ieses	hubieras venido
3. venga	vin-iera/iese	hubiera venido
1. vengamos	vin-iéramos/iésemos	hubiéramos venido
2. vengáis	vin-ierais/ieseis	hubierais venido
3. vengan	vin-ieran/iesen	hubieran venido

PERFECT   haya venido etc.

INFINITIVE	*PARTICIPLE*
PRESENT	**PRESENT**
venir	viniendo
PAST	**PAST**
haber venido	venido

16. VERBS AND THEIR OBJECTS

A number of verbs in Spanish cannot be used without a specific preposition if their object is expressed.

1. Verbs taking *a* before an object

acercarse a	to approach
aproximarse a	to approach
asistir a	to attend
asomarse a	to lean out of
dar a	to look out onto
faltar a	not to fulfil/keep
jugar a	to play at (game)
llegar a	to arrive at/in
oler a	to smell of
oponerse a	to oppose
parecerse a	to resemble
renunciar a	to give up
resistir a	to resist
saber a	to taste of
sobrevivir a	to outlive

faltó a su promesa
he didn't keep his promise

la ventana de mi cuarto daba a un matadero
the window of my room looked out onto a slaughterhouse

la pequeña se parece a su padre
the little girl looks like her father

2. Verbs taking *de* before an object

abusar de	to misuse
acordarse de	to remember
apoderarse de	to seize
asombrarse de	to wonder at
burlarse de	to make fun of

cambiar de	to change
carecer de	to lack
compadecerse de	to take pity on
depender de	to depend on
desconfiar de	to distrust
despedirse de	to say goodbye to
disfrutar de	to enjoy
dudar de	to doubt
enamorarse de	to fall in love with
enterarse de	to find out
gozar de	to enjoy
maravillarse de	to wonder at
mudar de	to change
ocuparse de	to attend to
olvidarse de	to forget
pasar de	to exceed
prescindir de	to do without
reírse de	to make fun of
responder de	to answer for
saber de	to know of
salir de	to leave (a place)
servirse de	to use
sospechar de	to distrust
tirar de	to pull
tratarse de	to be about
variar de	to change
vengarse de	to take revenge for/on

se trata de mi primo
it's about my cousin

afortunadamente gozamos de buena salud
fortunately we enjoy good health

dudar can be used with the direct object **lo** in cases like:

lo dudo	**no lo dude Vd.**
I doubt it	don't you doubt it

Otherwise it takes de:

dudo de su testimonio
I doubt his testimony

3. Verbs taking *con* before an object

acabar con	to put an end to
casarse con	to marry
contar con	to rely on

dar con	to come across
divertirse con	to be amused by
encontrarse con	to meet
hablar con	to talk to
portarse con	to behave towards
soñar con	to dream about

¡acabemos con estas mentiras!
let's put an end to these lies!

cuento contigo
I'm counting on you

4. Verbs taking *en* before an object

consentir en	to agree to
consistir en	to consist of
convenir en	to agree to
entrar en	to enter/go into
fijarse en	to look at
ingresar en	to enter
penetrar en	to penetrate
*pensar en	to think of
reparar en	to notice

consintió en ello
he agreed to it

¡fíjate en aquel edificio!
just look at that building!

*do not confuse **pensar en** with **pensar de** which means 'to have an opinion of'.

pensaba en sus vacaciones en España
she was thinking of her vacation in Spain

¿qué piensas de esta idea?
what do you think of this idea?

5. Verbs taking *por* before an object

asomarse por	to lean out of
felicitar por	to congratulate on
interesarse por	to take an interest in
preguntar por	to ask after

el cura preguntó por mi tía que está enferma
the priest asked after my aunt who is ill

6. Verbs which take no preposition before the object in Spanish though they do in English

agradecer	to be grateful for
aguantar	to put up with
aprobar	to approve of
aprovechar	to take advantage of
buscar	to look for
cuidar	to look after
escuchar	to listen to
esperar	to wait for
extrañar	to wonder at
lamentar	to be sorry about
mirar	to look at
pagar	to pay for
recordar	to remind of
regalar	to make a present of
rumiar	to ponder over
sentir	to be sorry about
soportar	to put up with

aprovecharon la ocasión para felicitar a Juan
they took advantage of the opportunity to congratulate Juan

le agradezco mucho el regalo
thank you very much for the gift

su historia me extraña
your story surprises me

17. VERBS FOLLOWED BY AN INFINITIVE

1. Verbs followed immediately by the infinitive

The direct infinitive is used after the following verbs, though they may also be followed by a clause with its verb in the subjunctive:

a) *Verbs of making, advising, ordering, preventing and permitting*

aconsejar	to advise to
amenazar	to threaten to
conceder	to concede to
dejar	to let/allow to
hacer	to make
impedir	to prevent from
mandar	to command/order to
ordenar	to command/order to
permitir	to permit/allow to
prohibir	to prohibit from/forbid to

mis padres no me dejan poner la radio después de medianoche
my parents don't allow me to play the radio after midnight
me mandó salir
he ordered me to leave

b) *Verbs of the senses: sentir, ver and oír*

oír	to hear
sentir	to feel
ver	to see

no te vi llegar
I didn't see you come in
le oí roncar
I heard him snoring

c) *Impersonal verbs, where the verb used in the infinitive is the subject of the impersonal verb*

alegrarse	**me alegra verte de nuevo**
	I am happy to see you again
gustar	**nos gusta mucho pasear en el campo**
	we love walking in the country
hacer falta	**te hace falta estudiar**
	you need to study
olvidarse	**se me olvidó ir al banco**
	I forgot to go to the bank
parecer	**¿te parece bien salir ahora?**
	do you think it's a good idea to leave now?
convenir	**no me conviene partir mañana**
	it doesn't suit me to leave tomorrow

d) *After the following verbs when the subject is the same as that of the infinitive*

acordar	to agree to
ansiar	to long to
concertar	to agree to
confesar	to confess to
conseguir	to succeed in -ing, manage to
creer	to believe
deber	to have to
decidir	to decide to
decir	to say, tell
descuidar	to neglect to
desear	to wish/want to
esperar	to hope/expect to
evitar	to avoid -ing
figurarse	to suppose, imagine
fingir	to pretend to
imaginar	to imagine -ing
intentar	to try to
lograr	to succeed in -ing, manage to
merecer	to merit -ing
necesitar	to need to
negar	to deny -ing
ofrecer	to offer to
olvidar	to forget to
osar	to dare to
parecer	to appear to
pedir	to ask to
pensar	to intend to
poder	to be able to
preferir	to prefer to
presumir	to presume to
pretender	to try/claim to

procurar	to endeavor to
prometer	to promise to
querer	to wish to
recordar	to remember to
resistir	to resist -ing
resolver	to resolve to
resultar	to turn out to (be)
saber	to know how to
sentir	to regret to, -ing
soler	to be accustomed to -ing
temer	to be afraid to

debemos pagar la cuenta ahora
we must pay the bill now

nuestro equipo consiguió ganar el partido
our team managed to win the match

el niño resultó ser el hijo del rey
the boy turned out to be the king's son

solemos merendar en el bosque los domingos
we usually go for a picinic in the woods on Sundays

2. Verbs followed by *a* + infinitive

The verbs given below take the preposition **a** before a following infinitive. In most cases the idea of 'in order to' is involved.

a) *Verbs of motion*

acercarse a	to come forward to
acudir a	to come to
adelantarse a	to go towards
andar a	to go to
apresurarse a	to hurry to
bajar a	to go down to
correr a	to run to
dirigirse a	to go towards ... to
entrar a	to go in to
enviar a	to send to
ir a	to go to
lanzarse a	to rush to
mandar a	to send to
precipitarse a	to rush to
salir a	to go out to
sentarse a	to sit down to
subir a	to go up to
traer a	to bring to
venir a	to come to
volver a	to do ... again

el mecánico se acercó a hablar conmigo
the mechanic came forward to speak to me

la chica se apresuró a hacer las camas
the maid rushed off to make the beds

el jefe mandó al chico a recoger las cartas
the boss sent the boy to pick up the mail

volveré a llamarte mañana
I'll call you again tomorrow

b) *Verbs of forcing, compelling, inviting*

animar a	to encourage to
conducir a	to lead to
convidar a	to invite to
empujar a	to push into
excitar a	to excite to
exhortar a	to exhort to
forzar a	to force to
impulsar a	to impel to
incitar a	to incite to
inducir a	to induce to
invitar a	to invite to
llamar a	to call to
llevar a	to bring/lead to
obligar a	to oblige to
persuadir a	to persuade to

animaron a la niña a montar al caballo
they encouraged the little girl to get on the horse

el dueño forzó al camarero a limpiar los platos
the owner forced the waiter to clean the plates

me invitó a pasar el fin de semana
he invited me to spend to weekend

c) *Verbs of beginning*

comenzar a	to begin to
echarse a	to start -ing
empezar a	to begin to
ponerse a	to begin to, set about -ing
romper a	to break into, do suddenly

el bebé se echó a llorar
the baby burst into tears

todos los alumnos se pusieron a trabajar
all the students started to work

d) *Verbs used reflexively to mean deciding or refusing*

decidirse a	to decide to
negarse a	to refuse to
resolverse a	to resolve to

el niño se negó a comer
the little boy refused to eat

e) *The following verbs*

acostumbrarse a	to get used to -ing
aguardar a	to wait to
alcanzar a	to manage to
aprender a	to learn to
arriesgarse a	to risk -ing
aspirar a	to aspire to
atreverse a	to dare to
autorizar a	to authorize to
aventurarse a	to venture to
ayudar a	to help to
comprometerse a	to undertake to
condenar a	to condemn to
contribuir a	to contribute to -ing
dedicarse a	to devote oneself to
detenerse a	to stop to
disponerse a	to get ready to
enseñar a	to teach to
entregarse a	to devote oneself to
exponerse a	to expose oneself to
habituarse a	to get used to -ing
limitarse a	to limit oneself to -ing
ofrecerse a	to offer oneself to
oponerse a	to object to -ing
prepararse a	to prepare to
pararse a	to stop to
quedarse a	to stay and
renunciar a	to give up -ing
resignarse a	to resign oneself to -ing
tender a	to tend to

los chicos no se arriesgaron a cruzar el río
the boys didn't dare cross the river

después del accidente, Juan se dedicó a cuidar de su mujer
after the accident, Juan devoted himself to looking after his wife

se detuvo a hablar conmigo
he stopped to speak to me

3. Verbs followed by *de* + infinitive

In these cases **de** is required before a following infinitive:

a) *Verbs of stopping or leaving off an action*

abstenerse de	to abstain from -ing
acabar de	to finish -ing, have just

cansarse de	to become tired of -ing
cesar de	to cease -ing
dejar de	to leave off -ing
desistir de	to desist from -ing
disuadir de	to dissuade from -ing
excusar de	to excuse from -ing
fatigarse de	to grow tired of -ing
guardarse de	to take care not to
hartarse de	to grow tired of -ing
librarse de	to escape from -ing
parar de	to stop -ing
saciarse de	to grow tired of -ing
terminar de	to finish -ing

When **dejar de** is used in the negative, it expresses the idea of 'not to fail to':

no dejes de devolverme los discos la semana que viene
make sure you give me back the records next week

b) *Also the following verbs*

acordarse de	to remember to
acusar de	to accuse of -ing
alegrarse de	to be glad to
arrepentirse de	to repent of -ing
avergonzarse de	to be ashamed of -ing
consolarse de	to console oneself for -ing
cuidar de	to be careful to
desconfiar de	to mistrust
desesperar de	to despair of -ing
dispensar de	to excuse from -ing
encargarse de	to undertake to, see to -ing
jactarse de	to boast of -ing
maravillarse de	to marvel at
olvidarse de	to forget to
no poder por menos de	not to be able to help -ing
tratar de	to try to
tratarse de	to be a question of

yo me encargo de hacer eso
I'll see to doing that

el joven se olvidó de acudir a la cita
the young man forgot to keep his appointment

se trata de trabajar más
it's a question of working more

no pude por menos de reírme
I couldn't help laughing

4. Verbs followed by *en* + infinitive

complacerse en	to take pleasure in -ing
consentir en	to consent to
consistir en	to consist in -ing
convenir en	to agree to
dudar en	to hesitate to
empeñarse en	to insist on -ing
entretenerse en	to amuse oneself in -ing
esforzarse en	to try hard to
hacer bien en	to do well/right to
hacer mal en	to do badly/wrong in
insistir en	to insist on -ing
interesarse en	to be interested in -ing
obstinarse en	to be determined to
pensar en	to think of -ing
persistir en	to persist in -ing
quedar en	to agree to
soñar en	to have in mind to
tardar en	to take (a long) time to
vacilar en	to hesitate to

la niña se esforzaba en montar en bicicleta
the little girl was trying hard to ride the bicycle

haces bien en ayudar a tu madre
you do well to help your mother

los amigos quedaron en verse a las ocho
the friends agreed to meet at eight o'clock

el tren tardó treinta minutos en llegar
the train took thirty minutes to come

5. Verbs followed by *con* + infinitive

amenazar con	to threaten to
contentarse con	to content oneself with -ing
soñar con	to dream of

el hombre de negocios soñaba con ir a Río de Janeiro
the business man dreamed of going off to Rio

6. Verbs followed by *por* + infinitive

a) *Verbs of beginning and ending, with the sense of the English 'by'*

acabar por	to end up by -ing
comenzar por	to begin by -ing
empezar por	to begin by -ing

acabó por comprarse el traje azul
she ended up buying the blue suit

b) *Verbs of longing / trying to etc*

esforzarse por	to make an effort to
luchar por	to struggle to
morirse por	to be dying to
rabiar por	to be dying to

la niña se moría por abrir los paquetes
the little girl was dying to open the packages

18. CONJUNCTIONS

1. Simple conjunctions

Simple conjunctions consist of one word only. The commonest are:

aunque	although
como	as (reason)
conforme	as (in proportion as)
conque	so, so then
cuando	when
e	and
***mas**	but
mientras	while
ni	neither/nor
o	or
pero	but
porque	because
pues	since, so
que	that, for (because)
según	according to
si	if, whether
sino	but
siquiera	if only
u	or
y	and

***mas** is old-fashioned nowadays, the everyday word for **but** being **pero**.

me fui al cine porque creía que ya no venías
I went to the movies because I thought you weren't coming

sabremos pronto si hemos ganado el premio
we'll soon know whether we've won the prize

se puso triste cuando se murió su perro
he became sad when his dog died

no grites tanto, que ya te oigo
don't shout so much, I can hear you

2. Compound conjunctions

These conjunctions consist of two or more words, the last one usually being **que**:

a condición de que	on condition that
a fin de que	so that

a medida que	as
a menos que	unless
a no ser que	unless
antes de que	before
a pesar de que	despite
así que	so (that)
con tal (de) que	provided that
de manera que	so (that)
de modo que	so (that)
desde que	since
después de que	after
en caso de que	in case
hasta que	until
luego que	as soon as
mientras	while
mientras que	whereas
para que	in order that
por lo que	for which reason
por si	in case
puesto que	since
salvo que	except that
siempre que	whenever, so long as
sino que	but
tan pronto como	as soon as
ya que	since

vamos a preparar la comida por si vienen pronto
let's get the meal ready in case they come soon

los niños jugaban mientras su madre se ocupaba de la casa
the children played while their mother took care of the house

llevo el paraguas por si llueve
I'll take my umbrella in case it rains

⚠ Note that, whereas *puesto que* and *ya que* refer to cause, *desde que* refers *only* to time in Spanish:

todo marcha bien desde que él llegó
everything has been fine since he arrived

puesto que las mercancías ya no están disponibles
since the goods are no longer available

3. Coordinating conjunctions

Coordinating conjunctions come in pairs and are used to link two closely associated ideas:

apenas . . . (cuando)	hardly . . . when
bien . . . bien	either . . . or
o . . . o	either . . . or

o bien . . . o bien	either . . . or
ni . . . ni	neither . . . nor
no sólo . . . sino también	not only . . . but also
que . . . o que	whether . . . or
ya . . . ya	sometimes . . . sometimes
tanto . . . como	both . . . and
no . . . sino	not . . . but
no . . . pero sí	not . . . but

ni los sindicatos ni los empresarios están contentos
neither the unions nor the employers are happy

tanto tú como yo
both you and I

19. NUMBERS

1. The Cardinal Numbers

0	cero	10	diez
1	uno, una	11	once
2	dos	12	doce
3	tres	13	trece
4	cuatro	14	catorce
5	cinco	15	quince
6	seis	16	dieciséis
7	siete	17	diecisiete
8	ocho	18	dieciocho
9	nueve	19	diecinueve
20	veinte	21	veintiuno
22	veintidós	23	veintitrés
24	veinticuatro	25	venticinco
26	veintiséis	27	veintisiete
28	veintiocho	29	veintinueve
30	treinta	31	treinta y uno/una
40	cuarenta	42	cuarenta y dos
50	cincuenta	53	cincuenta y tres
60	sesenta	64	sesenta y cuatro
70	setenta	75	setenta y cinco
80	ochenta	86	ochenta y seis
90	noventa	97	noventa y siete
100	ciento	101	ciento uno/una
105	ciento cinco	115	ciento quince
120	ciento veinte	123	ciento veintitrés
150	ciento cincuenta	176	ciento setenta y seis
200	doscientos/as	202	doscientos dos
300	trescientos/as	317	trescientos diecisiete
400	cuatrocientos/as	428	cuatrocientos veintiocho
500	quinientos/as	539	quinientos treinta y nueve
600	seiscientos/as	645	seiscientos cuarenta y cinco
700	setecientos/as	754	setecientos cincuenta y cuatro

800	**ochocientos/as**	863	**ochocientos sesenta y tres**
900	**novecientos/as**	971	**novecientos setenta y uno/una**
1,000	**mil**	2,000	**dos mil**
3,000	**tres mil**	4,000	**cuatro mil**
5,000	**cinco mil**	6,000	**seis mil**
7,000	**siete mil**	8,000	**ocho mil**
9,000	**nueve mil**	10,000	**diez mil**

200,000	**doscientos mil**
300,000	**trescientos mil**
600,000	**seiscientos mil**
1,000,000	**un millón**
2,000,000	**dos millones**

a) *Alternative forms*

There are alternative forms for 16 to 19 which are written as three separate words:

diez y seis, diez y siete etc.

b) *Shortened forms of certain numbers*

uno is shortened to **un** when followed by a noun or adjective + noun:

| **treinta y un meses** | **doscientos un días** |
| thirty-one months | two hundred and one days |

ciento is shortened to **cien** followed by (1) a noun, (2) an adjective + noun, (3) the numeral **mil**:

cien panes	**cien mil hojas**
a hundred loaves	a hundred thousand leaves
cien millones de pesetas	**cien buenos días**
a hundred million pesetas	a hundred good days

c) *Agreements*

Cardinal numbers are invariable except for the plural hundreds and numbers ending in **-uno**:

doscientas personas	**quinientas cincuenta libras**
two hundred people	five hundred and fifty pounds
veintiuna páginas	**ciento una cosas**
twenty-one pages	a hundred and one things

d) *Accents*

Written accents are necessary for some of the twenties:

| 22 | **veintidós** | 23 | **veintitrés** | 26 | **veintiséis** |

also: **ventiún años**   twenty-one years

e) *Counting by hundreds stops at 900:*

1966	**mil novecientos sesenta y seis**
	nineteen hundred and sixty-six
1200 pesetas	**mil doscientas pesetas**
	twelve hundred pesetas

2. The Ordinal Numbers

primero	first	**sexto**	sixth
segundo	second	**séptimo**	seventh
tercero	third	**octavo**	eighth
cuarto	fourth	**noveno**	ninth
quinto	fifth	**décimo**	tenth

a) Ordinals are adjectives and as such agree with their noun:

la segunda esquina   la séptima semana
the second corner   the seventh week

b) primero and **tercero** are shortened to **primer** and **tercer** before a masculine singular noun:

el primer tren   **el tercer coche**
the first train   the third coach

c) Ordinals are rarely used beyond the tenth, when cardinals are used instead:

el siglo once   **Luis XIV - Luis catorce**
the eleventh century   Louis the fourteenth

20. DAYS, MONTHS AND SEASONS

The names of the days of the week, the months and the seasons are written with small letters in Spanish.

Days of the week

el lunes	Monday
el martes	Tuesday
el miércoles	Wednesday
el jueves	Thursday
el viernes	Friday
el sábado	Saturday
el domingo	Sunday

Months

enero	January
febrero	February
marzo	March
abril	April
mayo	May
junio	June
julio	July
agosto	August
se(p)tiembre	September
octubre	October
noviembre	November
diciembre	December

Seasons

primavera	spring (March 21 to June 21)
verano	summer (June 21 to September 2)
otoño	autumn (September 21 to December 21)
invierno	winter (December 21 to March 21)

Index
to
Grammar

Part II
Exercises

Questions

1. ACCENTUATION

a) **All the accents are missing from these sentences. Where should they go?**

(1) El niño pidio mucho chocolate.

(2) El cantaro estaba medio vacio.

(3) No se pueden bañar en el rio.

(4) El tunel esta siempre atascado.

(5) No le gustan los platanos.

(6) ¿Como te van los negocios?

(7) Siempre escribe a lapiz.

(8) Cuando se rompio la pierna, compro unas muletas.

(9) No llameis despues de las nueve.

(10) ¿Que tal estais?

(11) Acercate a ellos.

(12) ¿Estas seguro de que estos arboles son viejos?

(13) Los jabalies no son faciles de cazar.

(14) Nos encantaria que estuvierais a gusto.

(15) ¡Atencion obras!

(16) ¿Por que no se dirigio a sus parientes?

(17) Estos jovenes estan de broma.

(18) En Mejico hay mucha contaminacion.

(19) Aqui esta el pueblo en donde se rodo la pelicula.

(20) Levantate de prisa.

score: ... × 5 = ◯

b) **Where should the accent go on these words?**

(1) brujula - (2) musica - (3) ambito - (4) razon - (5) energia - (6) ambicion - (7) Cordoba - (8) tia - (9) interprete - (10) sientate - (11) catedratico - (12) jovenes - (13) cortes - (14) azucar - (15) carcel - (16) metropoli - (17) levantese - (18) colera - (19) aguila - (20) matematicas.

score: ... × 5 = ◯

c) Which of the three words is correctly accented?

(1) duerméte, duérmete, dúermete - (2) asi, ási, así - (3) la alégria, la álegria, la alegría - (4) la ampliación, la ampliácion, la ámplia-cion - (5) muévase, muéváse, muevasé - (6) símpatico, simpático, simpatíco - (7) el frío, el frió, el frio - (8) increible, increíble, increiblé - (9) sábado, sabádo, sabadó - (10) pajáro, pájaro, pajaró.

score: ... × 10 = ◯

2. ARTICLES

A. THE DEFINITE ARTICLE

a) Add the definite article.

(1)	tesis	(6)	planeta
(2)	clima	(7)	teorema
(3)	árbol	(8)	hortalizas
(4)	tema	(9)	crisis
(5)	dentista	(10)	poema

score: ... × 10 =

b) Put these nouns into the plural and add the definite article.

(1)	actriz	(6)	crímen
(2)	interés	(7)	gris
(3)	jersey	(8)	crisis
(4)	maniquí	(9)	carmesí
(5)	nación	(10)	rubí

score: ... × 10 =

c) Complete by adding the correct definite article.

(1) ... aves cantan al amanecer.
(2) ... águila es a menudo imperial.
(3) ... agua de este río no está limpia.
(4) ... aula está llena de humo.
(5) Va por ... último curso.
(6) A ... una tenemos una cita.
(7) ... España del siglo 19 era atrasada.
(8) Se pasa ... mano por ... frente.
(9) Te gusta viajar per América ... Sur o por ... Indias.
(10) ... perro suele ser un animal muy fiel.

score: ... × 10 =

d) *El* or *la*?

   (1) Se corta la leña con **(el-la)** hacha.

   (2) **(El-La)** área de este terreno es muy amplia.

   (3) **(El-La)** alma es un problema metafísico.

   (4) Ya casí no existe **(el-la)** aldaba en las puertas.

   (5) El médico le dio **(el-la)** alta.

   (6) **(La-El)** hambre es una realidad insoportable.

   (7) A pesar de ser nativo de Salamanca, tiene **(el-la)** habla muy particular.

   (8) **(El-La)** anáfora es una forma poética.

   (9) No se debe comer en **(el-la)** aula.

   (10) **(El-La)** ama de casa siempre tiene algo que hacer.

score: ... × 10 = $\bigcirc$

e) Complete by using a definite article or the contraction of a preposition + article.

   (1) Vamos **(a el)** concierto.

   (2) No hablemos **(de el)** asunto.

   (3) No os fiéis **(de el)** seguro.

   (4) Mañana iré **(a el)** mercado.

   (5) Agachó ... cabeza.

   (6) Se dirige **(a el)** público.

   (7) Lleva ... equipaje.

   (8) Éste es ... retrato **(de el)** presidente.

   (9) No le gustan ... golosinas.

   (10) Apéese **(de el)** tren.

score: ... × 10 = $\bigcirc$

B. THE INDEFINITE ARTICLE

a) Complete using the indefinite article: un, uno, unos, una, unas.

   (1) Son ... estudiantes.

   (2) Ese alumno es ... empollón.

   (3) Son ... comadrejas.

   (4) Segovia está a ... seiscientos metros de altitud.

   (5) Su casa está a ... pasos de la de sus padres.

   (6) Son ... cuantos en examinarse.

     (7) Esos jóvenes tendrán ... quince años.

     (8) Volverán dentro de ... semanas.

     (9) Sólo me quedan ... mil pesetas.

     (10) Este coche lo adquirió por ... poco de dinero.

score: ... × 10 = ◯

b) **Translate these sentences, using the appropriate indefinite adjectives, if needed.**

     (1) There were only a few spectators left.

     (2) They observed the silence for a few minutes.

     (3) Some reporters questioned him.

     (4) Fruit and vegetables were on show.

     (5) I'll stay a few days at your house.

     (6) Some friends came to look for him.

     (7) There were some empty bottles lying on the floor.

     (8) They needed exercise books and pens.

     (9) Chess is not an easy game.

     (10) He still needed to make an effort.

score: ... × 10 = ◯

C. DEFINITE OR INDEFINITE ARTICLE?

a) **Complete using the definite or the indefinite article in the plural or the singular form.**

     (1) ... capataz vigila a ... peones.

     (2) En ... revista vienen las fotos de la boda.

     (3) Tengo ... cuantas horas por delante.

     (4) ... hábitos de ese pueblo son raros.

     (5) ... chicas preguntaron por él.

     (6) Han vuelto ... golondrinas.

     (7) ¿Quieres ... caramelos? Sí, dáme ... rojos.

     (8) Se vieron ... ratas por el metro.

     (9) Con este gobierno, se repiten ... crisis.

     (10) ... tesis de este estudiante es interesante.

score: ... × 10 = ◯

b) Add the definite or indefinite article.

(1) A ... veinte años se marchó.

(2) ... dia siguiente, vinieron a casa.

(3) La Exposición universal será en ... 92.

(4) A ... una y media es cuando cierran las tiendas.

(5) Para visitar este museo basta con ... buena guía.

(6) Se me han perdido ... pendientes.

(7) ... parte médico no era favorable.

(8) No obedece a ... orden.

(9) No parece que tengan ... margen de maniobra suficiente.

(10) ... editorial debe tener buenos autores.

(11) ... partida fue emocionante.

(12) ... capital de Chile es Santiago.

(13) No tengo ... menor idea.

(14) ... corte fue inesperado.

(15) Lo único que conoce de Marx es ... Capital.

(16) Hemos tenido ... guía muy amable.

(17) Dentro de ... minutos empezará ... partido de fútbol.

(18) Debió someterse a ... cura muy larga.

(19) En ... siglo quince fue cuando se creó el Tribunal de la Inquisición.

(20) ... paredes de esta casa son muy gruesas.

score: ... × 5 =

c) Translate the following.

(1) You *(tú)* like beer but not wine.

(2) I don't want milk but water.

(3) He took off his hat.

(4) A good number *(parte)* of his friends went abroad.

(5) I've a number of problems to solve.

(6) He wants to be a doctor.

(7) What a good idea!

(8) Do you *(tú)* have a house in the country?

(9) He lives in Paris, the capital of France.

(10) We have never been to such a place.

(11) I think of you *(tú)* as a brother.

(12) Spain is a country which is undergoing major development.

(13) The Director is waiting for you *(Vd)*.

(14) The European Community is really expanding.
(15) She always had very cold hands.
(16) Miss Garcia was delighted with her journey.
(17) He goes to mass every day.
(18) The most important thing is to decide quickly.
(19) The main thing is to know this author's work.
(20) I'm studying Spanish.

score: ... × 5 = ◯

3. LO, LO QUE

a) Complete these sentences using *lo* or *lo que*.

(1) ... bueno es pasear por la noche.
(2) No le gusta ... lúgubre de este film.
(3) ... sano sería ir a la montaña.
(4) ... raro era que asistiera a la cena.
(5) ... nos relata me interesa.
(6) No sabéis ... ingenioso que es.
(7) ... natural es beber agua.
(8) ... bien que lo estábamos haciendo.
(9) Es increíble ... tacaño que es.
(10) ... moderno no es siempre un logro.
(11) No oigo ... dice.
(12) Le ocultamos ... ocurrió.
(13) Di ... quieras.
(14) No lee ... escriben sobre ella.
(15) No puedes figurarte ... comprensivos que fueron.
(16) Es difícil creer ... bajos que son los salarios.
(17) ... peor es adoptar todas las creencias.
(18) ... más emocionante son las saetas.
(19) ... bonito es tomar el barco.
(20) ... peligroso le fascina.

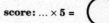

score: ... × 5 =

b) Translate these sentences using *lo* or *lo que*.

(1) What they did was a mistake.
(2) What you have explained *(exponer)* is not interesting.
(3) What we are planning will be communicated later.
(4) What you have bought is not very expensive.
(5) He is up to date with what you have decided.
(6) Do as you wish.
(7) He repeated what they had confided to him.

(8) What he is going to do will not please everybody.

(9) She doesn't know what is good.

(10) Be careful what you say *(tú)*.

score: ... × 10 = ◯

4. SHORTENED ADJECTIVES

a) Give the shortened form of the adjective where necessary.

(1) Hace (**bueno**) tiempo para pasear.
(2) Goya fue un (**grande**) pintor.
(3) (**Santo**) Antonio, es un santo muy famoso.
(4) No es (**cualquiera**) hombre.
(5) Son unos (**recientes**) casados.
(6) Dijo una (**grande**) mentira.
(7) Había una (**grande**) animación.
(8) Hace (**malo**) tiempo para ir a pasear.
(9) Siempre repite (**cualquiera**) cosa.
(10) Éste es un (**reciente**) nacido.

score: ... × 10 = ◯

b) Translate using the shortened form of the adjective, where appropriate.

(1) It's a big building.
(2) It's nice weather for going for a walk.
(3) St. Joseph is a famous saint in Spain.
(4) This newborn child cries a lot.
(5) I've got a hundred pesetas in my purse.
(6) If you (*tú*) have any problems come and see me.
(7) She has no information on this subject.
(8) This man has a bad character.
(9) She lives on the third floor.
(10) On the first day he visited the whole town.

score: ... × 10 = ◯

c) **Use the shortened form in the following sentences.**

(1) Es un **(grande)** acontecimiento.

(2) No tiene **(ninguno)** dinero en el banco.

(3) Los **(recientes)** nacidos están en una incubadora.

(4) **(Santo)** Antonio y **(Santo)** Sebastián son santos muy famosos.

(5) **(Cualquiera)** estudiante sabe eso.

(6) **(Ninguno)** amigo fue invitado.

(7) Vive en el **(primero)** piso.

(8) Es el **(tercero)** tren para Madrid.

(9) Es un **(bueno)** tema de debate.

(10) **(Alguno)** motivo habrá.

score: ... × 10 = ◯

5. GENDER AND NUMBER

a) What is the feminine of these words?

(1) actor
(2) estudiante
(3) alcalde
(4) catalán
(5) doctor

(6) senador
(7) maestro
(8) dentista
(9) gallo
(10) monje

score: ... × 10 =

b) What is the singular of these words?

(1) las afueras
(2) las bodas
(3) las narices
(4) las crisis
(5) los regímenes

(6) los andaluces
(7) los alrededores
(8) las tijeras
(9) los modales
(10) los equipajes

score: ... × 10 =

c) What is the plural of these words?

(1) nación
(2) pared
(3) joven
(4) nuez
(5) pez

(6) jabalí
(7) rubí
(8) martes
(9) tesis
(10) voz

score: ... × 10 =

d) Put these expressions into the plural.

    (1) El traje azul.

    (2) El Rey de España.

    (3) La ley de derecho.

    (4) La voz del pueblo.

    (5) El café está abierto.

    (6) La flor amarilla.

    (7) El jabalí no es fácil de cazar.

    (8) El lápiz está por el suelo.

    (9) Este pez es demasiado gordo.

    (10) La nación extranjera.

score: ... × 10 = ◯

e) Translate these words. Include the definite article and pay special attention to gender and number.

(1) chess	(6) hair
(2) people	(7) (facial) features
(3) harvest	(8) dentist
(4) back	(9) archives
(5) parents	(10) trash

score: ... × 10 = ◯

6. AUGMENTATIVES AND DIMINUTIVES

A. AUGMENTATIVES

a) Which is the correct augmentative?

(1) un hombre = hombrecete, hombrón, hombrecito.
(2) una mano = una manita, una manecita, una manaza.
(3) una voz = un vozón, una vocecita, un vozarrón.
(4) un puño = puñeton, puñetazo, puñón.
(5) un cánón = cañaza, cañonazo, cañoncito.
(6) un codo = codón, codazo, codacito.
(7) un señor = señorón, señorazo, señorcito.
(8) unos ojos = ojazones, ojazos, ojillos.
(9) un mozo = mozazón, mocetón, mozón.
(10) una cabeza = cabezón, cabezota, cabecita.

score: ... × 10 = ◯

b) Translate these sentences, using augmentatives.

(1) They bought a huge car.
(2) Don't use swear words *(tú)*.
(3) Sort out your papers *(tú)*.
(4) While repairing the table, he hit himself with a hammer.
(5) She slammed the door in a rage.
(6) They say she was killed by a punch.
(7) He pretends to be stupid so that nobody will bother him.
(8) This large wall is made of concrete.
(9) She woke him up by kicking him.
(10) It's a large house on the edge of the village.

score: ... × 10 = ◯

B. DIMINUTIVES

a) Change the words in brackets into diminutives.

    (1) Ésta es una casa (**nueva**).

    (2) Aqui está la (**vieja señora**) de la que te hablé.

    (3) Este juguete cuesta (**unas pesetas**).

    (4) Fuimos todos a dar un (**paseo**).

    (5) Este chico es un (**señor**).

    (6) ¿Te apetece un (**café**).

    (7) ¡Ojo! sube (**despacio**).

    (8) Ven con tu (**hermano pequeño**) y que te dé la (**mano**).

    (9) Es ella (**muy joven**) para casarse.

    (10) No podéis dormiros sin esa (**pequeña luz**).

score: ... × 10 = ◯

b) Which is the correct diminutive?

    (1) nuevo = nuevito, novecito, nuevecito.

    (2) casa = caseta, casucha, casita.

    (3) café = cafetito, cafelito, cafalito.

    (4) chico = chicote, chicito, chiquito.

    (5) pasea = pasito, paseíto, paseote.

    (6) joven = jovenito, jovencito, jovenzito.

    (7) hermano = hermanote, hermanastro, hermanito.

    (8) plaza = plazita, plazota, plazuela.

    (9) pez = pezito, pecito, pececito.

    (10) copa = copecita, copito, copita.

score: ... × 10 = ◯

7. COMPARATIVES AND SUPERLATIVES

A. COMPARATIVES

a) What would be the opposite of these comparatives?

(1) superior

(2) mayor

(3) mejor

(4) posterior

(5) anterior

(6) peor

(7) menor

(8) ulterior

(9) mayores

(10) peores

score: ... × 10 = ◯

b) Translate these sentences.

(1) He is more stubborn than his brother.

(2) The Basque Country is wetter than Catalonia.

(3) This job is better than the last one.

(4) You are a lot happier now that your projects are finished (Vd).

(5) These young boys are as tall as their father.

(6) This restaurant is worse than yesterday's.

(7) This bar is less crowded in the evening than in the morning.

(8) Our car is more comfortable than theirs.

(9) This bag is bigger than yours (tú).

(10) His research is more advanced than ours.

score: ... × 10 = ◯

c) **Add** *mas/mayores/menos/tanto/* **etc. to these sentences to make comparisons. The signs +, – and = indicate the type of comparison being made: 'more', 'less' or 'as ... as'.**

   (1) Las consecuencias fueron ... de lo que se esperaba. (+)
   (2) Mi vestido es ... estampado que el tuyo. (–)
   (3) Dormís ... vuestros hijos. (=)
   (4) Corres ... Pedro. (=)
   (5) No es ... autoritaria ... lo parece. (not =)
   (6) Posees ... libros ... ellos. (+)
   (7) El marido habla ... que su mujer. (–)
   (8) Este tablao flamenco es ... barato ... el anterior. (+)
   (9) El pueblo desea ... prohibiciones ... antes. (–)
   (10) El peligro es ... en coche. (+)

score: ... × 10 = ◯

d) **Use** *más, menos* **or** *tanto***, etc. to complete these sentences and make plausible comparisons.**

   (1) Una jirafa es ... alta ... una vaca.
   (2) Un gato es ... feroz ... un león.
   (3) Plácido Domingo es ... famoso ... mi hermano.
   (4) Toledo es ... grande ... Madrid.
   (5) El zorro suele ser ... astuto ... las gallinas.
   (6) El sol está ... lejos ... la luna.
   (7) Un kilo de ploma pesa ... ... un kilo de plumas.
   (8) Llueve ... en Andalucía ... en Galicia.
   (9) El Atlántico no es ... grande ... el Pacífico.
   (10) A los niños les gusta jugar ... ... estudiar.

score: ... × 10 = ◯

B. THE MORE ... THE LESS ...

Complete these sentences using the equivalent of 'the more/less ... the more/less ...' comparatives.

   (1) Está ... delgada ... come.
   (2) La casa es ... vieja ... se cuida.
   (3) Está ... contento ... asignaturas aprueba.

(4) Es ... culto ... lee.

(5) El perro es ... gracioso ... pequeño es.

(6) El velero va ... rápido ... sopla el viento.

(7) Es ... veloz ... corre.

(8) Está ... enfermo ... medicamentos toma.

(9) Es ... sensible ... inquietudes tiene.

(10) El pájaro es ... feliz ... libre es.

score: ... × 10 = ◯

C. SUPERLATIVES

a) **Replace the words in brackets with an adjective in the superlative.**

(1) Su tía es (**muy rica**).

(2) Es un cantante (**muy famoso**).

(3) Era una actriz (**muy guapa**).

(4) Es una noticia (**muy triste**).

(5) Fue una pareja (**muy feliz**).

(6) Es un río (**muy largo**).

(7) Eran unos padres (**muy simpáticos**).

(8) El destino fue (**muy duro**) para con ellos.

(9) Esta joya es (**muy antigua**).

(10) Fue una aldea (**muy pobre**).

score: ... × 10 = ◯

b) **Replace the word in brackets with an adjective in the superlative.**

(1) Es un chico (**muy bueno**).

(2) El Dos de Mayo es un cuadro (**muy famoso**).

(3) Hubo un estallido (**muy fuerte**).

(4) Su amiga está (**muy mala**).

(5) Esta región es un lugar (**muy antiguo**).

(6) Estaba (**muy blanca**) y (**muy pálida**).

(7) Este conferenciante es (**muy elocuente**).

(8) Es el (**más grande**) de la familia.

(9) Su provecho es (**muy grande**).

(10) Es el fracaso (**más grande**).

score: ... × 10 = ◯

c) Complete the sentences below with these superlatives:

menor, mayor, último, mínimo, mayores, máximo, óptimos, mejor, peor, ínfima.

(1) Esto es lo ... que puedo hacer por ti.

(2) Jaime nunca aprueba los exámenes. Es el ... alumno de todos.

(3) Ana es la ... de la familia. Sólo tiene dos meses.

(4) Hay que tener 17 años como ... par conducir un coche.

(5) Es una película para ... .

(6) Estudia ... que antes.

(7) Los resultados son ... .

(8) La herida es ... .

(9) Acaba de publicarse el ... libro que ha escrito.

(10) La salud es el ... de los bienes.

score: ... × 10 = ◯

d) Give the superlative(s) of these words.

(1) bueno - **(2)** grande - **(3)** blanco - **(4)** agradable -
(5) amable - **(6)** malo - **(7)** pequeño - **(8)** famoso -
(9) simpático - **(10)** pobre.

score: ... × 10 = ◯

e) Translate the following.

(1) It's the friendliest town in the area.

(2) He is the most learned man at the moment.

(3) You *(tú)* are the smartest of the three sisters.

(4) It's the tallest tree in the garden.

(5) It's the lightest room.

(6) He was the most talkative boy in his class.

(7) That's the most serious daily paper.

(8) She's the most spoiled child I know.

(9) He was the most qualified worker in the factory.

(10) He will be the most talented sportsman in the club.

(11) You *(vosotros)* have put on your nicest dresses.

(12) Andalusia is the most popular region in Spain for tourists.

(13) Japan is the most industrialized nation.

(14) He's cleverer than he appears.

(15) She's a very nice person.

(16) He's a very strong man.

(17) As it's very big, the house can hold many people.

(18) They are very poor people.

(19) This story is really boring.

(20) I drank very strong coffee.

score: ... × 10 = ◯

f) Translate these sentences, using a superlative.

(1) Today must be the hottest day of the year.

(2) I have just done the most stupid thing.

(3) She is the tallest girl in the class.

(4) He gave me the most interesting book.

(5) I find politics the most boring subject.

(6) This isn't the hottest soup I've tasted.

(7) He's the most widely-read author in the country.

(8) It was the worst storm I'd ever seen.

(9) What I like best is to be with you.

(10) Isabel is the smartest child in the school.

(11) It is the most complex situation you can imagine.

(12) He met a most attractive woman while walking in the park.

(13) Arthur is my biggest worry at the moment.

(14) Have you *(tú)* heard the latest about that áctress?

(15) She's the most generous person I know.

(16) It was the most incredible story I'd ever heard.

(17) We are now coming to the poorest area of the city.

(18) It's the least I can do.

(19) She had the best vacation of her life.

(20) This must be the worst wine I've tasted in a long time.

score: ... × 5 = ◯

D. REVIEW TEST

Translate these sentences.

(1) A government spokesman is less famous than a minister.

(2) A stone wall is more solid than a concrete one.

(3) A new hat is more attractive than an old beret.

(4) He is the most popular member of the party.

(5) The daily newspaper published the closing dates for the exams.

(6) The famine is more widespread than one thinks.

(7) Violence is as dangerous as fanaticism.

(8) There is more unemployment in Spain than in Germany.

(9) The number of refugees is lower today.

(10) You *(tú)* are the oldest in the family.

score: ... × 10 = ◯

8. PRONOUNS

A. PERSONAL PRONOUNS

a) Which is the correct pronoun?

(1) Se fueron todos salvo (**me - yo - mí**).

(2) Esto es un regalo para (**tú - te - ti**).

(3) Eres más dotado que (**el - sí - él**).

(4) Habla siempre de (**ella mismo - sí mismo - el mismo**).

(5) Llegaron antes de (**nos - nosotros - nuestros**).

(6) (**Las - Les - Los**) ordenó que se sentaran.

(7) Era un cliente importante, pero no (**lo - la - le**) hizo caso.

(8) Por (**nosotros - nuestros - nos**) lo haría todo.

(9) Despµés de (**si - se - usted**) no vino nadie.

(10) (**Ellas - Las - Les**) reservaste una buena cena en el mejor restaurante.

score: ... × 10 = ◯

b) Put these words in order to make a correct phrase.

(1) Ven, Madrid, con nosotros, a, visitar.

(2) Salió, la noche, ellos, por, con.

(3) Dí, algo, nos, antes, cuanto.

(4) Oye, en, lo, pasa, la calle, que.

(5) Rió, se, voz, de, alta, en, chistes, los.

(6) No hagan, se, lo, que, debe, no.

(7) Salir, de, se, abrigo, puso, antes, el.

(8) No conduzcas, rápida, a, velocidad, mucha.

(9) Vete, pan, a, por, el.

(10) A, plátanos, gustan, mi, me, no, los.

score: ... × 10 = ◯

c) Find the mistake and correct it.

(1) A ti les gustan las fiestas.

(2) Allá, nosotros os aburristeis mucho.

    (3) Hazlo y que te se repita más.
    (4) Él veremos cuando vayamos de vacaciones.
    (5) A vosotros nos encanta reunimos con ellos.
    (6) A ustedes os duele la cabeza.
    (7) Mañana, hablaremos con las.
    (8) Los diremos que se callen.
    (9) No vos contó lo que pasó.
   (10) A tú te dan miedo las películas policíacas.

score: ... × 10 = ◯

d) Fill in the gaps with suitable pronouns.

    (1) Te quedaste en casa pero ... se fueron a cenar fuera.
    (2) Todo aquello ... pareció extraño a nosotros.
    (3) Nos lo repitió ... misma.
    (4) ¿Te enteraste de ... que pasó? Sí, ... enteré.
    (5) Vosotros estáis sorprendidos y nosotros ... estamos también.
    (6) A ... os apetece un bocadillo.
    (7) Corrió detrás de ... para anunciarme la noticia.
    (8) ¿Los billetes ? no ... tengo.
    (9) A ustedes, ... vi durante la última feria.
   (10) Nos avisaron a ... y no a su hermana.
   (11) Después de ... no vi a nadie.
   (12) ¿Hablaron con mi familia ? Sí, hablamos con ...
   (13) A ... te encantan las fiestas.
   (14) ... no podemos hacerlo todo.
   (15) Quieres explicar ... todo.
   (16) A ... ... encantaría beber un granizado de limón.
   (17) ¿... fijaste en ...?
   (18) ... duele la cabeza.
   (19) ¿Por qué tipo de films se interesan ...?
   (20) No ... da la gana ir de compras.

score: ... × 5 = ◯

e) Choose the correct form.

    (1) El estanco se sitúa detrás de (**te, tu, ti**).
    (2) Todos estaban conformes, salvo (**mí, me, yo**).

(3) Ven (**comme, conmi, conmigo**).

(4) Júntate (**con se, con ellos, consigo**).

(5) Eligió el menú antes que (**vos, os, vosotros**).

(6) El accidente ocurrió delante de (**nuestro, nos, nosotros**).

(7) Acudieron todos menos (**te, ti, tú**).

(8) (**Escápati, escápatu, escápate**) por ese lado.

(9) Después de (**nos, nosotros**) no vino nadie más.

(10) Pasaba las vacaciones (**bañándose, bañando a sí**) y tomando el sol.

score: ... × 10 = ◯

f) Choose the correct form.

(1) Jugad con (**usted, les, él**).

(2) No (**lo, la, le**) arranque la página.

(3) Ve y (**confiésaselo, confiésasele, confiésaseos**).

(4) No (**le, la, lo**) neguéis.

(5) (**Enséñalos, Enséñalas, Enséñales**) todo lo que tienes guardado.

(6) (**Apuntadlos, Apuntadles, Apuntadlo**) en un papel.

(7) (**Tu, te, ti**) miraba tanto que (**la, te, ti**) llamó la atención.

(8) Estas paredes (**píntales, píntalos, píntalas**) de verde.

(9) Duerma (**usted, le, se**) pronto.

(10) A estas chicas, deberás (**acogerlos, acogerles, acogerlas**) con discreción.

score: ... × 10 = ◯

g) Translate these sentences.

(1) Who is it? Is it you *(tú)*?

(2) Will you hurry up *(tú)*!

(3) What do you *(tú)* think of all that?

(4) He admitted it to us himself.

(5) One can get used to anything given time.

(6) You *(Vd.)* always had a gift for languages.

(7) If you *(tú)* speak badly *(chapurrear)*, you can't be understood.

(8) Most people know at least one language.

(9) The problem is the difficult grammar points.

(10) She lent a dictionary to her colleague; he left it in the library.

257

(11) One can't help smiling when words are pronounced badly.

(12) He's already told me about that.

(13) You *(tú)* love plants.

(14) Are you *(Vd)* thinking about the exams? - Yes, I very often think about them.

(15) Learning Catalan and Galician did not seem important to him.

(16) It's certain that she won't come.

(17) They have often given him advice.

(18) There's only one solution for them *(ellas)*: to correct their faults.

(19) Your *(tú)* friends, I don't understand them *(ellas)*.

(20) Has she given him an answer? - No, she has not given him one.

score: ... × 5 = 〇

h) Translate these sentences.

(1) The mayor inaugurated the monument.

(2) I don't want water, I want milk.

(3) He took off his overcoat.

(4) His father is a famous architect.

(5) Have you *(tú)* got a house in the country?

(6) He lives in Madrid, the capital of Spain.

(7) Catalonia is a province that is developing greatly.

(8) The Director is waiting for you *(Vd)* in his office.

(9) The poor man is completely worn out.

(10) The main thing is to get an appointment.

(11) The EC is expanding rapidly.

(12) I'm asking you *(Vd)* to sit down.

(13) Miss, you *(Vd)* have a number of problems to sort out.

(14) You *(tú)* like beer, but you don't like wine.

(15) They *(ellas)* have no idea how much people love them.

(16) You *(tú)* put your jacket on.

(17) The important thing is to understand.

(18) I hate hypocrisy.

(19) That place has never been visited.

(20) It occurred to him to change the lock.

score: ... × 5 = 〇

B. ATTACHED PRONOUNS

a) **Attach the pronouns given to the verbs.**

   (1) Pon el sombrero (**te**).

   (2) Ve a la cama (**te**).

   (3) Están riendo de ti (**se**).

   (4) Irá a devolver (**telo**).

   (5) Sigue mirando (**la**).

   (6) Va buscando por todas partes (**los**).

   (7) Relaja cuando puedes (**te**).

   (8) Quiere imitar (**lo**).

   (9) Venid a visitar (**los**).

   (10) Estaban bañando (**se**).

score: ... × 10 =

b) **Translate the following sentences, using attached pronouns.**

   (1) *(Vd)* Say it to him.

   (2) Take *(tú)* your queen and put her there.

   (3) Come *(tú)* and tell me it.

   (4) He asked us to choose it.

   (5) I dare not tell him.

   (6) *(Vd)* Show us what you have painted.

   (7) I see you want to leave it.

   (8) Repeat *(vosotros)* the phrase to me.

   (9) Cover *(Vd)* them all.

   (10) He wants to do it all.

score: ... × 10 =

C. INDEFINITE PRONOUNS

a) **Complete the following sentences.**

   (1) ¿Vino ...? No, no vino ...

   (2) ¿Quieres ...? No, no quiero ...

   (3) Tenemos ... biografía sobre este autor.

    (4) No podemos darles … información.
    (5) Te apetece …? No, gracias … me apetece …
    (6) No tenéis dinero, ellos… .
    (7) … sabe …
    (8) Siempre están de acuerdo y ustedes …
    (9) No tiene recelo …
    (10) La obra de teatro no les gustó …

score: … × 10 = $\bigcirc$

b) Choose the correct form.

    (1) ¿Hay alguien en casa? No, no hay **(nada, alguien, nadie)**.
    (2) ¿Queda algún retrato de él? No, no queda **(nada, ninguno, ningún)**.
    (3) ¿Hay algún sitio para aparcar? No, no hay **(alguno, nada, ninguno)**.
    (4) ¿Hay algunos alumnos en el patio? No, no hay **(ninguno, nadie, ningún)**.
    (5) No quiero **(ningún, alguna, ninguna)** ayuda.
    (6) Sin duda **(alguna, ninguna, algún)**, no van a venir.
    (7) En el campeonato de esgrima, no le ganará **(alguien, algún, nadie)**.
    (8) Permaneció **(alguno, algo, algún)** tiempo en el hotel.
    (9) Sus postales estarán en **(ninguna, alguna, cualquiera)** parte.
    (10) No se me ocurre **(nada, alguna, ninguna)** respuesta.

score: … × 10 = $\bigcirc$

c) Use negative indefinites in the following sentences.

    (1) … conoce su paradero.
    (2) … viene a verlos.
    (3) … estaba informado sobre lo que pasaba.
    (4) … visitó Italia.
    (5) No suele … sacar a su perro.
    (6) No quisieron acoger a … .
    (7) No aprobaron a … alumno.
    (8) No estamos … cansados.

(9) ... coche pasa por aquí.

(10) ... otro niño contestó.

score: ... × 10 = $\bigcirc$

d) Translate the following sentences.

(1) He never speaks to anyone.

(2) You *(tú)* do not have to open the door.

(3) There's no point in you *(Vds)* giving anything at all.

(4) It would not be good for you *(Vd)* to drive.

(5) They did not have any change for the tip.

(6) I do not like the way he behaves at all.

(7) They are not in the least frightened.

(8) He has no more gasoline left.

(9) You never do anything *(tú)*.

(10) He doesn't have the least desire to go out.

score: ... × 10 = $\bigcirc$

e) Translate the following sentences.

(1) Do you *(tú)* see anything?

(2) There is nothing interesting on TV.

(3) She doesn't like snow either.

(4) Nobody asked about you *(Vd)*.

(5) He never helps his parents.

(6) We too visited the Prado.

(7) You *(tú)* will have seen some marvelous works of art.

(8) They have a few suspicions about us.

(9) You *(Vd)* supplied him with some goods.

(10) Which outfits will you *(Vd)* choose? Whichever. *(Present tense)*.

score: ... × 10 = $\bigcirc$

f) Translate the following sentences.

(1) I have no time left.

(2) He does not feel at all embarrassed.

261

(3) There is no more coffee left for me.

(4) I am not afraid.

(5) They have no work at all.

(6) You *(vosotros)* have absolutely no money.

(7) You *(Vd)* have absolutely no idea of that.

(8) He didn't eat any of that.

(9) You *(tú)* don't understand anything about that.

(10) Do you *(tú)* agree? Not at all.

score: ... × 10 = ◯

D. DEMONSTRATIVE PRONOUNS AND ADJECTIVES

a) **Complete, using *éste, ésta, éstos, éstas, ésto* or *este, esta, estos, estas*.**

(1) ... animales no están en buena salud.

(2) ... amigas no dejan de hablar.

(3) ... no es válido.

(4) Mis jerseyes son más cómodos que... .

(5) Ignoro ... dirección.

(6) Conozco de memoria ... réplicas.

(7) ... chica presume de rica.

(8) No me gustan ... plantas.

(9) ... niños son bien educados.

(10) Lo importante no es ... sino ... trabajo.

score: ... × 10 = ◯

b) **Complete, using demonstrative pronouns *ése, ésa, éso, ésos, ésas* or demonstrative adjectives *ese, esa, esos, esas*.**

(1) No te enseño ... billete sino ...

(2) Aquí están ...

(3) Voy a hablar con ...

(4) ¡Cuidado! ¿No has visto ... señal?

(5) ... amigos siempre llegaban tarde.

(6) ... habitación es muy amplia.

(7) Las ventanas ... están cerradas desde algún tiempo.

(8) ... edificio es una ruina.

(9) ... vecinos dan mucha lata.

(10) No les interesan ... tipo de películas

score: ... × 10 = ◯

c) **Complete, using demonstrative pronouns *aquél, aquélla, aquéllo, aquéllos, aquéllas* or demonstrative adjectives *aquel, aquella, aquellos, aquellas*.**

(1) ... camino era más asequible que éste.

(2) ... profesores eran competentes.

(3) Disfrutamos mucho durante ... vacaciones.

(4) ... mujeres eran muy raras.

(5) Recorríamos ... parajes solos.

(6) ... relojes sonaban todos al mismo tiempo.

(7) Mi casa no es ésta sino... .

(8) ... postales fueron difíciles de conseguir.

(9) ... fue conocido muy tarde.

(10) No os hablaron de él sino de ... asuntos.

score: ... × 10 = ◯

E. TRANSLATING 'HERE IS', 'THERE ARE' ETC

How would you translate these sentences?

(1) Here is my brother - (2) Here is the most important thing - (3) There is the classroom - (4) Here is Juan - (5) Here are the dried fruits - (6) There is the mechanic - (7) Here are the details - (8) Here are the reservations - (9) There is some beautiful scenery - (10) There are your neighbors.

score: ... × 5 = ◯

F. POSSESSIVES

a) **Replace the forms in brackets with a possessive and rearrange the sentences.**

(1) ¿Este libro es **(de él)**? No, es **(de tí)**.

(2) Los padres **(de nosotros)** nos esperan a las ocho.

(3) El cuaderno **(de mí)** está terminado.

(4) ¡Hijo **(de mí)** no seas cabezota!

(5) El piso **(de usted)** es muy amplio.

(6) Nunca lleva la documentación **(de ella)**.

(7) Las fotos **(de vosotros)** son interesantes.

(8) Los consejos **(de ustedes)** no sirven de nada.

(9) Los comentarios **(de ellos)** no me gustan.

(10) Juan no ha fotocopiado los documentos **(de él)**, sino los **(de usted)**.

score: ... × 10 = ◯

b) **Translate the following sentences.**

(1) One of his fingers is in a plaster cast.

(2) The pupils were chatting to their gymnastics teacher.

(3) When you *(Vd)* are six years old you lose some of your milk teeth.

(4) He became angry with you because you were moving too much.

(5) This prescription is not his but yours *(tú)*.

(6) Do you *(tú)* want his?

(7) Are these tablets hers?

(8) She has a toothache.

(9) Where does it hurt *(tú)*?

(10) My knee is hurting.

(11) They have an appointment with the doctor this afternoon.

(12) They took his tonsils out.

(13) I broke my leg.

(14) Whose hat is this?

(15) She put a scarf on.

(16) He's not our father, he's theirs.

(17) You *(tú)* hurt your wrist.

(18) Who does this house belong to? It is the dentist's.

(19) His mother washed his hands.

(20) They were not your *(vosotros)* gloves, they were theirs.

score: ... × 5 = ◯

c) **Translate the following sentences.**

    (1) Where is our baggage?

    (2) Where have you *(tú)* left your purse?

    (3) I haven't got your *(Vd)* keys.

    (4) They did not see your *(Vds)* friends, but ours.

    (5) Our town is very beautiful.

    (6) My dog hates cats.

    (7) He does not speak to his uncle but to his brother-in-law.

    (8) They are not patient with their mother.

    (9) My friend, we're going to climb the mountain.

    (10) Some of their relations stayed at home.

    (11) Where have you *(Vd)* left your coat?

    (12) One of your *(Vd)* sons wanted to know where his sister was.

    (13) Your *(tú)* car is a lot more comfortable than theirs.

    (14) William did not read his comics but he read yours *(vosotros)*.

    (15) Is this book yours *(Vd)*?

    (16) This girl is a friend of my daughter's.

    (17) Whose is this eraser? It's mine.

    (18) The owner of the hotel which burned down is furious.

    (19) *One Hundred Years of Solitude* is a novel by García Márquez.

    (20) Whose is this file? It is theirs.

score: ... × 5 =

d) **Complete, using the correct possessive.**

    (1) Este amigo conoce a ... familia **(de ti)**.

    (2) Lo que es ... **(de ti)** es también ... **(de él)**.

    (3) ... fábrica iba de mal en peor **(de él)**.

    (4) ... dependientes **(de mí)** son más activos que los ...
         (de usted).

    (5) Est jardín se parece al ... **(de mí)**.

    (6) Indíqueme ... dirección **(la de ella)**.

    (7) ¿Son ... **(de vosotros)** estos guantes ?

    (8) ... **(de él)** punto de vista es muy logíco.

    (9) ... (de ellos) deseos son demasiados importantes.

    (10) ... **(de ustedes)** niños son muy agradables.

    (11) ¡Elisa vida ...! **(de mí)**.

    (12) Este manuscrito ... **(de ti)** es muy largo.

    (13) ... **(de ti)** oficio es estupendo, pero el ... **(de usted)** es mejor.

(14) ... **(de nosotros)** amigos, llegaron pronto.

(15) Ya no marchan ... proyectos **(de usted)**.

(16) ... **(de mí)** diccionario es muy completo.

(17) ... **(de ustedes)** finca está apartada del pueblo.

(18) ... **(de mí)** novela está por escribir.

(19) El restaurante ... **(de usted)** acoge a toda clase de gente.

(20) ... **(de ellos)** familiares les esperan en la estación.

score: ... × 5 = $\bigcirc$

G. INTERROGATIVE PRONOUNS AND ADVERBS

a) **Change the following sentences into questions using interrogative pronouns or adverbs.**

(1) Suelen cenar tarde en España.

(2) Veraneamos a orillas del mar.

(3) Juega con sus primos.

(4) En esta familia, muchas personas tocan el piano.

(5) Escribe libros de clase.

(6) Su abuela viene a quedarse con ellos.

(7) Leo novelas policíacas.

(8) Mis vecinos son ruidosos.

(9) Miguel de Cervantes escribió *Don Quijote de la Mancha*.

(10) Rocinante era el nombre de su caballo.

(11) Sancho Panza era su criado.

(12) Don Quijote nació en un lugar de la Mancha.

(13) Sus aficiones eran leer y pelear.

(14) Iba siempre a caballo.

(15) Actuaba con mucho valor.

(16) El apodo de Don Quijote era « el Caballero a la triste figura ».

(17) Visita la meseta castellana en coche.

(18) Nos encanta bañarnos en el mar.

(19) Esos chavales tendrán unos diez años.

(20) Lee los periódicos para informarse.

score: ... × 5 = ◯

b) Change the following statements into questions using interrogative pronouns or adverbs.

(1) Tengo cita a las seis de la tarde.

(2) El domingo suele ir a pasear.

(3) Mi amigo es arquitecto.

(4) Tus padres viven en las afueras de Barcelona.

(5) He telefoneado a Ana.

(6) Tu primo es muy divertido.

(7) Está leyendo la última novela de García Márquez.

(8) Este tren pasa siempre por su ciudad.

(9) Vendió el cuadro por miles de pesetas.

(10) Los idiomas y las matemáticas son las asignaturas que prefiero.

score: ... × 10 = ◯

c) Translate these sentences using interrogative pronouns.

(1) You *(Vd)* have given them money, haven't you?

(2) Which is the one that you *(tú)* liked the most?

(3) Which of those shirts do you *(tú)* prefer?

(4) I don't know which one I prefer.

(5) Which of those parties calls itself right-wing?

(6) Did they greet each other?

(7) Do they mutually help each other?

(8) Did you *(Vd)* say "See you tomorrow" to him?

(9) Did he repeat a year *(repetir un curso)*?

(10) Did they choose several subjects?

score: ... × 10 = ◯

H. RELATIVE PRONOUNS

a) Match parts of sentences in A with B to make complete sentences.

	A		**B**
(1)	Viste la película	**a)**	a quien lo dice.
(2)	El chico	**b)**	detrás de la cual hay un parque.
(3)	Es una gran mansión	**c)**	a la cual dedico unos versos.
(4)	Debe comprometerse	**d)**	debajo de los cuales nos gusta cobijarnos.
(5)	Los clientes	**e)**	a quienes he pregonado las ventajas de este coche están satisfechos.
(6)	Es un café	**f)**	que se estrenó ayer.
(7)	Los amigos	**g)**	que está delante de ti es madrileño.
(8)	Fue un compañero	**h)**	en que se reúnen los famosos.
(9)	Son unos soportales	**i)**	con el que se carteó muchas veces.
(10)	Es la chica	**j)**	con quienes más te diviertes son muy abiertos.

score: ... × 10 = ◯

b) Choose the correct relative pronoun.

(1) Me encanta ir a las rebajas (**cuyas - de las cuales - que**) son numerosas en ciertas épocas del año.

(2) Estos jerseyes (**quienes - cuyos - que**) están de oferta, te los voy a comprar.

(3) El huésped (**el que - que - quien**) te acogió es muy simpático.

(4) Los guateques (**por los que - a los que - quienes**) acudimos son muy animados.

(5) Los automovilistas (**cuales - que - quienes**) conducen un cacharro son unos inconscientes.

(6) El cruce (**ante que - a donde - en el que**) se pararon es un peligro.

(7) La obra (**de cuyo - del que - cuyo**) autor es desconocido, es sin embargo famosa.

(8) El disco (**cuyo - el cual - que**) acabas de comprar es mi favorito

(9) En España hay unos monarcas (**los cuales - de los que - cuyos**) hijos son mayores.

(10) La vendedora (**por la que - para la cual - a la cual**) te diriges no te puede atender.

score: ... × 10 = ◯

c) **Complete using** *cuyo, cuya, cuyos* **or** *cuyas*, **preceded by a preposition where necessary.**

(1) Es un barrio ... vecinos desconozco.

(2) Era un pueblo ... tiendas eran buenas.

(3) Es una habitación ... ventana se ve el mar.

(4) Es un niño ... hermanos son todos mayores.

(5) Era una alfombra ... dibujo le encantaba.

(6) Fue un pueblo ... costumbres ignoraba.

(7) Es una región ... montañas subimos.

(8) Son unas flores ... olores me recuerdan mi niñez.

(9) Es un lugar de la Mancha ... nombre no recuerdo.

(10) Fueron unos personajes ... amigos no había nada que decir.

(11) Es una teoría ... contenido nos indigna.

(12) Fue una obra de teatro ... fama se acordaban todos.

(13) Es una película ... director es catalán.

(14) Es una casa ... tejado suelen anidar las cigüeñas.

(15) Es una habitación ... balcones se ve el parque.

(16) Es un escritor ... libros están muy de moda.

(17) Es una gramática ... reglas desconozco.

(18) Es una lección ... interés no veo.

(19) Es un parque ... alamedas me gusta pasear.

(20) Es una máquina ... cinta está gastada.

score: ... × 5 = ◯

d) **Translate these sentences using a suitable relative pronoun.**

(1) It is a country whose government is not neutral.

(2) It is a law which we will hear a lot about.

(3) It's a crisis the consequences of which we are ignorant.

(4) It's a campaign which the middle class is pleased about (*alegrarse*).

269

(5) The shop, in front of whose window there is a fir tree, belongs to my father.

(6) There was a group of young people amongst whom was my brother.

(7) The concert which you *(tú)* told me about was not recorded.

(8) The friend whose footsteps I was following has not been found (begin **No ha sido encontrado** ...).

(9) The city whose buildings you can glimpse is Seville.

(10) The farmhouse, which has a door open, is owned by my uncle.

(11) The bank, whose employees you know, has been closed since midday.

(12) She was a child whom all the others made fun of.

(13) It is an event that will be talked about for a long time.

(14) It's a language that she doesn't know a word of.

(15) It's a newspaper *(diario)* whose articles are varied.

(16) It was an animal whose owner was bad.

(17) It's a rented house whose comfort is dubioius.

(18) It's a beach with a friendly atmosphere (use *cuyo*)

(19) That was a year we shall always remember.

(20) The owner of the shop is from Aragon (begin *Es una tienda* ...)

score: ... × 5 = ◯

e) **Translate the following sentences using suitable pronouns.**

(1) I don't know anybody who can tell you *(Vd)*.

(2) Those who do not wish to take part can leave.

(3) Whoever is setting the table, don't forget the napkins.

(4) What they didn't like was his pride.

(5) Those who do not arrive on time will be sent away.

(6) I don't know a country where that is allowed.

(7) Are you *(Vd)* looking for someone to come with you?

(8) We don't have any books which would be useful to you *(vosotros)*.

(9) There is nobody who knows how to convince them.

(10) She is a pupil who has a gift for languages.

(11) The man who lost his job is unhappy.

(12) It's good news which doesn't surprise me.

(13) The desk on which you work is full of papers.

(14) Choose the film which you *(tú)* like most.
(15) What interests them most is leisure time.
(16) He was an actor whose past we knew.
(17) She went to the attic which was full of old boxes.
(18) The person whom he addressed is his aunt.
(19) This is a forest in which you *(vosotros)* like walking.
(20) The friends who had got together did not recognize her.

score: ... × 5 = ◯

f) **Complete each sentence using the correct relative pronoun.**

(1) Es una canción ... conozco de memoria.
(2) Fueron ellos ... denunciaron el suceso.
(3) Era una revista ... no le gustaba.
(4) Aquí está la ventana por ... se cayó.
(5) Se paseó por unos barrios en ... había mucha gente.
(6) Le gustaba recorrer los sitios por ... había estado.
(7) Dudaba de ... le contaban.
(8) Esta es la fila por ... se coló.
(9) Es un sitio de ... se ve toda la costa.
(10) Era una época en ... había muchas injusticias.
(11) No había nadie ... pudiera acompañarme.
(12) Es un proyecto ... propósito desconozco.
(13) Nos encantaba volver al café en ... había una tertulia.
(14) Sabe influir ... le escucha.
(15) La gente a ... se han dirigido es muy amable.
(16) Espero que salgan pronto del trance en ... están.
(17) Que venga ... quiera.
(18) Dime ... fue la victima.
(19) Es una enciclopedia ... le interesa mucho.
(20) Aquí están los amigos de ... te hablé.

score: ... × 10 = ◯

g) Match parts of sentences in A with B to make complete sentences.

A	B
(1) No soportan que, no digan la verdad	**a)** que tomen medidas autoritarias.
(2) España está en plena expansión,	**b)** lo cual es legítimo.
(3) La guerra civil duró tres años,	**c)** lo que se verifica a diario.
(4) Es un edificio	**d)** de los que hablaron juntos.
(5) No nos parece prudente	**e)** que saca buenas notas.
(6) Fueron unos acontecimientos	**f)** sobre el cual se pusieron do acuerdo.
(7) Es una alumna	**g)** lo que fue una tragedia para todos.
(8) Es una revista	**h)** delante del cual nos citamos a menudo.
(9) Firmará un acuerdo	**i)** que compro a menudo.
(10) Es en verano	**j)** cuando suelo ir a la playa.

score: ... × 10 = ◯

9. VERB FORMS

Give yourself one point for each verb conjugation which you give correctly.

a) Conjugate these verbs in the present tense.

   (1) aportar
   (2) cubrir
   (3) conocer
   (4) distribuir
   (5) costar

b) Conjugate these verbs in the imperfect tense.

   (6) ser
   (7) sentir
   (8) ver
   (9) disolver
   (10) soñar

   score: ... × 10 = ◯

c) Conjugate these verbs in the present subjunctive.

   (1) haber
   (2) reconocer
   (3) despertarse
   (4) adquirir
   (5) hacer

d) Conjugate these verbs in the future tense.

   (6) poner
   (7) tener
   (8) salir
   (9) haber
   (10) hacer

   score: ... × 10 = ◯

e) **For each verb give** *(a)* **the first person singular present indicative and** *(b)* **the third person singular of the preterite.**

(1) hacer		(11) poner	
(2) caer		(12) proponer	
(3) ir		(13) disponer	
(4) traer		(14) detener	
(5) ser		(15) convenir	
(6) dar		(16) oír	
(7) poder		(17) conducir	
(8) haber		(18) venir	
(9) estar		(19) tener	
(10) salir		(20) querer	

score: ... × 5 = ◯

f) **For each verb give** *(a)* **the first person singular present indicative and** *(b)* **the first person plural present subjunctive.**

(1) conducir		(11) permanecer	
(2) desaparecer		(12) pertenecer	
(3) favorecer		(13) reducir	
(4) amanecer		(14) aborrecer	
(5) establecer		(15) traducir	
(6) producir		(16) nacer	
(7) aparecer		(17) obedecer	
(8) conocer		(18) ofrecer	
(9) carecer		(19) merecer	
(10) introducir		(20) crecer	

score: ... × 5 = ◯

g) **For each verb give** *(a)* **the first person singular and** *(b)* **the third person plural of the present indicative.**

(1) acordar		(6) demostrar	
(2) rendir		(7) divertirse	
(3) mover		(8) mostrar	
(4) acentuar		(9) rodar	
(5) contar		(10) herirse	

(11) colgar

(12) envolver

(13) morder

(14) rogar

(15) convertirse

(16) volverse

(17) soñar

(18) soler

(19) dormir

(20) adquirir

score: ... × 5 = ◯

h) **For each verb give (a) the second person singular and (b) the second person plural of the present indicative.**

(1) cocer

(2) costar

(3) acostar

(4) advertir

(5) resolver

(6) doler

(7) encontrar

(8) devolver

(9) esforzarse

(10) jugar

(11) remover

(12) consentir

(13) hervir

(14) sonar

(15) soltarse

(16) mentir

(17) preferir

(18) volar

(19) recordar

(20) referirse

score: ... × 5 = ◯

i) **For each verb give (a) the first person singular present indicative and (b) the third person singular of the preterite.**

(1) huir

(2) atribuir

(3) distribuir

(4) retribuir

(5) afluir

(6) incluir

(7) restituir

(8) instituir

(9) disminuir

(10) substituir

(11) contribuir

(12) constituir

(13) excluir

(14) obstruir

(15) instruir

(16) influir

(17) destruir

(18) seducir

(19) producir

(20) reducir

score: ... × 5 = ◯

j) For each verb give the first person singular of *(a)* the present indicative and *(b)* the preterite.

(1)	salir	(11)	oír
(2)	haber	(12)	valer
(3)	caber	(13)	dar
(4)	deshacer	(14)	poder
(5)	poner	(15)	hacer
(6)	querer	(16)	tener
(7)	decir	(17)	traer
(8)	saber	(18)	obtener
(9)	ser	(19)	proponer
(10)	ir	(20)	venir

score: ... × 5 =

k) For each verb give *(a)* the first person singular present indicative, *(b)* the third person singular of the preterite and *(c)* the third person plural present subjunctive.

(1)	asombrarse	(11)	reunirse
(2)	dormirse	(12)	peinarse
(3)	asearse	(13)	entristecerse
(4)	levantarse	(14)	caerse
(5)	casarse	(15)	disgustarse
(6)	convertirse	(16)	cansarse
(7)	preocuparse	(17)	endurecerse
(8)	sentarse	(18)	decidirse
(9)	alegrarse	(19)	acostarse
(10)	mirarse	(20)	reflejarse

score: ... × 5 =

l) For each verb give *(a)* the third person singular of the preterite, *(b)* the first person plural of the future and *(c)* the first person plural of the conditional.

(1)	informar	(7)	moverse
(2)	acordarse	(8)	conducir
(3)	dormirse	(9)	preferir
(4)	resolver	(10)	volar
(5)	obedecer	(11)	rodar
(6)	reducir	(12)	excluir

    (13) establecer   **(17)** producir

    (14) repetir   **(18)** jugar

    (15) soler   **(19)** demostrar

    (16) pedir   **(20)** escribir

score: ... × 5 = ◯

m) Which is the correct verb form?

    (1) cantar: **(cantió - cantó - canti)**.

    (2) comer: **(comi - comie - comí)**.

    (3) agotar: **(agotaba - agotia - agotiase)**.

    (4) esconder: **(escondaré - esconderes - esconderé)**.

    (5) tocar: **(toco - toquo - tuoco)**.

    (6) tomar: **(tomiste - tomastes - tomaste)**.

    (7) notar: **(notastis - notastéis - notasteis)**.

    (8) responder: **(respondías - respondabas - responderas)**.

    (9) coger: **(cojos - cogo - cojo)**.

    (10) abrir: **(abrito - abrido - abierto)**.

    (11) romper: **(rompeido - rompido - roto)**.

    (12) ver: **(veíemos - viamos - veíamos)**.

    (13) inquirir: **(inquirís - inquires - inquieris)**.

    (14) borrar: **(borréis - bueráis - borráis)**.

    (15) esconder: **(escondiería - escondiera - escondiesies)**.

    (16) llorar: **(lloreron - lloron - lloraron)**.

    (17) aparecer: **(aparezo - apareza - aparezca)**.

    (18) nombrar: **(nombreriáis - nombraráis - nombrieséis)**.

    (19) nacer: **(naco - nació - nazió)**.

    (20) destruir: **(destruyas - destruilla - destrullas)**.

score: ... × 5 = ◯

n) Conjugate the following verbs.

    (1) nevar - third person singular, present indicative.

    (2) encender - second person singular, present subjunctive.

    (3) impedir - third person plural, present subjunctive.

    (4) reñir - first person singular, present indicative.

    (5) perder - first person singular, preterite.

    (6) extenderse - imperative (all persons).

(7) **agradecer** - first person singular, preterite.

(8) **acostarse** - imperative (all persons).

(9) **merendar** - second person plural, present subjunctive.

(10) **jugar** - first person plural, present subjunctive.

(11) **cenar** - first person plural, preterite.

(12) **mentir** - second person singular, imperfect subjunctive.

(13) **saber** - negative imperative (all persons).

(14) **conferir** - first person plural, present subjunctive.

(15) **conducir** - third person plural, preterite.

(16) **divertirse** - negative imperative (all persons).

(17) **tener** - third person singular, future.

(18) **haber** - second person plural, conditional.

(19) **rodar** - second person plural, imperfect subjunctive.

(20) **ser** - first person plural, imperfect indicative.

score: ... × 5 = $\bigcirc$

o) **Conjugate the following verbs.**

(1) **poder** - first person singular, present indicative.

(2) **helarse** - third person singular, preterite.

(3) **herir** - second person singular, preterite.

(4) **andar** - third person plural, imperfect subjunctive.

(5) **soñar** - first person plural, present subjunctive.

(6) **plegar** - second person plural, imperfect indicative.

(7) **moverse** - imperative (all persons).

(8) **reírse** - negative imperative (all persons).

(9) **caber** - first person singular, present indicative.

(10) **carecer** - first person singular, present subjunctive.

(11) **vestirse** - third person plural, imperfect subjunctive.

(12) **querer** - first person plural, future.

(13) **poder** - second person singular, present indicative.

(14) **perder** - third person plural, preterite.

(15) **ir** - gerund.

(16) **caerse** - negative imperative (all persons).

(17) **seguir** - third person singular, preterite.

(18) **defender** - second person plural, conditional.

(19) **decir** - imperative (all persons).

(20) **parecer** - first person singular, present subjunctive.

(21) **coger** - third person plural, imperfect subjunctive.

(22) poner - imperative (all persons).

(23) despedir - second person plural, present indicative.

(24) ser - preterite (give the whole tense).

(25) haber - first person singular, present indicative.

score: ... × 4 = ◯

p) Give the person, tense and mood of each verb.

(1) calientan   (11) empiezo

(2) aciertes   (12) sueles

(3) negasteis   (13) sueñen

(4) acreciendo   (14) ruego

(5) gobernamos   (15) compruebes

(6) confiesa   (16) desplieguen

(7) calentad   (17) resuelve

(8) aprietas   (18) juegan

(9) atravesé   (19) duele

(10) desconciertan   (20) pienso

score: ... × 5 = ◯

q) Give the person, tense and mood of each verb.

(1) parezco   (11) favorezcan

(2) ofrezcas   (12) pertenecía

(3) carecemos   (13) permanezcan

(4) naciste   (14) conozco

(5) obedeció   (15) condujeron

(6) merecisteis   (16) amanece

(7) entristece   (17) obedezco

(8) aparezcáis   (18) produjera

(9) establezca   (19) traduzcamos

(10) conduzco   (20) enriquezcan

score: ... × 5 = ◯

r) Give the person, tense and mood of each verb.

(1) perdéis   (4) tiemblo

(2) meriendas   (5) piensa

(3) friegue   (6) recomiendan

(7)	analicemos	(14)	entendemos
(8)	adquiramos	(15)	siega
(9)	sintáis	(16)	remueves
(10)	enciendo	(17)	discernís
(11)	llueve	(18)	nieva
(12)	huele	(19)	sentís
(13)	defiendas	(20)	tienden

score: ... × 5 = ◯

s) **Give the person, tense and mood of each verb.**

(1)	adquiero	(11)	apuesten
(2)	sienta	(12)	acuérdense
(3)	truena	(13)	difiero
(4)	absuelve	(14)	encierre
(5)	disuelvo	(15)	defiendas
(6)	remueve	(16)	conduélase
(7)	conmovieron	(17)	envuelvan
(8)	discierna	(18)	volvierais
(9)	cuelgan	(19)	sintamos
(10)	recomienda	(20)	revolvisteis

score: ... × 5 = ◯

t) **Give the person, tense and mood of each verb.**

(1)	sentís	(11)	asolaban
(2)	revolvías	(12)	comprobaré
(3)	discernís	(13)	disuena
(4)	segaron	(14)	sintieses
(5)	llueve	(15)	renovamos
(6)	huela	(16)	huelga
(7)	encomendaron	(17)	resollaras
(8)	vuelo	(18)	pensemos
(9)	aprobabas	(19)	mordía
(10)	encuentres	(20)	esfuérzate

score: ... × 5 = ◯

u) Which of these verbs has a radical change?

(1) acortar	(11) robar
(2) controlar	(12) mostrar
(3) envolver	(13) divertir
(4) correr	(14) sentir
(5) recordar	(15) montar
(6) esconder	(16) preferir
(7) mejorar	(17) costar
(8) soñar	(18) constar
(9) toser	(19) demostrar
(10) soler	(20) pedir

score: ... × 5 =

v) Express the following in Spanish.

(1) come! *(tú)*	(10) go away! *(tú)*
(2) you will do it *(tú)*	(11) let's get up
(3) he asked *(preterite)*	(12) they drove *(preterite)*
(4) they concluded *(preterite)*	(13) I have
	(14) we would like
(5) ... that he has written *(subjunctive)*	(15) move away
	(16) I'm coming back
(6) I light	(17) stop! *(tú)*
(7) rest! *(tú)*	(18) I put ... *(present)*
(8) she will put	(19) she is coming back
(9) they will go out	(20) you *(tú)* are waking up

score: ... × 5 =

w) Express the following in Spanish.

(1) I would ask	(6) I say
(2) they show	(7) everyone went quiet
(3) we will stay	(8) let go! *(tú)*
(4) you close *(tú)*	(9) we will leave
(5) you *(vosotros)* were spending	(10) that you *(tú)* are *(subjunctive)*

(11)	I do	(16)	they have died
(12)	I know	(17)	I'm coming
(13)	she has got up	(18)	that they put *(subjunctive)*
(14)	bring! *(tú)*	(19)	I distinguish
(15)	sit down! *(tú)*	(20)	he resolves

score: ... × 5 = ◯

x) Complete the impersonal expressions in brackets.

(1) **(A vosotros gustar)** el vine y el teatro.
(2) **(A ti encantar)** las puestas de sol.
(3) **(A ellos ilusionar)** viajar a Méjico.
(4) **(A usted ocurrirse)** muchos proyectos.
(5) **(A mí antojarse)** escribirte.
(6) **(A nosotros dar ganas)** hacer un guateque.
(7) **(A ustedes figurarse)** que todo es fácil.
(8) **(A ella dar vergüenza)** tener mal acento.
(9) **(A los niños dar pena)** los animales abandonados.
(10) **(A él doler)** las piernas.

score: ... × 10 = ◯

y) Give the past participle of the following verbs.

(1)	decir	(11)	imprimir
(2)	disponer	(12)	descubrir
(3)	escribir	(13)	abrir
(4)	cubrir	(14)	proponer
(5)	deshacer	(15)	resolver
(6)	devolver	(16)	ver
(7)	hacer	(17)	proveer
(8)	morir	(18)	freír
(9)	romper	(19)	bendecir
(10)	poner	(20)	distinguir

score: ... × 5 = ◯

10. THE VERB 'TO BE'

a) **Complete these sentences using the appropriate part of the verbs *ser* or *estar*, in the present indicative.**

(1) Ustedes … María y Juan.

(2) ¿Quién … tú? … Elena.

(3) Vosotras … guatemaltecas.

(4) Nosotros … madrileños.

(5) ¿Quién de ustedes … la madre?

(6) Granada … en Andalucía.

(7) ¿Dónde … ustedes? … de vacaciones.

(8) La escuela … enfrente del metro.

(9) Nosotros … cansados.

(10) … los últimos en salir.

score: … × 10 = ◯

b) **Complete these sentences using the appropriate part of the verbs *ser* or *estar* in the present tense.**

(1) Nosotros … veinticinco en clase.

(2) Hoy … el seis de enero.

(3) Ellas … dormidas.

(4) ¿Dónde … el coche?

(5) Mis padres … profesores.

(6) Yo … contenta.

(7) Ellos … a gusto.

(8) Usted … rubio.

(9) Estas llaves … del jardín.

(10) Los recuerdos … de su familia.

score: … × 10 = ◯

c) **Add the present tense form of the verbs *ser* or *estar*.**

    (1) Esto no … mío.

    (2) El … de guardia.

    (3) Vosotros … agitados.

    (4) Aquellos monumentos … de mármol.

    (5) Tú … el primero en llegar.

    (6) Ellas … de empleadas.

    (7) Yo … feliz.

    (8) Ustedes … inquietos.

    (9) Yo … enfermo.

    (10) Nosotros … muy acogedores.

score: … × 10 =

d) **Answer the questions using *ser* or *estar* in the appropriate person of the present tense.**

    (1) ¿Quién eres?

    (2) ¿Cuándo es tu santo?

    (3) ¿De dónde son?

    (4) ¿Están ustèdes bien?

    (5) ¿Cuáles son tus colores preferidos?

    (6) ¿A cuántos estamos?

    (7) ¿Cuántos sois en clase?

    (8) ¿A dónde vais?

    (9) ¿En qué partido político milita?

    (10) ¿Estás segura de lo que dices?

score: … × 10 =

e) **Which is the correct verb in these sentences?**

    (1) (Somos - Estamos) sentados en un sofá.

    (2) (Está - Es) simpática desde siempre.

    (3) (Somos - Estamos) bronceados en verano.

    (4) (Fueron - Estuvieron) detenidos por los guardias.

    (5) El garage (es - está) cerca del centro.

    (6) El niño (está - es) llorando.

    (7) El público (es - está) atenta al discurso.

(8) El incendio (**fue - estuvo**) apagado.

(9) La mesa (**era - estaba**) llena de papeles.

(10) La ropa (**es - está**) sin planchar.

(11) Desde su accidente (**es - está**) malo.

(12) Este coche deportivo (**está - es**) rápido.

(13) El diccionario (**está - es**) en inglés.

(14) El espectáculo no (**estaba - era**) bueno.

(15) El collar (**está - es**) de plata.

(16) Sus suegros (**estaban - son**) de Lima

(17) (**Eran - estaban**) de pie desde temprano.

(18) (**Es - está**) mediodía cuando comen.

(19) Este anuncio (**está - es**) para usted.

(20) (**Estuvieron - Fueron**) miles en manifestarse.

score: ... × 5 =

f) **Complete the following sentences, using *ser* or *estar*.**

(1) No ... tantos (*vosotros*).

(2) Isabel ... muy inteligente.

(3) Yo no ... preparado para el examen.

(4) ¿... lista? todavía, no (*tú*).

(5) ¿Cúanto ... esto?

(6) Ustedes no ... de buen humor.

(7) El cielo ... azul pero el mar ... verde.

(8) ¿Dónde ... la estatua?

(9) ¿Cuándo ... de regreso?

(10) ... quietos (*vosotros*).

(11) Este barrio no ... seguro.

(12) El plátano ... verde.

(13) Ustedes ... felices.

(14) Con cinco años ... aún pequeños.

(15) ... segura de lo que dices.

(16) ... franceses desde siglos.

(17) Estos zapatos ... de cuero.

(18) Siempre ... cansado.

(19) En verano ... de músico en una cabaré.

(20) ... felices cuando se ven

score: ... × 5 =

g) Complete these sentences using *ser* or *estar*.

(1) El bar ... en la esquina.

(2) Lo primero ... informarse.

(3) Vosotros ... hartos de esperar.

(4) El tren ... acercándose.

(5) El niño ... jugando en la arena.

(6) ¿En dónde ... alojados? *(vostros)*.

(7) De momento ... en un hotel *(nosotros)*.

(8) ¿... puesto el homo?

(9) Todo ... dicho en un momento.

(10) ¿Dónde ... el buzón?

(11) ... en aquella acera.

(12) El paseo ... lleno de turistas.

(13) ¿Qué ... haciendo? *(vosotros)*.

(14) ... protegiéndonos del sol *(nosotros)*.

(15) Todas las luces ... encendidas.

(16) En este sitio el aire ... húmedo.

(17) La mujer ... atracada por unos carteristas.

(18) El edificio ... derribado por la grúa.

(19) ¡Qué morenos ...! *(ellos)*.

(20) ... agobiados por el trabajo *(ustedes)*.

score: ... × 5 = ◯

h) Choose between *ser* or *estar*.

(1) El árbol **es/está** cargado de hojas.

(2) El jardín **es/está** repleto de flores.

(3) La nieve **es/está** derritiéndose con el sol.

(4) El barco **está/es** surcando el mar.

(5) El sol **está/es** en el oeste.

(6) El gato **está/es** en el tejado.

(7) El león **es/está** el rey de la selva.

(8) El elefante **está/es** bañándose.

(9) **¿Está/es** el hombre un animal racional?

(10) **Es/está** un espectáculo divertido.

(11) La conferencia **es/está** dada por el ministro de educación.

(12) Vargas Llosa **está/es** un escritor que me gusta.

(13) **Está/es** un cuadro surrealista.

(14) El apartamento **está/es** descuidado.

(15) El jardín **está/es** una monada.

(16) Tu jersey **es/está** manchado.

(17) Las sombrillas **son/están** como hongos en la playa.

(18) **Es/está** enferma desde ayer.

(19) **Está/es** un ser muy independiente.

(20) **Es/está** de aprendiz en una carpintería durante las vacaciones.

score: ... × 5 = ◯

i) **Complete these sentences using *ser* or *estar*.**

(1) La noticia ... difundida por la radio.

(2) Los vasos ... vacíos.

(3) La carretera ... pavimentada por los obreros.

(4) *Eva Luna* de Isabel Allende ...una novela muy divertida.

(5) ... a uno de agosto.

(6) ¿Cuántos ... ? ... una veintena.

(7) ... ellos que se quejaban siempre.

(8) ... enfermo desde algunos días *(tú)*.

(9) ¿... loco?

(10) Todos los platos ... rotos.

(11) ¿Qué tal ... ? ... bien, gracias.

(12) ... sentadas en la terraza de un café *(ellas)*.

(13) ... de vacaciones *(vosotros)*.

(14) El toldo ... echado.

(15) El castillo ... en un acantilado.

(16) ¿Cuál ... su altura?

(17) ... unos alumnos rebeldes.

(18) ... de pie desde muy temprano.

(19) Lo que le gustan ... las novelas policíacas.

(20) ... inútil protestar.

score: ... × 5 = ◯

j) Complete this letter, using the verbs *ser* or *estar*.

¡Querida María!:

(1) Hoy … lunes, … las diez de la noche, … sentada a mi escritorio y … pensando en ti y en tu familia. (2) Antes de todo … feliz que tú … bien y que tu hermano haya aprobado; Luis … un chico serio, … listo y … siempre atento a los demás, o sea que … muy agradable, también … abierto. (3) En cuanto a ti en tu última carta me contabas que … en forma y que sobre todo … enamorada. (4) Esto … una noticia estupenda; espero conocer pronto a tu novio; me gustaría saber cómo …, quién …, de dónde …, cómo … fisicamente; … unas preguntas un tanto indiscretas, pero tú … mi amiga. (5) Ya sabes cuán grande … mi cariño por ti y los tuyos. (6) Por mi parte, últimamente … de maestra en un pueblo; éste … cerca de la ciudad y de la autopista, por lo tanto las combinaciones … fáciles. (7) Los alumnos … serios y … divertidos; mis colegas … amenos y dinámicos, siempre … listos para emprender nuevos métodos. (8) A veces al acabar la jornada … cansada porque … de pie a lo largo del día. (9) Los fines de semana … muy ajetreada entre las tareas caseras y las salidas con los amigos. (10) En fin, … bien, deseo que también lo … todos vosotros.

Amistosamente, Julia.

score: … × 5 = ⬭

k) Translate these sentences, using *ser* or *estar*.

(1) Andalusia is a region in the south of Spain.
(2) Your *(tú)* father's car is grey.
(3) This door is made of glass.
(4) You *(vosotros)* are Chilean, but you come from Cuba.
(5) This house does not belong to them.
(6) It was one o'clock in the morning when they left.
(7) He is an engineer in a big firm.
(8) It is necessary to do it today.
(9) I think that Spanish is very easy to learn.
(10) You *(tú)* had red eyes.
(11) Her dress was yellow.
(12) The lock was broken by the thieves.
(13) She was given a warm welcome.
(14) The grape harvest was damaged by the bad weather.

(15) When you *(tú)* went into the attic you saw that the skylight was broken.

(16) The parcels can be sent by mail.

(17) The palace was built in 1492.

(18) The Alps are on the Franco-Italian border.

(19) We are against pollution.

(20) The mistake is due to the bad accoustics.

score: ... × 5 =

11. THE VERB 'TO HAVE'

a) **Choose the correct form in the following sentences.**

    (1) **(Tiene - He)** andado por la playa.

    (2) Este castillo **(no había - no tenía)** calefacción.

    (3) **(Has habido - Has tenido)** buen tiempo.

    (4) **(Habrán tenido - Habrán habido)** una multa.

    (5) **(Había - Tenía)** mucho tiempo por delante.

    (6) **(Tendrías - Habrías)** que visitar esa feria.

    (7) **(Habéis - Tenéis)** valentia.

    (8) **(No había - No tenía)** demasiadas huelgas.

    (9) **(He - Tengo)** alumnos mayores.

    (10) **(Tuvieron - Hubieron)** escogido aquel recuerdo.

score: ... × 10 = ◯

b) **Translate these sentences, using *haber* or *tener*.**

    (1) He has done a tour of old Madrid.

    (2) She was 24 when she married.

    (3) This morning we have taken the bus.

    (4) You *(tú)* never have money on you.

    (5) We have seen him in a café.

    (6) You *(vosotros)* have traveled a lot.

    (7) Some years ago he had an estate in Galicia.

    (8) This theater does not have enough seats.

    (9) She has written to him to announce his arrival.

    (10) They have chosen to remain silent.

    (11) We only had to cross the road to be on the beach.

    (12) I'm talking about the little boy who had a parrot.

    (13) You *(tú)* didn't tell them that he had died.

    (14) This company no longer has many employees.

    (15) This avenue has a lot of bookshops.

(16) Nobody has his address *(señas)*.

(17) They have a few hours to think about it.

(18) You *(Vd)* do not have all the singer's records.

(19) I have a few pre-Columbian statues.

(20) His apartment has few pieces of furniture.

score: ... × 5 = ◯

c) **Translate these sentences using *haber* or *tener*.**

(1) Our neighbor has a new car.

(2) Do you *(Vd)* have the means to leave?

(3) I have called him several times.

(4) They had gone to visit the cathedral.

(5) You *(tú)* have no information to give them.

(6) I have a lot to do.

(7) Have you *(tú)* bought his last novel?

(8) We have a lot of photos of them.

(9) In this cafeteria they don't have many waiters.

(10) We had followed his advice.

score: ... × 10 = ◯

12. THE SUBJUNCTIVE

a) **Give the correct forms of the verb in brackets.**

   (1) Tal vez (**dormir**) aún *(ellos)*.
   (2) Acaso (**estar**) en casa *(tú)*.
   (3) Es posible que (**tener**) mucho que hacer *(usted)*.
   (4) Es de suponer que (**haber**) perdido el tren *(él)*.
   (5) Quizá no (**saber**) nada *(ustedes)*.
   (6) Acaso (**preferir**) el cine *(ella)*.
   (7) Puede que no (**encontrar**) sitio para aparcar *(yo)*.
   (8) Quizás (**mentir**) *(ellos)*.
   (9) Sería posible que (**arrepentirse**) *(tú)*.
   (10) Era de suponer que (**volver**) a la madrugada *(ellos)*.
   (11) Tal vez (**pedirte**) dinero.
   (12) Sería conveniente que (**despedirse**) *(usted)*.
   (13) Quizá (**enfurecerse**) al enterarse de la noticia *(tú)*.
   (14) Era posible que (**conocer**) el idioma *(ella)*.
   (15) Acaso se (**encontrar**) en la plaza *(ellos)*.
   (16) Es posible que (**jugar**) en la playa *(él)*.
   (17) Tal vez (**sentir**) lo que ha hecho *(usted)*.
   (18) Quizás (**morder**) este perro.
   (19) Supongo que se (**haber**) conmovido mucho *(ustedes)*.
   (20) Fue de suponer que (**apostar**) dinero *(tú)*.

score: ... × 5 = ◯

b) **Put the verbs in brackets into the present and imperfect subjunctive.**

   (1) Yo quiero, quería que (**ellas volver**).
   (2) Yo quiero, quería que (**tu hacerlo**).
   (3) Yo quiero, quería que (**él pedirlo**).
   (4) Yo quiero, quería que (**usted dormir**).
   (5) Yo quiero, quería que (**nosotros levantarse**).

(6) Yo quiero, quería que **(vosotras reírse).**

(7) Yo quiero, quería que **(ellas conducir).**

(8) Yo quiero, quería que **(ustedes ir).**

(9) Yo quiero, quería clue **(ellos salir).**

(10) Yo quiero, quería que **(ella decirlo).**

score: ... × 10 = $\bigcirc$

c) **Put the verb in brackets into the correct tense of the subjunctive or indicative, as appropriate.**

(1) Dice que cuando usted **(venir)** los vio a todos.

(2) Dice que cuando usted **(venir)** los verá a todos.

(3) Dice que cuando usted **(venir)** los ve a todos.

(4) Dijo que cuando usted **(venir)** los vería a todos.

(5) Dice que aunque usted **(venir)** no los vio.

(6) Dice que aunque usted **(venir)** no los ve.

(7) Dice que aunque **(venir)** no los verá.

(8) Dijo que aunque **(venir)** no los vería.

(9) Temo que cuando **(encontrarme)** no me crea.

(10) Temí que cuando **(verme)** no me creería.

score: ... × 10 = $\bigcirc$

d) **Put the verb in brackets into the correct tense of the subjunctive or indicative, as appropriate.**

(1) Te pido que cuando **(tú salir)** me avises.

(2) Te pedí que cuando **(tú salir)** me avisaras.

(3) Te pido que aunque **(tú salir)** me avises.

(4) Te pido que aunque **(tú saberlo)** me avises.

(5) Te pedí que aunque **(tú saberlo)** me avisaras.

(6) Le aconseja que cuando **(él volver)** se lo diga.

(7) Le aconsejó que cuando **(él volver)** se lo dijera.

(8) Le aconseja que aunque **(él volver)** se lo diga.

score: ... × 10 = $\bigcirc$

e) Put the verb in brackets into the present or imperfect subjunctive.

(1) A menos que (**ellos correr**) mucho no te alcanzarán.

(2) Quien no (**haber comido**), que (**probar**) este plato.

(3) Se quedaba en casa como si no (**tener**) nada que hacer.

(4) Ojalá (**tú aprobar**) el examen.

(5) No hay nada que (**gustarme**) tanto como leer.

(6) Le aviso en el momento en que (**él volver**).

(7) Quienes (**conocerla**), no la reconocerían hoy.

(8) Temí que (**tú tener**) un accidente.

(9) No cree que (**tú absolverla**).

(10) No pienso que (**vosotros sentir**) su ida.

(11) Con tal que (**dormir**) mucho, te recuperarás.

(12) Por más que (**ustedes querer**) ayudarle, no conseguían hacer nada.

(13) Parece mentira que (**él tener**) dinero.

(14) No cabe duda de que éste (**ser**) muy famoso.

(15) No engordarás salvo que (**tú comer**) muchos pasteles.

(16) No nos parece que (**ir**) a llover.

(17) Tal vez (**ellos protegerla**) demasiado.

(18) Cuando (**ellos preguntarte**) contestarás en seguida.

(19) Es increíble que no (**saber**) ustedes estas fechas.

(20) Por mucho que (**tomar él**) medicamentos, no se mejora.

score: ... × 5 = ◯

f) Put the following sentences into the present or imperfect subjunctive.

(1) Le han ordenado que él (**presentarse**) hoy.

(2) Cuando (**venir**) ellos dígale que (**pasar**).

(3) Ruégale a Juan que (**atender**) mis razones.

(4) Espérame hasta que (**llegar**).

(5) Quiero que tú (**estar**) bien aquí.

(6) Es mejor que vosotros la (**conocer**).

(7) Conoces a alguien que (**hablar**) holandés.

(8) Ojalá (**pasar**) el autobús.

(9) No saldré hasta que Vd. (**desayunar**).

(10) No cree que tú (**leer**) este libro.

(11) Esperamos que ellos **(ver)** la nota que hemos dejado.

(12) Conoces a alguien que **(vivir)** en el Japón.

(13) Jamás permitía que ellos le **(interrumpir)** cuando hablaba.

(14) Nos gustaría que usted **(comer)** más.

(15) Sería mejor que vosotros **(terminar)** rápidamente vuestro trabajo.

(16) Les había pedido que me **(traer)** las fotos.

(17) Ojalá **(vivir)** ahora.

(18) No era capaz de matar una mosca ni aunque lo **(querer)**.

(19) Te encantaría que te **(acompañar)**.

(20) No había nada que me **(divertir)** en aquella época.

score: ... × 5 = ◯

g) **Put the verbs in brackets into either the present or the imperfect subjunctive.**

(1) Le pediré que me **(dejar)** las llaves.

(2) Os rogué que **(tener)** paciencia.

(3) Nos aconsejaba que **(reducir)** la velocidad.

(4) Les mandaba que **(esperar)** un momento.

(5) Me dijo que **(venir)**.

(6) Te recomendamos que **(tomar)** cita con el médico.

(7) Quisiera que nadie me **(seguir)**.

(8) Le advierto que **(estar)** atento a lo que pasa.

(9) Nos pidió que yo te **(decir)** la verdad.

(10) Nos avisó que no nos **(asomarse)** a la ventana.

(11) Hubiera deseado que todos me **(comprender)**.

(12) Os prohibe que **(fumar)**.

(13) Me gusta que ellas **(dormir)** tarde.

(14) No les permitía que **(salir)** por la noche.

(15) Te alegraba de que ellos **(tener)** éxito.

(16) Le ordeno que nos **(acoger)**.

(17) Os dicen que **(ser)** puntuales.

(18) Nos ruega que no **(destruir)** las pruebas.

(19) Me aconsejaba que **(elegir)** pronto mi carrera.

(20) Le pido que **(tener)** paciencia.

score: ... × 5 = ◯

h) Translate these sentences, using the subjunctive.

    (1) Much better that you *(tú)* do it tomorrow.

    (2) It would be fair if he were punished.

    (3) It's likely that he is going to leave.

    (4) It was surprising that you *(tú)* invited them.

    (5) It would be essential for us to listen to them.

    (6) It's time for him to go now.

    (7) It would be important for you *(tú)* to take part.

    (8) It's strange that she has not replied.

    (9) It would be urgent for her to get better.

    (10) It's not good that you *(Vd)* don't welcome them.

score: ... × 10 = $\bigcirc$

i) Translate these sentences, using the subjunctive where necessary.

    (1) She cannot work without your *(Vd)* interrupting her.

    (2) I am telephoning you *(tú)* so that you know.

    (3) It is difficult to correct her, all the more so as we do not know her.

    (4) You *(Vd)* were speaking in such a way *(de tal modo)* that nobody could follow you.

    (5) In order for everything to work out well, it will be necessary to be objective.

    (6) They have brought their books in order for you *(vosotros)* to sell them.

    (7) After you *(tú)* have read, you can amuse yourself.

    (8) As soon as she is here I will inform you *(Vd)*.

    (9) I will read these documents as *(a medida que)* I receive them.

    (10) Even if you *(Vd)* had spoken loudly, they would not have heard you.

score: ... × 10 = $\bigcirc$

j) Translate these sentences, using the subjunctive.

    (1) We are delighted that he is coming.

    (2) I am sorry that you *(Vd)* did not succeed.

    (3) It seemed important to me that you *(tú)* should take on your responsibilities.

(4) You *(tú)* would like it if everybody obeyed you.

(5) It would worry them if you *(Vd)* didn't find any lodgings.

(6) It will upset him if you *(Vd)* don't go with them.

(7) I wanted you *(vosotros)* to see each other again.

(8) We are pleased that you *(tú)* have your driver's licence.

(9) It would be a shame if you *(vosotros)* hesitated.

(10) It used to upset him if they did not pay attention.

score: ... × 10 =

k) Translate these sentences, using the subjunctive.

(1) I am asking you *(tú)* to eat at home.

(2) I had advised him that they would telephone.

(3) You *(tú)* don't think that she looks after them.

(4) She would have liked you *(tú)* to stay there.

(5) We have recommended that he buy this make.

(6) They will ask me to tell you it *(tú)*.

(7) Your *(vosotros)* mother prefers you to put on pants and a shirt.

(8) You *(Vd)* have stopped him from doing something silly.

(9) His commander *(jefe)* will order him to shoot.

(10) They do not allow them to smoke.

(11) You *(Vd)* didn't think they would undertake this journey.

(12) He would prefer you *(vosotros)* to spend the holidays in the country.

(13) You *(tú)* will give him the task of filling in these forms.

(14) I am telling you *(tú)* to come immediately.

(15) She was asking you *(tú)* to be patient.

(16) We are advising you *(tú)* to provide evidence.

(17) She would like him to take some vacation.

(18) You *(Vd)* will tell them to drive carefully.

(19) You *(tú)* advised him not to lie.

(20) He has asked them to keep the mail.

score: ... × 5 =

l) Translate these sentences.

(1) My father wants you *(tú)* to go with him.

(2) It is necessary for us to shut the windows.

(3) She thought that you *(tú)* were getting supper.

(4) You *(tú)* will recommend them to read old authors.

(5) I didn't want you *(Vd)* to do it.

(6) She will ask you *(tú)* to go swimming with her.

(7) He was afraid that you *(tú)* were not at home.

(8) It would hurt them if you *(tú)* did not come.

(9) It would be desirable if you *(vosotros)* got your tickets.

(10) I do not believe that you *(tú)* can see it.

(11) She insists that you *(tú)* go to see a doctor.

(12) We were pleased that you *(Vd)* too were invited.

(13) It's very good for you to *(tú)* obey.

(14) We would advise him to take the car.

(15) Nobody will believe him.

(16) They have advised you *(tú)* to type everything.

(17) You *(tú)* are sorry that they did not send you the document.

(18) You *(Vds)* will write to them so that they won't worry.

(19) It would please you *(Vd)* if she passed all her exams.

(20) We would like them to settle down at the seaside.

score: ... × **5** = ◯

13. SEQUENCE OF TENSES

a) **Put these sentences into the past tense.**

   (1) Insiste para que lo hagamos.
   (2) Dudo que acierte.
   (3) Es probable que hayan llegado.
   (4) Es inútil que se lo devuelva.
   (5) Siento mucho que no haya ganado.
   (6) No puedo admitir que no te escuchen.
   (7) Quiero que se recupere.
   (8) Nos extraña mucho que no contesten.
   (9) Estamos satisfechos con tal que aprueben.
 (10) Te espero hasta que me llames.
 (11) Le ruego que se despida.
 (12) Busco alguien que me aconseje.
 (13) Me temo que no estén.
 (14) Te avisa a fin de que tomes conciencia de esto.
 (15) Les pide que traigan sus discos.
 (16) Es normal que celebren el suceso.
 (17) Desea que se tranquilice.
 (18) Les parece raro que salgan tan tarde.
 (19) Nos gusta que vengan a vernos.
 (20) No soportan que hagan tanto ruido.

score: ... × 5 = ◯

b) **Put the verbs in brackets into the required form.**

   (1) Niega a que **(haber)** algo entre ellos.
   (2) Te rogué que **(ayudarme)**.
   (3) Me aburrió que **(tu repetir)** siempre lo mismo.
   (4) Le pediste que nos **(contestar)**.
   (5) Es estupendo que **(ellos poder)** venir.

    (6) Me disgustaba que Juan **(pensar)** en tonterías.
    (7) Nos dolió mucho que el perro **(escaparse)**.
    (8) Os fastidia que **(poner)** esta película en la televisión.
    (9) No estamos seguros de que **(vosotros conseguir)** convencerlo.
  (10) Ignoraban que su padre **(vivir)** en aquella ciudad.
  (11) Era una lástima que no **(ellos disfrutar)** del buen tiempo.
  (12) Era necesario que **(ellas vestirse)** bien.
  (13) Fue evidente que todos lo **(ver)**.
  (14) Es horrible que **(haber)** guerras.
  (15) En aquella época era normal que la población **(rendir)** homenaje al presidente.
  (16) Está visto que usted no **(querer)** recibirlos.
  (17) Fue una pena que no la **(él conocer)** antes.
  (18) Nos permitirá que le **(llamar)** por teléfono.
  (19) Es cierto que les **(haber)** tocado la lotería.
  (20) Sería imprescindible que le **(ellos atribuir)** el premio.

score: ... × 5 = $\bigcirc$

c) Put the verbs in brackets into the correct form.

    (1) ¡Ojalá **(seguir)** bien **(vosotros)**!
    (2) Tal vez **(rendirse)** el perso.
    (3) A lo mejor **(calentar)** la calefacción.
    (4) Hay muchos libros, con que **(escoger)** el que **(tú querer)**.
    (5) Viene a que el anticuario le **(restaurar)** el cuadro.
    (6) Puesto que te **(pertenecer)**, te lo dejo.
    (7) Te lo confiamos con objeto de que no lo **(repetir)**.
    (8) No os marchéis hasta que **(volver)** ellos.
    (9) Quita el coche antes de que te **(poner)** una multa.
  (10) Acaso **(haber)** suspendido este alumno.
  (11) Después de que te lo **(traer)**, se fue.
  (12) Deseamos que **(venir)** vosotros, de modo que os **(dar)** la dirección.
  (13) Te avisé para que lo **(adquirir)**.
  (14) El resultado del problema es falso, pues **(corregirlo tú)**.
  (15) Llámame tan pronto como lo **(saber)**.
  (16) Será probable que te **(atender)** tarde **(ella)**.
  (17) Dudo que **(ser)** elegido.

(18) Que (**aprobar**) la selectividad (**tú**).

(19) Cuando (**almorzar**) con nosotros, se lo diremos.

(20) Procurará trabajar bien con tal que sus padres (**animarle**).

score: ... × 5 = ◯

d) Put the verbs in brackets into the correct form.

(1) Me dices esto para que (**hacerlo**).

(2) Quiere hablarte porque (**ser**) necesario.

(3) Han acabado de estudiar, pues (**haber**) salido.

(4) He visto a quien quería, conque (**irme**).

(5) Mira a que (**decírtelo**) yo.

(6) Te avisé para que (**saberlo**).

(7) Me habló con objeto de que (**comprenderle**).

(8) Como no tienes ganas de irte, pues (**quedarse**) en casa.

(9) Venid a que (**verlos**).

(10) Se ha marchado porque (**desearlo**).

(11) Ya que ella lo hace, ¿por qué (**hacerlo**) él ?

(12) Hoy me da tiempo de ir de paseo contigo, asi que (**venirte**).

(13) Hablaba tres idiomas ya que (**viajar**) mucho.

(14) Escuchaba mucha música por lo tanto (**estar**) al corriente.

(15) Visto que todos (**salir**), pues yo también salí.

(16) No había quien (**oír**) lo que decía.

(17) No habíe nadie que (**informarme**).

(18) Irás a donde (**querer**).

(19) No hay ningún lugar donde (**vosotros poder**) aparcar.

(20) A tu padre no le gusta esta chica, de modo que no (**tú volver**) a verla.

score: ... × 5 = ◯

e) Put the verb in brackets into the correct form.

(1) Se marchó después de que le (**amenazar**) (**ellos**).

(2) Por mucho que te (**empeñar**) en convencerle, no lo conseguirás.

(3) Cuando tú (**salir**) de tu casa, pásate por la mía.

(4) A medida que (**yo ir**) pintando este cuadro, se lo explicaré.

(5) Huyó antes de que la policía lo (**coger**).

301

(6) Actúa como si **(estar)** solo.

(7) Se negaba a escuchar y eso que ella **(insistir)**.

(8) Por muy activo que usted **(ser)** no podrá hacerlo todo.

(9) Están tan alegres que **(pegar)** saltos.

(10) El que vosotros **(contar)** chistes, divertía a todos.

(11) Aunque ustedes **(ser)** cultos no lo seríais tanto como ellos.

(12) Tan pronto como **(colgar)** el teléfono, salió.

(13) Lo harás a no ser que ellos lo **(hacer)**.

(14) Quizá ustedes **(poder)** comprobarlo.

(15) Aunque **(haber)** mucha gente, no quiere perderse esta exposición.

(16) Por mal que él lo **(hacer)** se lo perdonará.

(17) No hay nada que **(gustarme)** tanto come leer.

(18) Con tal que **(acostarse)** temprano, recuperarás.

(19) No cabe duda de que este escritor **(obtener)** éxito.

(20) Parece mentira que ellos lo **(excluir)**.

score: ... × 5 = ◯

f) Translate the following sentences.

(1) I see we are not welcome.

(2) I heard that you *(vosotros)* arrived late.

(3) She had never noticed that it was strange.

(4) We didn't know that there were pine trees in that region.

(5) What you say *(tú)* does not go down well.

(6) He does not believe that you *(vosotros)* know them.

(7) I imagine that they are all happy.

(8) It seems that the weather is fine.

(9) You *(Vd)* suppose that they have done their homework.

(10) It didn't seem to me to be so cold last year.

(11) She didn't realize that you *(Vd)* had money.

(12) I didn't think that you *(vosotros)* would say it.

(13) They aren't promising that they will see you *(tú)*.

(14) We didn't think that everyone would have the same opinion.

(15) It wasn't usual for them to make a fuss.

(16) You *(tú)* order them to remain silent.

(17) You *(Vd)* doubted that he would turn up.

(18) It would be interesting if you took part in the research.

(19) I am pleased that you *(Vd)* had a good trip.

(20) We told you *(tú)* not to listen to her.

score: ... × 5 = $\bigcirc$

g) **Replace the infinitive in brackets with an indicative or a subjunctive verb, depending on the context.**

(1) Quieres que ellas (**ponerse**) a la ventana.

(2) Os encargaron que (**ordenar**) la casa.

(3) Nos ruega que (**ir**) a visitarla.

(4) Siempre te pedía que (**despertarla**) pronto.

(5) Le mandó que (**subir**) a su cuarto.

(6) Prefiero que tú (**callarse**).

(7) Dejaste que los jóvenes (**salir**) por la noche.

(8) Os alegraría que ellos (**venir**) en semana santa.

(9) Me temo que no (**haber**) abrir las tiendas.

(10) No me gusta que (**molestarme**).

(11) Nos permitirá que (**abrir**) la ventana.

(12) Les extraño que ella (**interrumpir**) el partido de ajedrez.

(13) Os gusta que los amigos (**reunirse**) con vosotros.

(14) Te molestará que ellos (**instalarse**) cerca de ti.

(15) Dudé que (**estar**) al corriente (**tú**).

(16) Les sorprendió que el conferenciante (**concluir**) así.

(17) Te esperabas a que él (**acordarse**) de tu santo.

(18) Nos fastidiaría que ellos no (**leer**) su libro.

(19) Me dolió que ustedes no (**asistir**) a la ceremonia.

(20) No os apetecerá que (**haber**) tanto de comer.

score: ... × 5 = $\bigcirc$

h) **Put the verbs in brackets into the correct tense.**

(1) Hablaré contigo cuando (**irse**) ellos.

(2) Por más que (**ocultar**) la verdad, se enterará un día (**usted**).

(3) Vendremos a hablarle después de que los (**haber**) saludado a todos (**nosotros**).

(4) No pensaba que (**hacer**) tanto frío.

(5) Es evidente que los españoles (**comer**) tarde.

(6) No es imposible que **(mudarse)** de casa **(ellos)**.

(7) El que **(sacar)** buenas notas, pasará al próximo curso.

(8) En cuanto **(aprobar)** la selectividad, tus padres te comprarán un coche.

(9) No cabe duda de que la estancia en un hotel **(costar)** mucho dinero.

(10) Aunque **(volver)** no te hablaría más.

(11) Es imposible que **(pagar)** un alquiler tan alto **(ellos)**.

(12) En cuanto **(tener)** la licencia jugaremos contigo.

(13) Quizá **(hacer)** la carrera de ingeniero.

(14) Quiso que **(dormir)** en su casa **(ellos)**.

(15) Actuaba como si todo le **(ser)** indiferente.

(16) Como **(nadar)** después de comer puede pasarte algo.

(17) Le rogaron que no **(fumar)** demasiado.

(18) Nos mandó que no **(hacer)** pronto el equipaje.

(19) Te pidió que le **(acompañar)** al aeropuerto.

(20) Deseé que **(juntarse)** todos.

score: ... × 5 = ◯

i) **Put the verbs in brackets into the correct tense.**

(1) Visto que no **(mirar)** la televisión, apágala.

(2) Estaré desvelado hasta que **(volver)** **(ellos)**.

(3) A pesar de que **(haberse)** comprometido, no cumplió **(él)**.

(4) A medida que **(ir)** creciendo, vas pareciendo a tu padre.

(5) Ya que lo **(saber)** todo, confesad la verdad.

(6) Antes de que me **(avisar)** ya lo sabía medio pueblo **(usted)**.

(7) Estuvo deprimido después de que **(marcharse)** **(ella)**.

(8) Tomarás los billetes cuando te **(dar)** los horarios **(ellos)**.

(9) A medida que **(ir)** nadando, te encontrarás mejor.

(10) Me instalé en aquel sitio a fin do que **(poder)** **(nosotros)** encontrar trabajo.

(11) Difundieron la noticia para que **(enterarse)** el pueblo.

(12) Hay personas que **(destacar)** por no seguir las tendencias.

(13) Estoy buscando un piano que **(sonar)** bien.

(14) Para que **(funcionar)** la democracia, es necesario un buen sistema parlamentario.

(15) Un día poseerás un coche que **(tener)** una tecnología de punta.

(16) Con que te **(relajar)** un par de horas, será suficiente.

(17) El que **(haber)** tantas protestas, es sintomático de un malestar social.

(18) No creían que esto os **(perjudicar)**.

(19) Me parece muy sano que **(practicar)** **(vosotros)** un deporte.

(20) No los veremos a no ser que **(insistir)**.

score: ... × 5 = $\bigcirc$

14. THE IMPERATIVE

a) Give the correct imperative of the verb in brackets.

(1) Señores **(sentarse)**.
(2) **(Irse)** de aquí **(tú)**.
(3) Este abrigo **(ponerselo)** **(usted)**.
(4) **(Ser)** atento con tu padre.
(5) **(Pensarlo)** antes de tomar una decisión **(vosotros)**.
(6) **(Despertarse)** **(ustedes)**.
(7) **(Decir)** lo que piensas.
(8) **(Tener)** cuidado **(nosotros)**
(9) **(Salir)** de este lugar **(usted)**
(10) **(Hacer)** lo que te mandan

score: ... × 10 = $\bigcirc$

b) Give all the negative command forms of these reflexive verbs.

(1) sentirse
(2) probarse
(3) condolerse
(4) volverse
(5) esforzarse
(6) pasearse
(7) arrepentirse
(8) vestirse
(9) asomarse
(10) despertarse

score: ... × 10 = $\bigcirc$

c) **Give all the positive command forms of these reflexive verbs.**

   (1) sentarse
   (2) reunirse
   (3) dormirse
   (4) moverse
   (5) caerse
   (6) echarse
   (7) irse
   (8) divertirse
   (9) reírse
   (10) acordarse

score: ... × 10 = ◯

d) **Choose the correct form to make a negative command.**

   (1) Contad el suceso (**No contad - No contéis - No cuenten - No cuentais**).
   (2) Durmámonos pronto (**No durmámonos - No os durmanos - No nos durmamos - No nos dormínos**).
   (3) Que traiga sus libros de estudios (**Que no se traigan - Que no traiga - Que no traen - Que no traeis**).
   (4) Di la verdad (**No dices - No decir - No digas - No di**).
   (5) Vuelvan pronto (**No volvan - No vuelva - No vuelvan - No volved**).
   (6) Tente en pie (**No te ten - No te tengas - No tente - No te tienes**).
   (7) Haz tu tarea (**No haz - No haces - No hagas - No hice**).
   (8) Buscad la solución (**No buscas - No busquéis - No busquen - No buscar**).
   (9) Sueña con tu porvenir (**No sueñes - No sueña - No soñar - No sueñan**).
   (10) Huyan frente al peligro (**No huid - No huyen - No huyan - No huir**).

score: ... × 10 = ◯

e) **Translate the following imperatives.**

   (1) Go *(tú)*.
   (2) Run *(Vd)*.

(3) Don't stay there *(tú)*.
(4) Come *(tú)*.
(5) Say *(tú)*.
(6) Set the table *(tú)*.
(7) Don't pay attention *(tú)*.
(8) Don't feel sorry *(tú)*.
(9) Don't fuss *(tú)*.
(10) Go out *(tú)*.
(11) Know *(tú)*.
(12) Don't move *(vosotros)*.
(13) Be good *(tú)*.
(14) Sit down *(tú)*.
(15) Get up *(Vd)*.
(16) Don't fall asleep *(tú)*.
(17) Let's sit down *(nosotros)*.
(18) Wash your hands *(tú)*.
(19) Wait for me *(Vds)*.
(20) Don't go for a walk *(vosotros)*.

score: ... × 5 = ◯

f) **Translate the following imperatives.**

(1) Let's see that.
(2) Try this pleated skirt *(tú)*.
(3) Go to his house *(tú)*.
(4) Devote yourself *(dedicarse)* to your studies *(vosotros)*.
(5) Don't dye your hair brown *(tú)*.
(6) Get changed—get dressed *(Vd)*.
(7) Let's begin.
(8) Excuse me for disturbing you, but I need some information.
(9) Let's go.
(10) Put on this blouse *(tú)*, it will suit you.
(11) Don't bring any cash *(tú)*.
(12) Let's not hurry, it's not our turn.
(13) Be patient *(tú)*.
(14) Come out and see them *(tú)*.
(15) Tell him what make the car is *(tú)*.
(16) Don't cross *(tú)* when the lights are green.

(17) Go away *(vosotros)*.

(18) Don't get lost *(Vds)*.

(19) Let's not have a race.

(20) Please fasten your seat belts *(Vds)*.

score: ... × 5 = ◯

g) Translate the following imperatives.

(1) Let's not fall.

(2) Bring *(tú)* it.

(3) Don't distribute them *(vosotros)*.

(4) Have money *(tú)*.

(5) Don't lean *(tú)* out of the window.

(6) Correct the problem *(tú)*.

(7) Come out *(salir) (tú)* to the garden.

(8) Let's laugh.

(9) Don't drive fast *(tú)*.

(10) Don't go on *(vosostros)*.

(11) Let's build the road.

(12) Translate this prose *(tú)*.

(13) Put the heater on *(tú)*.

(14) Don't walk in bare feet.

(15) Teach yourselves *(instruirse) (vosotros)*.

(16) Let's not get worked up.

(17) Ask *(tú)*.

(18) Choose *(Vds)*.

(19) Get dressed *(tú)*.

(20) Let's get dressed.

score: ... × 5 = ◯

15. THE PASSIVE

a) **Change these sentences from the passive to the active.**

   (1) El paquete no fue recibido por el empleado.
   (2) Se construyó una nueva calzada en la autopista.
   (3) Se plantó flores en el parque.
   (4) Se le puso una multa por estar en doble fila.
   (5) El plano fue ideado por el arquitecto.
   (6) Esta obra fue publicada por unos aficionados.
   (7) El cantante es aplaudido por el público.
   (8) Varias escuelas fueron cerradas por el alcalde.
   (9) El almacén fue abierto por el director.
   (10) El presidente fue elegido por los diputados.

   score: ... × 5 = ◯

b) **Which is the correct form? (In some cases both are possible.)**

   (1) Esta carta **(fue escrita-se escribió)** por mi amiga.
   (2) En casa **(es servida-se sirve)** la cena a las nueve.
   (3) En la escuela **(se recibían-eran recibidos)** alumnos extranjeros.
   (4) El instituto **(fue cerrado-se cerró)** en julio.
   (5) El regalo **(será enviado-se enviará)** por Correos.
   (6) El mueble **(fue comprado-se compró)** por un anti-cuario.
   (7) El delincuente **(fue detenido-se detuvo)** hace poco tiempo.
   (8) El cargo de primer ministro **(es dado-se dio)** por el presidente.
   (9) El chico **(fue cegado-se cegó)** por el rayo.
   (10) El castillo **(es protegido-se protege)** por unos perros.

   score: ... × 10 = ◯

c) **Change these passive phrases into the active.**

(1) Ha sido elegido presidente de la república por la mayoría de la población.
(2) Es una película muy vista por los jóvenes.
(3) Fue aplaudido por todos.
(4) El niño fue ayudado por los vecinos.
(5) El incendio fue apagado por los bomberos.
(6) Fue avisado por sus amigos.
(7) El cantante fue matado por un loco.
(8) El disco te será ofrecido por tus padres.
(9) El palacio es cerrado por el conserje.
(10) La casa es limpiada por la asistenta.

score: ... × 10 = ◯

d) **Translate the following sentences.**

(1) A week ago, they sent the letter.
(2) Before leaving the room, they opened the window.
(3) The news was given to them all.
(4) Several buildings were built there.
(5) A liberal régime was set up.
(6) Elections were planned for the spring.
(7) Some laws were announced.
(8) The Velazquez masterpiece was sold for a fortune.
(9) A hunter killed the deer.
(10) The room is empty.
(11) He was injured by a machine.
(12) He has been received by a famous author.
(13) All the boxes are closed.
(14) The pavements are very dirty.
(15) The police arrested them.
(16) Our host welcomed us.
(17) The artist didn't sign this picture.
(18) The house is silent.
(19) The flowers are withered.
(20) The jury approved it.

score: ... × 5 = ◯

16. THE GERUND

a) **Complete, using** *estar, ir, seguir, andar* **or** *venir*.

   (1) … unos ejercicios difíciles **(yo hacer)**.

   (2) … **(ella llorar)** a pesar de su presencia.

   (3) Cuando lo vimos … **(subir)** las escaleras.

   (4) … **(tu comer)** cuando te llamaron.

   (5) Con el cursillo … **(él mejorar)** su nivel.

   (6) La contaminación … **(crecer)** con tantos coches.

   (7) … **(él buscar)** sus señas por todas partes.

   (8) … **(nosotros proyectar)** un viaje desde muchos años.

   (9) No … **(tú decir)** la verdad.

   (10) Ya … **(tú ser)** mayor.

score: … × 10 =

b) **Choose the correct form to complete the sentences.**

   (1) A las doce de la mañana **(iba - seguía - estaba)** durmiendo.

   (2) Cuando llegamos **(seguía - iba - estaba)** vistiéndose.

   (3) A pesar de su accidente **(iba - seguía - estaba)** entrenándose.

   (4) Al anunciarle la noticia, **(estaba - iba - seguía)** leyendo.

   (5) Pese a los consejos **(estaba - iba - seguía)** desobedeciendo.

   (6) **(Ibas - estabas - seguías)** bebiendo demasiado.

   (7) **(Estabais - Ibais - seguiais)** diciendo tonterías.

   (8) **(Iba siendo - seguía - estaba)** demasiado testarudo.

   (9) Cada día **(está - va - sigue)** repitiendo lo mismo.

   (10) Ya **(van - siguen - están)** distribuyendo los premios.

score: … × 10 =

c) **Translate these sentences. Remember that a gerund in English is not necessarily translated by a gerund in Spanish.**

   (1) Thinking that I was resting, they left.

   (2) By reading the instructions, you could understand what it was about.

(3) There being no route, we will have to devise one *(inventar)*.
(4) You *(vosotros)* have seen them doing their homework.
(5) Although you are offering him a good present, he doesn't deserve it.
(6) Thinking that you would not go, he didn't get the tickets.
(7) As soon as it was light, they got up.
(8) When out walking, she took photos.
(9) He manages *(arreglárselas)* by working.
(10) He was making his way towards them.

score: ... × 10 = ◯

17. CONDITIONS

a) Which verb is the correct one in these conditional sentences?

(1) Si desalojan a los inquilinos, **(edificarían, edificarán, edifican)** otro inmueble.

(2) Si llevaras zapatos planos, te **(dolían, dolerán, dolerían)** menos los pies.

(3) Si estudia más atentamente, le **(estimarán, estiman, estimarían)** los profesores.

(4) Si invitaran a sus amigos, **(es, será, sería)** una velada agradable.

(5) Si vas a la playa, no **(olviden, olvidarás, olvides)** tu traje de baño.

(6) De confiarse, **(tenga, tendría, tendré)** menos problemas.

(7) De leer más, **(estariámos, seremos, seríamos)** más cultos.

(8) De tener más tiempo, **(poderé, podríamos, podrían)** ver a sus amigos.

(9) De haber descansado, no le **(duelen, dolerán, dolerían)** las piernas.

(10) Si fuera más centrada, **(será, serán, sería)** más feliz.

score: ... × 10 =

b) Fill in the gaps using the verb shown in brackets.

(1) Si el médico me diera de baja, ... a México **(viajar)**.

(2) Si tuvieras un equipo, ... escuchar música **(poder)**.

(3) Si hubieras sido más atento, no ... ido **(haberse)**.

(4) Si no estuvieras tan resfriada, ... a pasear **(salir)**.

(5) Si anduvieras más rápido, no ... el tren **(perder)**.

(6) Si fueran más veloces, ... la carrera **(ganar)**.

(7) Si vistiese mejor, ... más éxito **(tener)**.

(8) Si fuese más serio, ... más proyectos **(emprender)**.

(9) Si fueran más tolerantes, ... más amistades **(entablar)**.

(10) Si supieras montar a caballo, ... con ellos **(ir)**.

score: ... × 10 =

c) Translate these sentences.

(1) If you *(tú)* don't want to have any problems, be quiet.

(2) If this one doesn't please you *(tú)*, you may take another.

(3) If she comes tomorrow, she will see it.

(4) If you *(vosotros)* cause a commotion *(meter ruido)*, the neighbors will complain.

(5) If you *(vosotros)* are cold, go into the house.

(6) If they leave early, they will go and see you *(vosotros)*.

(7) If I go to the theater, I will bring you *(tú)* back the program.

(8) If you *(usted)* know their address, show it to us.

(9) If you *(tú)* know your lessons, you will pass the exam.

(10) If he meets up with them, he will return with them.

(11) If they dissolve the Cortes, there will be new elections.

(12) If you *(tú)* get dressed quickly, you will arrive on time.

(13) If we can't work out his intentions, we will have difficulties.

(14) If they distribute prizes, he will get one.

(15) If you *(vosotros)* don't open the door, they will break it down.

(16) If we go to say goodbye to them, we will stay for dinner.

(17) If you *(tú)* knock your glass over, you will have to clean the table.

(18) If the snow melts, they will not be able to ski anymore.

(19) If you *(Vd)* sneak in, people will not be happy.

(20) If you *(tú)* adapt, it will be easier for you.

score: ... × 5 =

d) Translate these sentences.

(1) If I knew his address, I would be able to write to him.

(2) If you *(vosotros)* drove less quickly, you would see the countryside.

(3) If we slept more, we wouldn't be so tired.

(4) If she sat up properly, she would not get a backache.

(5) If it snowed, we would be able to ski.

(6) If we knew the laws, we would have fewer problems.

(7) If you *(tú)* knew, you would tell her.

(8) If he didn't go out so much, he would get better grades.

(9) If the weather was good, we could get a suntan.

(10) If it rained, we would get wet.

(11) If you *(vosotros)* went to bed earlier, you would be more rested.

(12) If we told them the truth, they would be disappointed.

(13) If you *(tú)* asked me, I would do it.
(14) If there were more of you *(vosotros)*, you would play cards.
(15) If I had the time, I would go with you *(vosotros)*.
(16) If she had money, she would often travel.
(17) If we went out with them, we would have a good time.
(18) If you *(tú)* put this pullover on, you wouldn't be cold.
(19) If you *(Vd)* lived in the countryside, you would have less pollution.
(20) If you *(Vd)* telephoned them, they would tell you that they are ready.

score: ... × 5 = ◯

e) **Translate these sentences.**

(1) If you *(tú)* had disobeyed, you would have been punished.
(2) If he had been born a year earlier, he would not have done his military service.
(3) If you *(vosotros)* had become rich, you would have helped your parents.
(4) If they had stayed longer, they would have met him.
(5) If you *(Vd)* had given *(regalar)* him a record, that would have given him a great deal of pleasure.
(6) If that country had more grains, it would not be in deficit.
(7) If you *(tú)* had restricted your life style, you would not have debts now.
(8) If he had repented, everyone would have forgiven him.
(9) If she had managed to persuade him, I would have been satisfied.
(10) If he had missed them, he would have come back.
(11) If we had seen this movie, we would have been able to talk about it.
(12) If *(Vd)* you had written to them, they would have been very pleased.
(13) If he had come back to see her, she would have been very happy.
(14) If you *(Vd)* had told us what it was about, we would not have been surprised.
(15) If she had done her work, she would have been able to go out.
(16) If they had seen us, they would have waited for us.
(17) If you *(vosotros)* had been dressed up, perhaps you would have gotten a prize *(premio)*.

(18) If you *(tú)* had not broken your leg, you would have been able to take part in sports.

(19) If we had taken the cassette back, we would have gotten our money back.

(20) If I had set the table, they would have settled down.

score: ... × 5 = ◯

f) Translate these sentences.

(1) If we were to eat earlier, we would make the most of the afternoon.

(2) If you *(tú)* were placing a bet, I would win.

(3) If he passed his exam, he would be relieved.

(4) If you *(Vd)* comforted him, he would have more courage.

(5) If you *(tú)* thought more about your future, you would forget about your grief.

(6) If we redecorated the apartment, it would be more comfortable.

(7) If they swapped addresses, they would write to each other.

(8) If you *(Vd)* did them a favor, they would be able to count on you.

(9) If she did some exercise, she would feel like working.

(10) If you *(Vd)* corrected their homework, they would understand their mistakes.

(11) If I were wearing evening dress, I would go into the casino.

(12) If they served us quickly, we would get back soon.

(13) If they discovered new remains *(vestigios)*, they would exhibit them.

(14) If the snow melted, we would have to leave again.

(15) If the government exiled the king, the people would be disappointed.

(16) If you *(tú)* took the subway, you would not arrive late.

(17) If we elected a new president, the stock exchange would undergo changes.

(18) If you *(Vd)* find the solution, telephone me.

(19) If she said fewer stupid things, we would believe her.

(20) If there were more justice, the people would be satisfied.

score: ... × 5 = ◯

g)   Replace *si* by *de* + the infinitive of the verb.

(1) Si me lo hubieras dicho, lo habría hecho.

(2) Si fuera su padre, le castigaría.

(3) Si hubiera tenido más tiempo, habría ido a visitarles.

(4) Si lo hubiera sabido, no habríais cometido ese error.

(5) Si tuviéramos un barco, haríamos un crucero.

(6) Si alcanzaran a sus amigos, sería estupendo.

(7) Si durmiera más, estaría más atento en clase.

(8) Si soltáramos el perro, haría tonterías.

(9) Si lloviera, iría al cine.

(10) Si nevara, tendríamos que comprar cadenas para el coche.

score: ... × 10 =

18. OBLIGATION

a) Complete the following sentences, using the appropriate verb expressing obligation.

    (1) Este niño no ... madrugar tanto.

    (2) Usted ... firmar cuanto antes.

    (3) Nosotros ... ayudar a los minusválidos.

    (4) ... permanecer en tu habitación.

    (5) Para entenderse ... escuchar al otro.

    (6) ... ser tolerantes.

    (7) ¿Por qué ... regañarte tanto?

    (8) ... notar que están mejorando los negocios.

    (9) A quién ... dirigirme para esta información.

    (10) Has corrido mucho, ... descansar.

score: ... × 10 = ◯

b) Choose the correct form in the following sentences.

    (1) **(Han de - Tienen que)** mirar al guardia antes de cruzar la calle.

    (2) **(Es menester - Hay que)** conocer la región, antes de marcharnos.

    (3) **(Hace falta - Debe)** llover para la agricultura.

    (4) **(Deberíamos - Tendríamos que)** participar a la colecta.

    (5) **(Tenías que - Habías de)** acompañar a tus padres a la estación.

    (6) Si usted **(debiera - tuviera que)** escoger ¿ qué escogería?

    (7) **(Hará falta - Tendrá que)** comer alguna fruta.

    (8) **(He de - es necesario)** aprender la consigna de seguridad.

    (9) Es posible que **(tengan que - deban)** alquilar otro piso.

    (10) **(Debéis - tenéis que)** examinaros a la vuelta del verano.

score: ... × 10 = ◯

c) Choose the correct form. (Sometimes there is more than one correct answer.)

(1) En clase **(debe, hay que, tienes que)** prestar atención.

(2) El empleado **(hay que, ha de, debe)** llegar a la hora.

(3) Los vigilantes **(hay que, tienen que, deben)** estar atentos a lo que pasa.

(4) Isabel **(debió, hubo que, tenía que)** repasar su lección.

(5) Los coches no **(debieron, hubieron de, tenían que)** acelerar.

(6) Antes de comer **(has de, deben, hay que)** asegurar que todos están servidos.

(7) **(Ha de, hay que, tengo que)** ir a buscar a mi hijo a la escuela.

(8) **(No debe, no tiene que, no hay que)** circular a toda velocidad.

(9) Si estás enferma **(has de, debes, tienes que)** avisar al médico.

(10) Siempre **(has de, debes, hay que)** contestar cortesmente.

score: ... × 10 = ◯

d) Translate the following sentences.

(1) You **(vosotros)** must return what doesn't belong to you.

(2) She must be operated on.

(3) One has to respect traffic regulation.

(4) He has to study every evening.

(5) They should respect the neighborhood.

(6) A lot of patience is needed to put up with them.

(7) They need clean clothes.

(8) One must be polite with everyone.

(9) You **(tú)** must not read without understanding.

(10) He must write better.

(11) You **(tú)** have to ring the bell several times if you want them to hear you.

(12) She must not dress like this.

(13) They shouldn't be so insolent.

(14) This child shouldn't have left his parents' side.

(15) You **(tú)** mustn't stay up late.

(16) What must one do?

(17) She must not mix the medicines.

(18) You **(vosotros)** must not tear pages out of the books.
(19) They must behave like everyone else.
(20) You **(tú)** have to warn them.

score: ... × 5 = ◯

19. THE INFINITIVE

a) **Replace *cuando* + verb with *al* + the verb in the infinitive.**

    (1) Cuando apareció, nos saludó.

    (2) Cuando entramos en la habitación, vimos que la ventana estaba abierta.

    (3) Cuando se vieron, se abrazaron.

    (4) Cuando lo encuentro, se puso pálida.

    (5) Cuando se puso a hablar, oyó un ruido extraño.

    (6) Cuando vuelve, se junta con sus amigos.

    (7) Cuando recibió la carta, estaba durmiendo aún.

    (8) Cuando se asomaron a la ventana, vieron el desfile.

    (9) Cuando da clase, se olvida de todo.

    (10) Cuando leyó el periódico, se enteró de la noticia.

score: ... × 10 = ◯

b) **Translate the following sentences, using the infinitive.**

    (1) They attended the ceremony without greeting anyone.

    (2) If they had listened to the talk, they would be up to date with the latest developments.

    (3) He fell while climbing up to the loft.

    (4) He plays the piano without looking at the music.

    (5) When she arrived, she noticed the change.

    (6) He was knocked down by a car as he was leaving his house.

    (7) Their house is a complete ruin because they don't look after it.

    (8) They accused him because he had stolen many things.

    (9) She had an accident because she didn't see the traffic lights.

    (10) They approved the budget without considering the consequences.

score: ... × 10 = ◯

20. THE VERB 'TO BECOME'

a) Which verb is the correct one in these sentences?

(1) (Llega a ser - Se hace - Se pone) viejo.

(2) Hernan Cortés (se convirtió - se hizo - se volvió) en famoso.

(3) El partido (llegó a ser - se puso - se volvió) una fiesta.

(4) Su confianza (se pone - se hace - se vuelve) recelo.

(5) El campo va (haciéndose - volviéndose - poniéndose) solitario.

(6) Las antigüedades (se convierten - se hacen - se vuelven) de moda.

(7) Esta tierra yerma (se convirtió en - se hizo - se volvió) fértil.

(8) Este chaval (llega a ser - se pone - se vuelve) grosero.

(9) La felicidad (se transforma - se hace - se vuelve) en infortunio.

(10) Esos pensamientos (llegaron a ser - se pusieron - se volvieron) proféticos.

score: ... × 10 = ◯

b) Complete the sentences using the appropriate verb for 'become'.

(1) En cuanto los ve ... alegre.

(2) Desde la muerte de su dictador, este pais ... libre.

(3) Al cabo de muchos años ... famoso.

(4) ... loco con lo que le contaron.

(5) Este campo ... un basurero.

(6) Después de la tormenta, el cielo ... azul.

(7) Este hombre ... jefe de su plantilla.

(8) Después de su estancia en Nueva York, ... un fanático de los Estados Unidos.

(9) Ustedes ... amigos durante las vacaciones.

(10) Aquel lugar … muy concurrido.

(11) La situación … pésima.

(12) El tráfico … una pesadilla.

(13) No os … los desentendidos.

(14) Los niños empezaron a … pesados.

(15) Aquel barrio … un lugar poco frecuentado.

(16) Goya … el enemigo de Fernando VII.

(17) Esta editorial … famosa al editar libros prohibidos.

(18) Con los años usted … cada vez más soñador.

(19) Durante la Guerra de Independencia, los españoles …
los enemigos de Napoleón y de los franceses.

(20) El sueño … realidad.

score: … × 5 = ◯

c) Put the verb in brackets into the correct form.

(1) **(Hacerse)** breve el tiempo contigo.

(2) Tú **(volverse)** furioso cuando alude a eso.

(3) Dejó de estudiar y **(hacerse)** vendedor.

(4) Ella **(ponerse)** mala cuando sube al coche.

(5) En poco tiempo, él **(convertirse)** en un cantante famoso.

(6) Nunca **(llegar ellos a ser)** lo que querían.

(7) Él **(volverse)** receloso a raíz de su fracaso.

(8) Esta aula **(convertirse)** en una pajarera.

(9) No **(ponerse tú)** tan inquieto.

(10) De tanto trabajar **(él llegar a ser)** rico.

score: … × 10 = ◯

d) Translate these sentences using the appropriate verb for 'become'.

(1) This teacher has become very strict.

(2) You **(vosotros)** have become rich.

(3) You **(tú)** will become very strong if you do sports.

(4) This country has become a great economic power.

(5) This house has become a museum.

(6) When she heard the news she became agitated.

(7) Since practising yoga, we have become calmer.

(8) Golf is becoming a fashionable sport.

(9) They became friends during the cruise.

(10) She turns red when she runs.

(11) He becomes aggressive when people don't agree with him.

(12) As we get older, we become more serious.

(13) This stray dog turned into a real wild animal.

(14) This business has become a real enterprise.

(15) One day, this statue will become a monument.

(16) Don't (**tú**) get impatient.

(17) This dance club has become very popular.

(18) Living with them is becoming a chore.

(19) If there were any more cars, it would be a nightmare.

(20) They became real music lovers.

score: ... × 5 =

21. TO GET, TELL SOMEONE TO DO SOMETHING

a) Choose the correct form in the following sentences.

(1) **(Pidió, hizo, mandó)** cortar un traje a la costurera.

(2) No me **(digas, preguntes, mandes)** ir de compras.

(3) **(Le pidieron, le hicieron, le mandaron)** hacer el plano de la casa.

(4) **(No le pida, no le dé, no le mande)** grabar esta canción.

(5) Nos **(dijeron, pidieron, mandaron)** corregir aquellas pruebas.

(6) Al niño **(le dirá, le mandará)** su madre forrar los libros.

(7) **(Os rogaban, Os mandaban, Os decían)** sacar siempre las mismas fotos.

(8) **(Te querrán, te mandarán)** echar mantequilla a los alimentos.

(9) Siempre le **(decían, mandaban)** apagar las luces.

(10) La maestra **(preguntó, pidió, mandó)** barrer el aula a los alumnos.

score: ... × 10 = 〇

b) Translate the following sentences.

(1) I told them to bring you some coffee.

(2) You have the clothes ironed.

(3) He makes them obey.

(4) You **(vosotros)** tell him to set the table.

(5) We got them to translate the text.

(6) You **(tú)** got him to clean the windows.

(7) She tells you **(tú)** to read lots of books.

(8) They make you clear out the attic.

(9) You (**tú**) will get us to tidy up the room.

(10) She will get him to type it.

score: ... × 10 = $\bigcirc$

22. ADVERBS

A. ADVERBS OF PLACE

Complete the following sentences with: *aquí, lejos, cerca, dentro, fuera, arriba, abajo, detrás, encima, en ninguna parte*.

(1) ¿Dónde están? Estamos …

(2) El campo se situa … del pueblo.

(3) Trabaja … su casa.

(4) Mis llaves se hallan … del bolso.

(5) … hace mucho calor.

(6) … se oyen voces.

(7) No te escondas … del árbol.

(8) Lo estoy buscando desde hace una hora, no lo veo …

(9) El frutero está … de la mesa.

(10) … del piso tenemos una bodega.

score: … × 10 = ◯

B. ADVERBS OF TIME

Complete the following sentences with: *ahora, siempre, todavía, mañana, pronto, luego, a menudo, acto seguido, dentro de poco*.

(1) … es de día tarde.

(2) … está enfadada.

(3) … no ha empezado a trabajar.

(4) … te traigo los papeles.

(5) … se reunirán.

(6) ¡Hasta …!

(7) . . dan una vuelta por la alameda.

(8) Empezaron a discutir, … se pegaron.

(9) … habrá menos polución.

(10) … come carne.

score: … × 10 = ◯

C. ADVERBS OF MANNER

a) Change the words in brackets into adverbs of manner.

(1) Se portó (**con cordialidad**).

(2) Respiraba (**con pena**).

(3) Habla (**con claridad**).

(4) Estudia (**con superficialidad**).

(5) Se propuso (**con espontaneidad**).

(6) Vive (**con alegría**).

(7) Camina (**con lentitud**).

(8) Actúa (**con mucha audacia**).

(9) Se las arregla (**con facilidad**).

(10) Se queja (**con frecuencia**).

score: ... × 10 = $\bigcirc$

b) Translate the following sentences using adverbs.

(1) She wants to leave at once, she isn't going to wait for you.

(2) He greeted us courteously.

(3) It is just what I was saying.

(4) He will certainly go.

(5) I'm just coming.

(6) They settled in comfortably.

(7) She speaks clearly and distinctly.

(8) Unfortunately, no one can come.

(9) She doesn't go anymore.

(10) I think therefore I am.

(11) They came in silently.

(12) The problem is extremely complicated.

(13) I have an appointment for the day after tomorrow.

(14) They fell on top of me.

(15) He was slightly wounded.

(16) They drove very fast.

(17) She lives intensely.

(18) They behave dangerously.

(19) We always answer politely.

(20) She looked at the photograph sadly.

score: ... × 5 = $\bigcirc$

c) **Choose the correct form in the following sentences.**

(1) Habla (**de propósito - con voracidad - de prisa**).

(2) Se comportaron (**con sus anchas - con gusto - con gravedad**).

(3) Se irán (**en realidad - en extremo - a hurtadillas**).

(4) Despedía a la clientela (**de verdad - de modo distinto - con gusto**).

(5) Compartiré mis vacaciones con vosotros (**con cortesía - por lo común - de buena gana**).

(6) Los niños juegan (**de verdad - a sus anchas - a hurtadillas**) con sus padres.

(7) Le gusta expresarse (**en público - de propósito - de buena gana**).

(8) Los árabes triunfaron sobre los españoles (**en realidad - con rapidez - con cortesía**).

(9) (**Desgraciadamente - En absoluto - En realidad**) se produjo el bombardeo de Guernica.

(10) Expuso el problema (**de seguro - de lado - con claridad**).

score: ... × 10 = ◯

d) **Give the opposite of the following adverbs.**

(1) despacio	(6) delante
(2) tarde	(7) dentro
(3) poco	(8) demasiado
(4) antes	(9) lejos
(5) aquí	(10) a menudo

score: ... × 10 = ◯

23. PREPOSITIONS

a) **Complete the following sentences using the prepositions *de* or *desde*.**

   (1) Vende un poco … todo.

   (2) … ayer, no come nada.

   (3) Los almacenes abren … diez a ocho de la tarde.

   (4) ¿ … dónde eres?

   (5) Procedo … padres españoles.

   (6) … que llueve, no sale.

   (7) Vivió en Buenos Aires … que cumplió los diez años.

   (8) Este paquete llega … Barcelona.

   (9) ¿ … cuándo sois amigos?

   (10) … la apertura des su librería, ni siquiera la vemos.

score: … × 10 = ◯

b) **Complete the following sentences using the prepositions *a* or *en*.**

   (1) … los negocios hay que ser prudente.

   (2) … lo mejor están … casa.

   (3) Acérquese … la ventana.

   (4) Llegaré … tren … las ocho.

   (5) ¿ … qué piensa usted?

   (6) Este conjunto está … cinco mil pesetas … Madrid.

   (7) ¿ … dónde vas?

   (8) … ver si contesta.

   (9) Anda … que salga.

   (10) Se empeña … quedarse.

score: … × 10 = ◯

c) **Choose the correct preposition in the following sentences.**

   (1) Está muy contenta (**por - de**) su viaje.

   (2) Posee una máquina (**para - de**) escribir.

(3) Tienen prejuicios (**de - sobre**) muchas cosas.

(4) Iremos (**a - de**) compras (**por - a**) eso de las nueve.

(5) No sabe contar (**de - sin**) su calculadora.

(6) Fue (**hacia - a por**) el pan.

(7) (**Por - Para**) ingresar en la universidad es necesario aprobar la selectividad.

(8) El dilema está (**por - en**) que no carecemos de pruebas.

(9) ¡(**A - de**) ver si se percata del error!

(10) Están (**con - en**) plan de fiesta desde ayer.

score: ... × 10 = ◯

d) **Complete the following sentences with:** *ante, antes de, delante de, debajo de, dentro de, después de, desde, encima de, según, detrás de, a, de, por, con.*

(1) Irás ... España en Navidades.

(2) La encontrarás ... aquel andén.

(3) ... el revisor, el tren tiene mucho retraso.

(4) El tablón de información está ... ti.

(5) ... reservar, infórmate bien.

(6) El próximo tren sale ... media hora.

(7) El tren de cercanías pasa ... el tren de largo recorrido.

(8) Dejó su carné de identidad ... la mochila.

(9) Presentaos ... el aduanero para declarar.

(10) Pusieron sus bolsas de viaje ... su asiento.

(11) Pasarás ... Granada.

(12) Desde muy joven, se aficionó ... las artes.

(13) No sabes nada ... ellos.

(14) No comparéis esta situación ... la anterior.

(15) Se contentan ... lo que le dan.

(16) Os marcháis ... vacaciones ... verano.

(17) Esta fruta sabe ... limón.

(18) Me permito insistir ... esta palabra.

(19) Sube a buscarte ... tu cuarto.

(20) Se hicieron mucho ... suplicar.

score: ... × 5 = ◯

e) **Complete the following sentences using the appropriate preposition.**

(1) No sueñes ... este viaje.

(2) ¿ ... qué piensas? No pienso ... nada.

(3) Nunca sale ... la calle.

(4) Se pasó la mano ... la frente.

(5) Bastaba ... decirlo ... convencerlos.

(6) Traducid este texto ... español.

(7) Llámalo ... teléfono.

(8) ... no escuchar sus consejos, fracasaron.

(9) Estudia ... médico.

(10) ... los niños, oiste los gritos.

(11) Esto es fácil ... hacer.

(12) Es un producto imposible ... encontrar aquí.

(13) ... este país no se soluciona nade.

(14) No puedes esquiar ... buenos esquíes.

(15) Sube ... la torre para ver el paisaje.

(16) No te asomes ... la ventana.

(17) Acércate ... los turistas ... ayudarles

(18) Se fue ... Colombia ... avión.

(19) No vuelvas ... cometer el mismo error.

(20) Por favor, hablen ... voz baja.

score: ... × 15 = ◯

f) **Complete the following sentences using the appropriate preposition.**

(1) Piensas ... tus amigos.

(2) Llegaste ... la estación demasiado temprano.

(3) Este cuadro consta ... dos partes.

(4) Se preocupa ... el bien de la humanidad.

(5) Su tarea consiste ... dar hora a los clientes.

(6) Insiste ... venir también.

(7) Aprovéchate ... las vacaciones.

(8) No se da cuenta ... que se trata de un exámen.

(9) No deja ... telefonear.

(10) Se interesa ... el teatro de vanguardia.

(11) No salgas ... dinero.

(12) … saberlo, no lo habría dicho.

(13) Esta novela es … tí.

(14) No sabe cómo reaccionar … tal situación.

(15) Experimento mucho cariño … él.

(16) Ha visto … sus familiares.

(17) Se porta muy bien … sus abuelos.

(18) Aparca el coche … la plaza.

(19) Fíjate … el semáforo … de cruzar la calle.

(20) Salieron … la cena.

score: … × 5 = ◯

g) Translate the following sentences.

(1) He left home at the age of twelve.

(2) In the café, she always sits at the bar.

(3) You (**tú**) can go there on foot, on horseback or by car.

(4) Yesterday you (**vosotros**) came into Segovia.

(5) As far as I know, he died the following day.

(6) We returned three days later.

(7) He goes down to the mailbox twice a day.

(8) She went out for the newspaper.

(9) The director called for him.

(10) In the face of so many responsibilities he abdicated.

(11) The Golden Age of drama was in the reign of Philip II.

(12) They are attentive to everyone.

(13) This dress is made of cotton.

(14) The young man with blue eyes is a friend of the family.

(15) They spoke out against the bill.

(16) In Spain, you usually have lunch at around three in the afternoon.

(17) As a child I dreamt a lot.

(18) Prices have gone up by ten percent.

(19) At least five hundred people came.

(20) You (**tú**) don't obey his orders.

score: … × 5 = ◯

h) Complete the following sentences with *por* or *para*.

    (1) ... culpa suya, llegamos tarde al concierto.

    (2) ... lo que escribe, está pasándolo bien.

    (3) No te asomes ... la ventana.

    (4) Te darán los billetes ... la ventanilla.

    (5) Estoy ... ir a bañarme, hace demasiado calor.

    (6) Estamos ... vosotros ya que queríamos ir al teatro.

    (7) ... honesto, prefiero rechazar la oferta.

    (8) ... Dios, no te asustes.

    (9) Vamos a brindar ... los novios.

    (10) ... fin he acabado la tarea.

    (11) Fue declarado inocente ... los jueces.

    (12) Su nuevo libro está ... publicarse.

    (13) Sube a ... noticias suyas.

    (14) Esta situación está ... reírse.

    (15) ... lo visto, no pinta nada.

    (16) Tienes un cheque ... cobrar.

    (17) Los ladrones merodearon ... los alrededores.

    (18) Pasa ... ser buen conductor.

    (19) Llamó por teléfono ... media hora.

    (20) ... la primavera, suele llover mucho.

score: ... × 5 = ◯

i) Translate the following sentences using the preposition *por* or *para*.

    (1) You (**Vd**) did it out of necessity.

    (2) You (**tú**) made this mistake because you were tired.

    (3) We have met together in order to review.

    (4) She is going to change this record for another.

    (5) Such a change would be welcome for Chile.

    (6) It is not for eating.

    (7) She was run over by a car.

    (8) He followed this course to be an engineer.

    (9) His parents scolded him for having lied.

    (10) She is interested in politics.

score: ... × 10 = ◯

24. CONJUNCTIONS

a) **Complete each sentence using the appropriate conjunction.**

    (1) Es un obrero más hábil ... el anterior.

    (2) Su amigo no baila tan bien ... ella.

    (3) Este deporte es más corriente ... los otros.

    (4) No durmió tanto ... ellos.

    (5) El mar está más agitado ... ayer.

    (6) Velázquez es más famoso ... Zurbarán.

    (7) Tu coche es menos rápido que ... el nuestro.

    (8) Este piso es tan cómodo ... el mio.

    (9) Es un niño de 18 meses ... todavia no sabe andar.

    (10) Tenemos dos coches ... habrá sitio para todos.

    (11) ... tiene ... un día de descanso.

    (12) No ve más ... películas policíacas.

    (13) No me divierto tanto ... mis hermanos.

    (14) Todos vinieron ... todos están invitados.

    (15) En esta playa no hay arena ... piedras.

    (16) No habla ... de si mismo.

    (17) Ni ... contesta a mis preguntas.

    (18) En el mercado no había más ... algunos tenderetes.

    (19) No memoriza ... está preocupada.

    (20) No hace buen tiempo ... jugaremos a las cartas en casa.

score: ... × 5 = ◯

b) **Complete the following sentences using the conjunctions:**
asi, o, sino, pero, por lo tanto, sin embargo, a pesar de, en lo tocante a, ante todo, por fin.

    (1) No me gusta el teatro ... la música.

    (2) Vi a mucha gente ... no a mis amigos.

    (3) No tienes dinero, ... no puedes comprar mucho.

    (4) Tenías toda la razón, ... no lo aceptaron.

    (5) Le gusta ir al cine ... a la discoteca.

    (6) Nos ilusionaría montar a caballo, ... sería estupendo.

(7) ... a la moda, esa deja mucho que desear.

(8) ... se abrió la verja.

(9) ... lo dejó todo ... los ruegos de su familia.

(10) ... ordena tu habitación.

score: ... × 10 = $\bigcirc$

25. DURATION

a) Change the following sentences using: *llevar, hace, desde, desde hace.*

   (1) Llevan dos meses trabajando en esta tienda.

   (2) Hace un año que se fue.

   (3) No he vuelto al cine desde hace seis meses.

   (4) Estudian en España desde hace cinco años.

   (5) Le aguardaba desde hacía media hora.

   (6) Hacía mucho tiempo que estaba con ellos.

   (7) Estaban edificando la casa desde hacía seis meses.

   (8) Hablé durante una hora y media por teléfono.

   (9) Llueve desde el viernes pasado.

  (10) Hace mucho tiempo que lo advierten.

score: ... × 10 = ◯

b) Translate the following sentences.

   (1) For years, women have been fighting for equal rights.

   (2) I haven't seen you for a long time.

   (3) They haven't worked for months.

   (4) You (**vosotros**) haven't been to mass for some time.

   (5) She has been going to the dentist for two years.

   (6) He'll have been going to the same school for four years in September.

   (7) It's weeks since I have been out.

   (8) He hasn't washed his hair for a week.

   (9) She had been waiting for him for hours.

  (10) They haven't spoken to each other for a year.

score: ... × 10 = ◯

26. NUMBERS

a) **Complete the following sentences, writing out the numbers in full.**

   (1) Colón descubrió América en ...
   (2) Diego Velázquez pintó *Las Meninas en* ...
   (3) El ... de mayo y el ... de mayo fueron días inolvidables para el pueblo madrileño.
   (4) El Rey Juan Carlos nació en ...
   (5) El bombardeo de Guernica tuvo lugar en ...
   (6) En ... Fidel Castro tomó el poder.
   (7) La guerra civil española duró ... años.
   (8) La constitución expañola fue votada en ...
   (9) Federico García Lorca murió en ...
   (10) El « Tejerazo » fue el ...

score: ... × 10 = ◯

b) **Translate the following sentences, writing out the numbers in full.**

   (1) It is August 1st
   (2) There were 15 in the class.
   (3) There were thousands of people at the demonstrations.
   (4) From here to your house by bus there are 20 stops.
   (5) You (**tú**) are the 5th child.
   (6) The English alphabet consists of 26 letters.
   (7) I bought 6 records for his birthday.
   (8) Every day, 10 of you sit down to eat.
   (9) This man's library has 3,000 books.
   (10) This dealer sells 5 meters of material for 5000 pesetas.
   (11) Cecilia is twice as old as her daughter.
   (12) With 10,000 pesetas you have enough money.
   (13) The summer of '76 was very hot.
   (14) They have won millions, hitting the jackpot.
   (15) Their address is: 2 Veracruz Street, Madrid.
   (16) America was discovered in 1492.

    (17) The 1st of November is All Saints' Day.
    (18) The 31st of December is a night of celebration.
    (19) The Spanish Civil War lasted from 1936 to 1939.
    (20) In Seville, the temperature reaches 30° in May.

score: ... × 5 = ◯

c) **Translate the following sentences, writing out the numbers in full.**

    (1) This car costs $10,000.
    (2) You are never first, but second.
    (3) This firm has about 30 employees.
    (4) They have always liked "The Arabian Nights".
    (5) Three quarters of the people were against this law.
    (6) This old book is worth several thousand pesetas.
    (7) It takes him half an hour to park.
    (8) There are a thousand people in this theater.
    (9) Alfonso XIII was the grandfather of King Juan Carlos.
   (10) Call the ninth floor.

score: ... × 10 = ◯

d) **Translate the following sentences, writing out the numbers in full.**

    (1) For her twentieth birthday, she invited about 30 friends.
    (2) I have only got a few thousand pesetas left.
    (3) He celebrated reaching one hundred.
    (4) When he was 15, he went to America.
    (5) You (**vosotros**) have given him 13 roses.
    (6) These shelves hold about a hundred books.
    (7) Prices have increased by 10 percent.
    (8) In order to teach a language well, there should be no more than 12 students in the group.
    (9) You (**tú**) only take 50 drops of this medicine.
   (10) Seven o'clock is when the family gets up.

score: ... × 10 = ◯

Answers

1. ACCENTUATION

a) (1) pidió - (2) cántaro, vacío - (3) río - (4) túnel, está -
(5) plátanos - (6) cómo - (7) lápiz - (8) rompió, compró - (9)
llaméis, después - (10) qué, estáis - (11) acércate - (12) estás,
árboles - (13) jabalíes, fáciles - (14) encantaría, estuviérais - (15)
atención - (16) qué, se dirigió - (17) jóvenes, están - (18) Méjico,
polución - (19) aquí, está, rodó, película - (20) levántate.

b) (1) brújula - (2) música - (3) ámbito - (4) razón - (5) energía -
(6) ambición - (7) Córdoba - (8) tí - a (9) intérprete - (10) siéntate
- (11) Catedrático - (12) jóvenes - (13) cortés - (14) azúcar -
(15) cárcel - (16) metrópoli - (17) levántese - (18) cólera -
(19) águila - (20) matemáticas.

c) (1) duérmete - (2) así - (3) la alegría - (4) la ampliación -
(5) muévase - (6) simpático - (7) el frío - (8) increíble -
(9) sábado - (10) pájaro.

2. ARTICLES

A. THE DEFINITE ARTICLE

a) (1) la - (2) el - (3) el - (4) el - (5) el - (6) el - (7) el - (8) las - (9) el - (10) el.

b) (1) las actrices - (2) los intereses - (3) los jerseyes - (4) los - maniquíes (= mannequins), las maniquíes (= models) - (5) las naciones - (6) los crímenes - (7) los grises - (8) los crisis - (9) los carmesíes - (10) los rubíes.

c) (1) las - (2) el - (3) el - (4) el - (5) el - (6) la - (7) la - (8) la, la - (9) del, las - (10) el.

d) (1) el - (2) el - (3) el - (4) la - (5) el - (6) el - (7) el - (8) la - (9) el - (10) el.

e) (1) al - (2) del - (3) del - (4) al - (5) la - (6) al - (7) el - (8) el, del - (9) las - (10) del.

B. THE INDEFINITE ARTICLE

a) (1) unos - (2) un - (3) unas - (4) unos - (5) unos - (6) unos - (7) unos - (8) unas - (9) unas - (10) un.

b) (1) Sólo quedaban algunos espectadores - (2) Observaron el silencio algunos minutos - (3) Le interrogaron unos reporteros - (4) Estaban expuestas frutas y hortalizas - (5) Me quedaré algunos días en su casa - (6) Unos amigos vinieron a buscarle - 7) Hubo unas botellas vacías tiradas por el suelo. - 8) Necesitaban cuadernos y bolígrafos - (9) El ajedrez no es un juego fácil - (10) Aun tenía que hacer algunos esfuerzos.

C. DEFINITE OR INDEFINITE ARTICLE?

a) (1) el, los - (2) la - (3) unas - (4) los - (5) las - (6) las - (7) unos, los - (8) unas - (9) las - (10) la.

b) (1) los - (2) al - (3) el - (4) la - (5) una - (6) los - (7) el - (8) la - (9) un - (10) la - (11) la - (12) la - (13) el - (14) el - (15) el - (16) un - (17) unos, el - (18) una - (19) el - (20) las.

c) (1) Te gusta la cerveza, pero el vino no - (2) No quiero leche sino agua - (3) Se quitó el sombrero - (4) Buena parte de sus amigos se fueron al extranjero - (5) Tengo unos problemas que resolver - (6) Quiere ser médico - (7) ¡ Qué idea más buena ! - (8) ¿ Tienes

una casa de campo? - **(9)** Vive en Paris, capital de Francia -
(10) No hemos ido nunca a tal sitio - **(11)** Yo te considero
como un hermano - **(12)** España es un país que se desarrolla
mucho últimamente - **(13)** Le espera el señor Director -
(14) La comunidad europea está en plena expansión -
(15) Siempre tenía las manos muy frías - **(16)** A la señorita
Garcia le encantó su viaje -
17) Va a misa todos los días - **(18)** Lo más importante es decidirse
rápidamente - **(19)** Lo esencial es conocer la obra de este autor -
(20) Estudio el español.

3. LO, LO QUE

a) **(1)** Lo - **(2)** lo - **(3)** Lo - **(4)** lo - **(5)** Lo que - **(6)** lo - **(7)** Lo -
(8) Lo - **(9)** lo - **(10)** Lo - **(11)** lo que - **(12)** lo que - **(13)** lo que -
(14) lo que - **(15)** lo - **(16)** lo - **(17)** Lo - **(18)** Lo - **(19)** Lo -
(20) Lo.

b) **(1)** Lo que hicieron fue un error - **(2)** Lo que ha expuesto no es
interesante - **(3)** Lo que proyectemos será comunicado más
adelante - **(4)** Lo que has comprado no es muy caro - **(5)** Está al
tanto de lo que has decidido - **(6)** Haz lo que quieras - **(7)** Repitió
lo que le habían confiado - **(8)** Lo que va a hacer no les gustará a
todos - **(9)** Desconoce lo bueno - **(10)** Ten cuidado con lo que dices.

4. SHORTENED ADJECTIVES

a) (1) buen - (2) gran - (3) San - (4) cualquier - (5) recién -
(6) gran - (7) gran - (8) mal - (9) cualquier - (10) recién.

b) (1) Es un gran edificio - (2) Hace buen tiempo para pasear -
(3) San José es un santo famoso en España - (4) Grita mucho
este recién nacido - (5) Tengo cien pesetas en mi monedero -
(6) Si tienes algún problema, ven a verme - (7) No tiene ningún
dato sobre este tema - (8) Este hombre tiene mal carácter -
(9) Vive en el tercer piso - (10) El primer día, visitó toda la ciudad.

c) (1) gran - (2) ningún - (3) recién - (4) San, San - (5) Cualquier -
(6) Ningún - (7) primer - (8) tercer - (9) buen - (10) Algún.

5. GENDER AND NUMBER

a) **(1)** La actriz - **(2)** La estudiante - **(3)** La alcaldesa - **(4)** La catalana - **(5)** La doctora - **(6)** La senadora - **(7)** La maestra -**(8)** La dentista - **(9)** La gallina - **(10)** La monja.

b) **(1)** no singular - **(2)** La boda - **(3)** La nariz - **(4)** La crisis - **(5)** El régimen - **(6)** El andaluz - **(7)** no singular - **(8)** no singular - **(9)** no singular - **(10)** El equipaje.

c) **(1)** Las naciones - **(2)** Las paredes - **(3)** Los jóvenes - **(4)** Las nueces - **(5)** Los peces - **(6)** Los jabalíes - **(7)** Los rubíes - **(8)** Los martes - **(9)** Las tesis - **(10)** Las voces.

d) **(1)** Los trajes azules - **(2)** Los reyes de España - **(3)** Las leyes de derecho - **(4)** Las voces del pueblo - **(5)** Los cafés están abiertos - **(6)** Las flores amarillas - **(7)** Los jabalíes no son fáciles de cazar - **(8)** Los lápices están por el suelo - **(9)** Estos peces son demasiado gordos - **(10)** Las naciones extranjeras.

e) **(1)** El ajedrez - **(2)** La gente - **(3)** La cosecha - **(4)** La espalda - **(5)** Los padres - **(6)** El pelo - **(7)** Los rasgos - **(8)** El or la dentista - **(9)** Los archivos - **(10)** La basura.

6. AUGMENTATIVES AND DIMINUTIVES

A. AUGMENTATIVES

a) **(1)** un hombrón - **(2)** una manaza - **(3)** un vozarrón -
(4) un puñetazo - **(5)** un cañonazo - **(6)** un codazo -
(7) un señorón - **(8)** unos ojazos - **(9)** un mocetón -
(10) un cabezón.

b) **(1)** Compraron un cochazo - **(2)** No digas palabrotas - **(3)** Ordena
tus papelotes - **(4)** Mientras arreglaba la mesa, se dió un
martillazo - **(5)** Furiosa, dio un portazo - **(6)** Dicen que la
asesinaron de un puñetazo - **(7)** Se hace el simplón para que
nadie le moleste - **(8)** Este paredón es de hormigón - **(9)** Le des-
pertó con una patada - **(10)** Es una casona a la salida del pueblo.

B. DIMINUTIVES

a) **(1)** nuevecita - **(2)** la viejecita - **(3)** unas pesetillas -
(4) un paseíto - **(5)** un señorito - **(6)** un cafelito - **(7)** despacito -
(8) hermanito, manita - **(9)** jovencita - **(10)** lucecita.

b) **(1)** nuevecito - **(2)** casita - **(3)** cafelito *or* cafetito - **(4)** chiquito -
(5) paseíto - **(6)** jovencito - **(7)** hermanito - **(8)** plazita *or* plazuela -
(9) pececito - **(10)** copita.

7. COMPARATIVES AND SUPERLATIVES

A. COMPARATIVES

a) (1) inferior - (2) menor - (3) peor - (4) anterior - (5) posterior - (6) mejor - (7) mayor - (8) anterior - (9) menores - (10) mejores.

b) (1) Es más terco que su hermano - (2) El País Vasco es más húmedo que Cataluña - (3) Este trabajo es mejor que el anterior - (4) Vd está mucho más feliz ahora que se han terminado los proyectos - (5) Estos chicos son tan altos como su padre - (6) Este restaurante es peor que él de ayer - (7) Este bar es menos concurrido por la noche que por la mañana - (8) Nuestro coche es más cómodo que el suyo - (9) Este bolso es más grande que el tuyo - (10) Sus investigaciones están más adelantados que los nuestros.

c) (1) Las consecuencias fueron mayores de lo que se esperaba - (2) Mi vestido es menos estampado que el tuyo - (3) Dormís tanto como vuestros hijos - (4) Corres tanto como Pedro - (5) No es tan autoritaria como lo parece - (6) Posees más libros que ellos - (7) El marido habla menos que su mujer - (8) Este tablao flamenco es más barato que el anterior - (9) El pueblo desea menos prohibiciones que antes - (10) El peligro es mayor en coche.

d) (1) Una jirafa es más alta que una vaca - (2) Un gato es menos feroz que un león - (3) Plácido Domingo es más famoso que mi hermano - (4) Toledo es menos grande que Madrid - (5) El zorro suele ser más astuto que la gallina - (6) El sol está más lejos que la luna - (7) Un kilo de plomo pesa tanto como un kilo de plumas - (8) Llueve menos en Andalucía que en Galicia - (9) El Atlántico no es tan grande como el Pacifico - (10) A los niños les gusta jugar más que estudiar.

B. THE MORE ... THE LESS ...

(1) Está tanto más delgada cuanto menos come - (2) La casa es tanto más vieja cuanto menos se cuida - (3) Está tanto más contento cuanto más asignaturas aprueba - (4) Es tanto más culto cuanto más lee - (5) El perro es tanto más gracioso cuanto más

pequeño es - **(6)** El velero va tanto más rápido cuanto más sopla el viento - **(7)** Es tanto más veloz cuanto más corre - **(8)** Está tanto más enfermo cuanto más medicamentos toma - **(9)** Es tanto más sensible cuanto más inquietudes tiene - **(10)** El pájaro es tanto más sensible cuanto más libre es.

C. SUPERLATIVES

a) **(1)** riquísima - **(2)** famosísimo - **(3)** guapísima - **(4)** tristísima - **(5)** felicísima - **(6)** larguísimo - **(7)** simpatiquísimos - **(8)** durísimo - **(9)** antiquísima - **(10)** pobrísima or paupérrima.

b) **(1)** bonísimo - **(2)** famosísimo - **(3)** fortísimo - **(4)** malísima - **(5)** antiquísimo - **(6)** blanquísima, palidísima - **(7)** elocuentísimo - **(8)** el mayor - **(9)** grandísimo - **(10)** mayor.

c) **(1)** máximo - **(2)** peor - **(3)** menor - **(4)** mínimo - **(5)** mayores - **(6)** mejor - **(7)** óptimos - **(8)** ínfima - **(9)** último - **(10)** mayor.

d) **(1)** el mejor or bonísimo - **(2)** el mayor - **(3)** blanquísimo - **(4)** agradabilísimo - **(5)** amabilísimo - **(6)** el peor or malísimo - **(7)** el menor or pequeñísimo - **(8)** famosísimo - **(9)** simpatiquísimo - **(10)** paupérrimo or pobrísimo.

e) **(1)** Es la ciudad más acogedora de la región - **(2)** Es el hombre más culto del momento - **(3)** De las tres hermanas, eres la más hábil - **(4)** Es el árbol más alto del jardín - **(5)** Es la habitación más clara - **(6)** Era el chico más hablador de su clase - **(7)** Es el diario más serio - **(8)** Es la niña más mimada que conozca - **(9)** Era el obrero más cualificado de la fábrica - **(10)** Será el deportista más dotado del club - **(11)** Os habéis puesto los vestidos más monos - **(12)** Andalucía es la región más turística de España - **(13)** Japón es el país más industrializado - **(14)** Es más listo de lo que aparenta - **(15)** Es una persona amabilísima - **(16)** Es un hombre fortísimo - **(17)** Cabe mucha gente en la casa porque es grandísima - **(18)** Es una gente pobrísima - **(19)** Este relato es aburridísimo - **(20)** Bebí un café muy fuerte!.

f) **(1)** Hoy debe ser el día más caluroso del año - **(2)** Acabo de hacer una cosa tontísima - **(3)** Ella es la más alta de la clase - **(4)** Me dio un libro interesantísimo - **(5)** La política lo encuentro aburridísimo - **(6)** Esta sopa no es la más caliente que haya probado - **(7)** Es el autor que más se lee en el país - **(8)** Fue la tormenta más violenta que jamás había visto - **(9)** Lo que más me gusta es estar contigo - **(10)** Isabel es la niña más lista del colegio - **(11)** Es la situación más compleja que te puedas imaginar - **(12)** Conoció a una mujer guapísima mientras paseaba por el parque - **(13)** Arturo es mi mayor preocupación en este momento - **(14)** ¿Has oído lo último sobre esa actriz - **(15)** Es la persona más generosa que conozco - **(16)** Fue la historia más increíble que había oído jamás - **(17)** Ahora llegamos a la zona más pobre de la ciudad

- **(18)** Es lo menos que puedo hacer - **(19)** Ella pasó las mejores vacaciones de su vida. - **(20)** Este tiene que ser el peor vino que pruebo desde hace mucho tiempo.

D. REVIEW TEST

(1) Un portavoz del gobierno es menos famoso que un ministro - **(2)** Una pared de piedra es más sólida que una de hormigón - **(3)** Un sombrero nuevo es más bonito que una boina vieja - **(4)** Es el socio más popular del partido - **(5)** El diario publicó las fechas límite de los exámenes. - **(6)** El hambre está más extendida de lo que se piensa - **(7)** La violencia es tan peligrosa como el fanatismo - **(8)** Hay más desempleo en España que en Alemania - **(9)** Hoy el número de refugiados es menor - **(10)** Eres el mayor de la familia.

8. PRONOUNS

A. PERSONAL PRONOUNS

a) (1) yo - (2) ti - (3) él - (4) sí mismo - (5) nosotros - (6) les -
(7) le - (8) nosotros - (9) usted - (10) les.

b) (1) Ven a visitar Madrid con nosotros - (2) Salió por la noche con
ellos - (3) Dínos algo cuanto antes - (4) Oye lo que pasa en la calle
- (5) Se rió de los chistes en voz alta - (6) No hagan lo que no se
debe - (7) Se puso el abrigo antes de salir - (8) No conduzcas a
mucha velocidad - (9) Vete a por el pan - (10) A mí no me gustan
los plátmos.

c) (1) A ti te - (2) Vosotros os - (3) se te - (4) A él lo -
(5) A vosotros os encanta reuniros - (6) a vosotros os -
(7) con ellas - (8) Les - (9) os - (10) A ti te.

d) (1) ellos - (2) nos - (3) ella - (4) lo, me - (5) Lo - (6) a vosotros -
(7) mí - (8) los - (9) les - (10) nosotros - (11) mí - (12) ella -
(13) a ti - (14) Nosotros - (15) lo - (16) ellos, les - (17) Te, él -
(18) Me - (19) Ustedes - (20) les.

e) (1) ti - (2) yo - (3) conmigo - (4) con ellos - (5) vosotros -
(6) nosotros - (7) tú - (8) escápate - (9) nosotros -
(10) bañándose.

f) (1) él - (2) le - (3) confiésaselo - (4) lo - (5) enséñales -
(6) apuntadlo - (7) te, te - (8) píntalas - (9) duérmase -
(10) acogerlas.

g) (1) ¿Quién es? ¿Eres tú? - (2) ¡ Quieres darte prisa! -
(3) ¿Qué opinas de todo eso? - (4) Nos lo confesó él mismo -
(5) Con el tiempo, uno se acostumbra a todo - (6) Usted siempre
ha tenido don de lenguas - (7) Si chapurreas, no se te entiende -
(8) La mayoria de la gente sabe por lo menos una lengua -
(9) El problema son los puntos de gramática dificiles -
(10) Le prestó un diccionario a su colega; éste lo dejó en la
biblioteca - (11) Uno no puede dejar de sonreír cuando se pronun-
cian mal las palabras - (12) De eso, ya me habló -
(13) A ti te encantan las plantas - (14) ¿Piensa usted en los
exámenes? Sí, pienso muy a menudo en ellos - (15) No le parecía
importante aprender el catalán ni el gallego - (16) Es cierto que no
vendrá - (17) Se lo han aconsejado a menudo - (18) Para ellos sólo
hay una solución: la de corregir sus faltas - (19) Tus amigas, no las
comprendo - (20) ¿Le ha dado una respuesta? No, no se la dio.

h) (1) El señor alcalde inauguró el monumento - (2) No quiero agua,
sino leche - (3) Se quitó el abrigo - (4) Su padre es un arquitecto
famoso - (5) ¿Tienes casa de campo? - (6) Vive en Madrid, capital

de España - **(7)** Cataluña es una provincia que se desarrolla mucho - **(8)** El señor director le espera en su despacho - **(9)** El pobre hombre está agotado del todo - **(10)** Lo importante es citarse - **(11)** La Comunidad europea está en plena expansión - **(12)** Le pido que se siente - **(13)** Señorita, tiene usted unas cuantas problemas que resolver - **(14)** Te gusta la cerveza pero no te gusta el vino - **(15)** No tienen idea de cuánto las quiere la gente - **(16)** Te pusiste (*or* pones) la chaqueta - **(17)** Lo importante es comprender - **(18)** Odio la hipocresía - **(19)** No se ha visitado nunca ese lugar - **(20)** Se le ocurrió cambiar la cerradura.

B. ATTACHED PRONOUNS

a) **(1)** ponte - **(2)** vete - **(3)** riéndose - **(4)** devolvértelo - **(5)** mirándola - **(6)** buscándolos - **(7)** relájate - **(8)** imitarlo - **(9)** visitarlos - **(10)** bañándose.

b) **(1)** Dígaselo - **(2)** Toma la reina y ponla ahí - **(3)** Ven a decírmelo - **(4)** Nos pidió escogerlo - **(5)** No me atrevo a decirselo - **(6)** Enséñenos lo que ha pintado? - **(7)** Veo que quieres dejarlo - **(8)** Repetidme la frase - **(9)** Tápelos todos - **(10)** Quiere hacerlo todo.

C. INDEFINITE PRONOUNS

a) **(1)** alguien, nadie - **(2)** algo, nada - **(3)** alguna - **(4)** ninguna - **(5)** algo, no, nada - **(6)** tampoco - **(7)** nadie, nada - **(8)** también - **(9)** alguno - **(10)** nada.

b) **(1)** nadie - **(2)** ninguno - **(3)** ninguno - **(4)** ninguno - **(5)** ninguna - **(6)** alguna - **(7)** nadie - **(8)** algún - **(9)** alguna - **(10)** ninguna.

c) **(1)** nadie - **(2)** nadie - **(3)** nadie - **(4)** no - **(5)** jamás - **(6)** nadie - **(7)** ningún - **(8)** nada - **(9)** ningún - **(10)** ningún.

d) **(1)** Nunca habla con nadie - **(2)** No tienes que abrir la puerta - **(3)** No es útil que den algo - **(4)** No sería bueno que condujera - **(5)** No tenían ningún cambio para la propina - **(6)** No me gusta nada su forma de ser - **(7)** No tienen ningún miedo - **(8)** no le queda nada de gasolina - **(9)** Nunca haces nada - **(10)** No tiene la menor gana de salir.

e) **(1)** ¿Ves algo ? - **(2)** No ponen nada interesante en la telé - **(3)** A ella tampoco ponen le gusta la nieve - **(4)** Nadie preguntó por usted - **(5)** Nunca ayuda a sus padres - **(6)** Nosotros también visitamos el Prado - **(7)** ¿ Habrás visto algunas obras de arte maravillosas ? - **(8)** Tienen algunas sospechas acerca de nosotros - **(9)** Le suministró algunas mercancías - **(10)** ¿ Qué trajes escogerán ? No importa cuales.

f) **(1)** Ya no me queda tiempo - **(2)** No se siente molesto en absoluto - **(3)** No me queda más café - **(4)** No tengo miedo -

(5) No tienen nada de trabajo - **(6)** No tenéis dinero en absoluto - **(7)** No tiene la menor idea de eso - **(8)** No comió nada de eso - **(9)** No comprendes nada de eso - **(10)** ¿ Estás de acuerdo ? En absoluto.

D. DEMONSTRATIVE PRONOUNS AND ADJECTIVES

a) **(1)** estos - **(2)** estas - **(3)** ésto - **(4)** éstos - **(5)** esta - **(6)** estas - **(7)** esta - **(8)** estas - **(9)** estos - **(10)** ésto, este.

b) **(1)** Ese, ése - **(2)** ésos *or* ésas - **(3)** ésos - **(4)** esa - **(5)** esos - **(6)** esa - **(7)** esas - **(8)** ese - **(9)** Esos - **(10)** ese.

c) **(1)** aquel - **(2)** aquellos - **(3)** aquellas **(4)** aquellas - **(5)** aquellos - **(6)** aquellos - **(7)** aquélla - **(8)** aquellas - **(9)** aquéllo - **(10)** aquellos.

E. TRANSLATING 'HERE IS', 'THERE ARE' ETC

(1) Aquí está mi hermano - **(2)** aquí está lo esencial - **(3)** Ahí está el aula - **(4)** éste es Juan - **(5)** Aquí están los frutos secos - **(6)** Ahí viene el mecánico - **(7)** Aquí hay todos los detalles - **(8)** Aquí están las reservas - **(9)** He ahí un paisaje hermoso - **(10)** Ahí vienen sus vecinos.

F. POSSESSIVES

a) **(1)** suyo, tuyo - **(2)** Nuestros padres - **(3)** Mi cuaderno - **(4)** ¡Hijo mío! - **(5)** Su piso - **(6)** su documentación - **(7)** Vuestras fotos - **(8)** Sus consejos - **(9)** Sus comentarios - **(10)** sus documentos de él, los de usted.

b) **(1)** Tiene uno de los dedos enyesado - **(2)** Los alumnos charlaban con su profesor de gimnasia - **(3)** A los seis años, se pierde algunos de los dientes de leche - **(4)** Se enfadó contigo porque te movías demasiado - **(5)** Esta receta no es suya, sino tuya - **(6)** ¿Quieres el o suyo la suya? - **(7)** ¿ Son suyas (de ella) esas pastillas? - **(8)** Le duelen las muelas **(9)** ¿ Dónde te duele? - **(10)** Me duele la rodilla - **(11)** Esta tarde tienen hora para el médico - **(12)** Le sacaron las amígdalas - **(13)** Se me rompió la pierna - **(14)** ¿De quién es este sombrero? - **(15)** Se puso una bufanda - **(16)** No es nuestro padre sino el suyo - **(17)** Te hiciste daño en la muñeca - **(18)** ¿De quién es esta casa? Es del dentista - **(19)** Su madre le lavó las manos - **(20)** No eran vuestros guantes sino los suyos.

c) **(1)** ¿Dónde está nuestro equipaje? - **(2)** ¿ Dónde dejaste tu monedero? - **(3)** No tengo sus llaves - **(4)** No vieron a sus amigos sino a los nuestros - **(5)** Nuestra ciudad es bellísima - **(6)** Mi perro

odia los gatos - **(7)** El no habla con su tío, sino con su cuñado -
(8) No tienen paciencia con su madre - **(9)** Amigo mío, vamos a
escalar la montaña - **(10)** Algunos parientes suyos se quedaron en
casa - **(11)** ¿ Dónde dejó su abrigo? - **(12)** Un hijo suyo quería
saber el paradero de su hermana - **(13)** Tu coche es mucho más
cómodo que el suyo - **(14)** Guillermo no leyó sus tebeos sino los
vuestros - **(15)** ¿ Ese libro es suyo? - **(16)** Esta chica es amiga de
mi hija - **(17)** De quién es esta goma de borrar? Es mía -
(18) El dueño cuyo hotel se incendió está furioso - **(19)** *Cien Años
de Soledad* es una novela de García Márquez - **(20)** ¿ De quién es
esta carpeta? Es suya.

d) **(1)** tu - **(2)** tuyo, suyo - **(3)** Su - **(4)** Mis, suyos - **(5)** mío -
(6) su - **(79)** vuestros - **(8)** su - **(9)** sus - **(10)** sus - **(11)** mía -
(12) tuyo - **(13)** tu, suyo - **(14)** Nuestros - **(15)** sus - **(16)** Mi -
(17) Su - **(18)** Mi - **(19)** suyo - **20)** Sus.

G. INTERROGATIVE PRONOUNS AND ADVERBS

a) **(1)** ¿ Dónde suelen cenar tarde? - **(2)** ¿ Dónde veraneáis? -
(3) ¿Con quién juega? - **(4)** ¿ Qué instrumento tocan muchas
personas? - **(5)** ¿ Qué escribe? - **(6)** ¿ Quién viene a quedarse con
ellos? - **(7)** ¿ Qué lees? - **(8)** ¿ Cómo son tus vecinos? - **(9)** ¿ Quién
escribió *Don Quijote de la Mancha*? - **(10)** ¿ Cómo se llamaba su
caballo? - **(11)** ¿ Quién era Sancho Panza? - **(12)** ¿ Dónde nació
Don Quijote? - **(13)** ¿ Cuáles eran sus aficiones? - **(14)** ¿ Cómo solía
ir? - **(15)** ¿ Cómo actuaba? - **(16)** ¿ Cuál era su apodo? - **(17)** ¿ Qué
visita en coche? - **(18)** ¿ Dónde os encanta bañaros? -
(19) ¿ Cuántos años tendrán? - **(20)** ¿ Por qué lee los periódicos?

b) **(1)** ¿ A qué hora tienes cita? - **(2)** ¿ Cuándo suele ir a pasear? -
(3) ¿ Qué oficio tiene tu amigo? - **(4)** ¿ Dónde viven tus padres? -
(5) A quién has telefoneado? - **(6)** ¿ Cómo es tu primo? - **(7)** ¿ Qué
está leyendo? - **(8)** Por dónde pasa este tren? - **(9)** ¿ Por cuánto
vendió el cuadro - **(10)** ¿ Qué asignaturas prefieres?

c) **(1)** ¿ Les ha dado dinero, no? - **(2)** ¿ Cuál es la que más te gustó? -
(3) ¿ Cuál de esas camisas prefieres? - **(4)** No sé cual prefiero -
(5) ¿ Cuál de esos partidos se llama de derechas? - **(6)** ¿ Se
saludaron? - **(7)** ¿ Se ayudan mutuamente? - **(8)** ¿ Le dijo "Hasta
mañana"? - **(9)** ¿ Repitió un curso? - **(10)** ¿ Escogieron varias
asignaturas?

H. RELATIVE PRONOUNS

a) **(1)** f) - **(2)** g) - **(3)** b) - **(4)** a) - **(5)** e) - **(6)** h) - **(7)** j) - **(8)** i) -
(9) d) - **(10)** c).

b) **(1)** que - **(2)** que - **(3)** que - **(4)** a los que - **(5)** que - **(6)** en el que -
(7) cuyo - **(8)** que - **(9)** cuyos - **(10)** a la cual.

c) (1) cuyos - (2) cuyas - (3) por cuya - (4) cuyos - (5) cuyo -
(6) cuyas - (7) cuyos - (8) cuyos - (9) cuyo - (10) de cuyos -
(11) cuyo - (12) de cuya - (13) cuya - (14) en cuyo -
(15) por cuyos - (16) cuyos - (17) cuyas - (18) cuyo -
(19) por cuyas - (20) cuya.

d) (1) Es un país cuyo gobierno no es neutro - (2) Es una ley de la
cual oiremos hablar - (3) Es una crisis cuya trascendencia
ignoramos - (4) Es una campaña do la que se alegra la clase media
- (5) La tienda delante de cuyo escaparate hay un abeto, es de mi
padre - (6) Había un grupo de jóvenes entre los cuales figuraba mi
hermano - (7) El concierto del que me hablaste no fue grabado -
(8) No ha sido encontrado el amigo cuyas huellas seguía yo -
(9) La ciudad cuyos edificios vislumbráis es Sevilla - (10) La finca
que tiene una de las puertas abiertas es propiedad de mi tío -
(11) El banco cuyos empleados conoces está cerrado desde
mediodía - (12) Fue una niña de la que se burlaban los demás -
(13) Es un acontecimiento del cual se hablará mucho tiempo -
(14) Es un idioma del cual no sabe ni una palabra - (15) Es un
diario cuyos articulos son variados - (16) Era un animal cuyo
dueño era malo - (17) Es una casa alquilada cuyo confort es
dudoso - (18) Es una playa cuyo ambiente es acogedor -
(19) Aquel fue un año del cual nos acordaremos siempre -
(20) Es una tienda cuyo dueño es aragonés.

e) (1) No conozco a nadie que pueda informarle - (2) Quienes no
deseen participar, pueden irse - (3) Al que ponga la mesa, que no
se le olviden las servilletas - (4) Lo que no les gustó fue su orgullo
- (5) Serán despedidas las que no lleguen a tiempo - (6) No conozco
un país en el que eso sea permitido - (7) ¿ Busca a alguien que
venga con usted? - (8) No tenemos libros que sean útiles para
vosotros - (9) No hay quien sepa convencerles - (10) Es una
alumna que tiene don de lenguas - (11) El hombre que perdió su
trabajo es infeliz - (12) Es una buena noticia que no me extraña -
(13) El escritorio sobre el cual trabaja usted está lleno de papeles -
(14) Escoge la película que te guste - (15) Lo que más les interesa
son los ratos libres - (16) Era un actor cuyo pasado conocíamos -
(17) Se fue a la buhardilla en la cual estaban amontonados
muchos objetos - (18) La persona a quien se dirigió es su tía -
(19) Es un bosque por el cual os gusta pasear -
(20) No la reconocían los amigos que se habían reunido.

f) (1) que - (2) que - (3) que - (4) por la cual/que - (5) en los
cuales/que - (6) por los que - (7) lo que - (8) por la cual/que -
(9) de donde - (10) la cual/que - (11) que - (12) cuyo -
(13) el cual/que - (14) al que *or* a quien - (15) quien -
(16) el cual *or* el que - (17) quien (18) quién - (19) que -
(20) quienes.

9. VERB FORMS

a) The present tense

(1) aportar: aporto, aportas, aporta, aportamos, aportáis, aportan

(2) cubrir: cubro, cubres, cubre, cubrimos, cubrís, cubren

(3) conocer: conozco, conoces, conoce, conocemos, conocéis, conocen

(4) distribuir: distribuyo, distribuyes, distribuye, distribuimos, distribuís, distribuyen

(5) costar: cuesto, cuestas, cuesta, costamos, costáis, cuestan

b) The imperfect

(6) ser: era, eras, era, éramos, erais, eran

(7) sentir: sentía sentías, sentía, sentíamos, sentíais, sentían

(8) ver: veía, veías, veía, veíamos, veíais, veían

(9) disolver: disolvía, disolvías, disolvía, disolvíamos, disolvíais, disolvían

(10) soñar: soñaba, soñabas, soñaba, soñábamos, soñabais, soñaban

c) The present subjunctive

(1) haber: haya, hayas, haya, hayamos, hayáis, hayan

(2) reconocer: reconozca, reconozcas, reconozca, reconozcamos, reconozcáis, reconozcan

(3) despertarse: me despierte, te despiertes, se despierte, nos despertemos, os despertéis, se despierten

(4) adquirir: adquiera, adquieras, adquiera, adquiramos, adquiráis, adquieran

(5) hacer: haga, hagas, haga, hagamos, hagáis, hagan

d) The future

(6) poner: pondré, pondrás, pondrá, pondremos, pondréis, pondrán

(7) tener: tendré, tendrás, tendrá, tendremos, tendréis, tendrán

(8) salir: saldré, saldrás, saldrá, saldremos, saldréis, saldrán

(9) haber: habré, habrás, habrá, habremos, habréis, habrán

(10) hacer: haré, harás, hará, haremos, haréis, harán

e) (1) hago, hizo - (2) caigo, cayó - (3) voy, fue - (4) traigo, trajo - (5) soy, fue - (6) doy, dio - (7) puedo, pudo - (8) he, hubo - (9) estoy, estuvo - (10) salgo, salió - (11) pongo, puso - (12) propongo, propuso - (13) dispongo, dispuso - (14) detengo, detuvo - (15) convengo, convino - (16) oigo, oyó - (17) conduzco, condujo - (18) vengo, vino - (19) tengo, tuvo - (20) quiero, quiso.

f) (1) conduzco, conduzcamos - (2) desaparezco, desaparezcamos - (3) favorezco, favorezcamos - (4) amanezco, amanezcamos -

(5) establezco, establezcamos - (6) produzco, produzcamos - (7) aparezco, aparezcamos - (8) conozco, conozcamos - (9) carezco, carezcamos - (10) introduzco, introduzcamos - (11) permanezco, permanezcamos - (12) pertenezco, pertenezcamos - (13) reduzco, reduzcamos - (14) aborrezco, aborrezcamos - (15) traduzco, traduzcamos - (16) nazco, nazcamos - (17) obedezco, obedezcamos - (18) ofrezco, ofrezcamos - (19) merezco, merezcamos - (20) crezco, crezcamos.

g) (1) me acuerdo, se acuerdan - (2) rindo, se rinden - (3) muevo, mueven - (4) acentúo, acentúan - (5) cuento, cuentan - (6) demuestro, demuestran - (7) me divierto, se divierten - (8) muestro, muestran - (9) ruedo, ruedan - (10) me hiero, se hieren - (11) cuelgo, cuelgan - (12) envuelvo, envuelven - (13) muerdo, muerden - (14) ruego, ruegan - (15) me convierto, se convierten - (16) me vuelvo, se vuelven - (17) sueño, sueñan - (18) suelo, suelen - (19) duermo, duermen - (20) adquiero, adquieren.

h) (1) cueces, cocéis - (2) cuestas, costáis - (3) acuestas, acostáis - (4) adviertes, advertís - (5) resuelves, resolvéis - (6) dueles, doléis - (7) encuentras, encontráis - (8) devuelves, devolvéis - (9) te esfuerzas, os esforzáis - (10) juegas, jugáis - (11) remueves, removéis - (12) consientes, consentís - (13) hierves, hervís - (14) suenas, sonáis - (15) te sueltas, os soltáis - (16) mientes, mentís - (17) prefieres, preferís - (18) vuelas, voláis - (19) recuerdas, recordáis - (20) te refieres, os referís.

i) (1) huyo, huyó - (2) atribuyo, atribuyó - (3) distribuyo, distribuyó - (4) retribuyo, retribuyó - (5) afluyo, afluyó - (6) incluyo, incluyó - (7) restituyo, restituyó - (8) instituyo, instituyó - (9) disminuyo, disminuyó - (10) substituyo, substituyó - (11) contribuyo, contribuyó - (12) constituyo, constituyó - (13) excluyo, excluyó - (14) obstruyo, obstruyó - (15) instruyo, instruyó - (16) influyo, influyó - (17) destruyo, destruyó - (18) seduzco, sedujo - (19) produzco, produjo - (20) reduzco, redujo.

j) (1) salgo, salí - (2) he, hube - (3) quepo, cupe - (4) deshago, deshice - (5) pongo, puse - (6) quiero, quise - (7) digo, dije - (8) sé, supe - (9) soy, fui - (10) voy, fui - (11) oigo, oí - (12) valgo, valí - (13) doy, di - (14) puedo, pude - (15) hago, hice - (16) tengo, tuve - (17) traigo, traje - (18) obtengo, obtuve - (19) propongo, propuse - (20) vengo, vine.

k) (1) me asombro, se asombró, se asombren - (2) me duermo, se durmió, se duerman - (3) me aseo, se aseó, se aseen - (4) me levanto, se levantó, se levanten - (5) me caso, se casó, se casen - (6) me convierto, se convirtió, se conviertan - (7) me preocupo, se preocupó, se preocupen - (8) me siento, se sentó, se sienten - (9) me alegro, se alegró, se alegren - (10) me miro, se miró,

se miren - **(11)** me reúno, se reunió, se reúnan - **(12)** me peino,
se peinó, se peinen - **(13)** me entristezco, se entristeció, se
entristezcan - **(14)** me caigo, se cayó, se caigan -
(15) me disgusto, se disgustó, se disgusten - **(16)** me canso, se
cansó, se cansen - **(17)** me endurezco, se endureció, se endurezcan
- **(18)** me decido, se decidió, se decidan - **(19)** me acuesto, se
acostó, se acuesten - **(20)** me reflejo, se reflejó, se reflejen.

l) **(1)** informó, informaremos, inforimaríamos - **(2)** se acordó, nos
acordaremos, nos acordaríamos - **(3)** se durmió, nos dormiremos,
nos dormiríamos - **(4)** resolvió, resolveremos, resolveríamos -
(5) obedeció, obedeceremos, obedeceríamos - **(6)** redujo, reducire-
mos, reduciríamos - **(7)** se movió, nos moveremos, nos moveríamos
- **(8)** condujo, conduciremos, conduciríamos - **(9)** prefirió, preferire-
mos, preferiríamos - **(10)** voló, volaremos, volaríamos -
(11) rodó, rodaremos, rodaríamos - **(12)** excluyó, excluiremos,
excluiríamos - **(13)** estableció, estableceremos, estableceríamos -
(14) repitió, repetiremos, repetiríamos - **(15)** solió, soleremos, sol-
eríamos - **(16)** pidió, pediremos, pediríamos - **(17)** produjo,
produciremos, produciríamos - **(18)** jugó, jugaremos, jugaríamos -
(19) demostró, demostraremos, demostraríamos - **(20)** escribió,
escribiremos, escribiríamos.

m) **(1)** cantó - **(2)** comi - **(3)** agotaba - **(4)** esconderé - **(5)** toco -
(6) tomaste - **(7)** notasteis - **(8)** respondías - **(9)** cojo - **(10)** abierto
- **(11)** roto - **(12)** veíamos - **(13)** inquirís - **(14)** borráis -
(15) escondiera - **(16)** lloraron - **(17)** aparezca - **(18)** nombraráis -
(19) nació - **(20)** destruyas.

n) **(1)** nieva - **(2)** enciendas - **(3)** impidan - **(4)** riño - **(5)** perdi -
(6) extiéndete, extiéndase, extendámonos, extendeos, extiéndanse -
(7) agradecí - **(8)** acuéstate, acuéstese, acostémonos, acostaos,
acuéstense - **(9)** merendéis - **(10)** juguemos - **(11)** cenamos -
(12) mintieras - **(13)** no sepas, no sepa, no sepamos, no sepáis, no
sepan - **(14)** confiramos - **(15)** condujeron - **(16)** no te diviertas, no
se divierta, no nos divirtamos, no os divirtáis, no se diviertan -
(17) tendrá - **(18)** habríais - **(19)** rodaráis - **(20)** éramos.

o) **(1)** puedo - **(2)** se heló - **(3)** heriste - **(4)** anduvieran - **(5)** soñemos -
(6) plegabais - **(7)** muévete, muévase, movámonos, moveos, mué-
vanse - **(8)** no te rías, no se ría, no nos ríamos, no os ríais, no se
rían - **(9)** quepo - **(10)** carezca - **(11)** se vistieran - **(12)** querremos -
(13) puedes - **(14)** perdieron - **(15)** yendo - **(16)** no te caigas, no se
caiga, no nos caigamos, no os caigáis, no se caigan - **(17)** siguió -
(18) defenderíais - **(19)** di, diga, digamos, decid, digan -
(20) parezca - **(21)** cogieran - **(22)** pon, ponga, pongamos,
poned, pongan - **(23)** despedís - **(24)** fui, fuiste, fue, fuimos,
fuisteis, fueron - **(25)** he.

p) **(1)** calientan: 3rd person plural, present indicative *(calentar)* -
(2) aciertes: 2nd person plural, present subjunctive *(acertar)* -
(3) negasteis: 2nd person plural, preterite *(negar)* - **(4)** acreciendo:

gerund *(acrecer)* - **(5)** gobernamos: 1st person plural, present indicative *(gobernar)* - **(6)** confiesa: 3rd person singular, present indicative *(confesar)* - **(7)** calentad: imperative, 2nd person plural *(calentar)* - **(8)** aprietas: 2nd person singular, present indicative *(apretar)* - **(9)** atravesé: 1st person singular, preterite *(atravesar)* - **(10)** desconciertan: 3rd person plural, present indicative *(desconcertar)* - **(11)** empiezo: 1st person singular, present indicative *(empezar)* - **(12)** sueles: 2nd person singular, present indicative *(soler)* - **(13)** sueñen: 3rd person plural, present subjunctive *(soñar)* - **(14)** ruego: 1st person singular, present indicative *(rogar)* - **(15)** compruebes: 2nd person singular, present subjunctive *(comprobar)* - **(16)** desplieguen: 3rd person plural, present subjunctive *(desplegar)* - **(17)** resuelve: 3rd person singular, present indicative *(resolver)* - **(18)** juegan: 3rd person plural, present indicative *(jugar)* - **(19)** duele: 3rd person singular, present indicative *(doler)* - **(20)** pienso: 1st person singular, present indicative *(pensar)*.

q) **(1)** parezco: 1st person singular, present indicative *(parecer)* - **(2)** ofrezcas: 2nd person singular, present subjunctive *(ofrecer)* - **(3)** carecemos: 1st person plural, present indicative *(carecer)* - **(4)** naciste: 2nd person singular, preterite *(nacer)* - **(5)** obedeció: 3rd person singular, preterite *(obedecer)* - **(6)** merecisteis: 2nd person plural, preterite *(merecer)* - **(7)** entristece: 3rd person singular, present indicative *(entristecer)* - **(8)** aparezcáis: 2nd person plural, present subjunctive *(aparecer)* - **(9)** establezca: 1st or 3rd person singular, present subjunctive *(establecer)* - **(10)** conduzco: 1st person singular, present indicative *(conducir)* - **(11)** favorezcan: 3rd person plural, present subjunctive *(favorecer)* - **(12)** pertenecía: 1st or 3rd person singular, imperfect indicative *(pertenecer)* - **(13)** permanezcan: 3rd person plural, present subjunctive *(permanecer)* - **(14)** conozco: 1st person singular, present indicative *(conocer)* - **(15)** condujeron: 3rd person plural, preterite *(conducir)* - **(16)** amanece: 3rd person singular, present indicative *(amanecer)* - **(17)** obedezco: 1st person singular, present indicative *(obedecer)* - **(18)** produjera: 1st or 3rd person singular, imperfect subjunctive *(producir)* - **(19)** traduzcamos: 1st person plural, present subjunctive *(traducir)* - **(20)** enriquezcan: 3rd person plural, present subjunctive *(enriquecer)*.

r) **(1)** perdéis: 2nd person plural, present indicative *(perder)* - **(2)** meriendas: 2nd person singular, present indicative *(merendar)* - **(3)** friegue: 3rd person singular, present subjunctive *(fregar)* - **(4)** tiemblo: 1st person singular, present indicative *(temblar)* - **(5)** piensa: 3rd person singular, present indicative *(pensar)* - **(6)** recomiendan: 3rd person plural, present indicative *(recomendar)* - **(7)** analicemos: 1st person plural, present subjunctive *(analizar)* - **(8)** adquiramos: 1st person plural, present subjunctive *(adquirir)* - **(9)** sintáis: 2nd person plural, present subjunctive *(sentir)* - **(10)** enciendo: 1st person singular, present indicative *(encendar)* - **(11)** llueve: 3rd person singular, present indicative *(llover)* - **(12)** huele: 3rd person singular, present indicative *(oler)* - **(13)** defiendas: 2nd person singular, present subjunctive *(defender)* - **(14)** entendemos: 1st person plural, present indicative *(entender)* - **(15)** siega: 3rd person singular, present indicative *(segar)* - **(16)** remueves: 2nd person singular, present indicative *(remover)* - **(17)** discernís: 2nd person plural, present indicative *(discernir)* - **(18)** nieva: 3rd person singular, present indicative *(nevar)* - **(19)** sentís: 2nd person plural, present indicative *(sentir)* - **(20)** tienden: 3rd person plural, present indicative *(tender)*.

s) **(1)** adquiero: 1st person singular, present indicative *(adquirir)* - **(2)** sienta: 1st or 3rd person singular, present subjunctive *(sentir)* - also 3rd person singular, present indicative *(sentar)* - **(3)** truena: 3rd person singular, present indicative *(tronar)* - **(4)** absuelve: 3rd person singular, present indicative *(absolver)* - **(5)** disuelvo: 1st person singular, present indicative *(disolver)* - **(6)** remueve: 3rd person singular, present indicative *(remover)* - **(7)** conmovieron: 3rd person plural, preterite *(conmover)* - **(8)** discierna: 1st or 3rd person singular, present subjunctive *(discernir)* - **(9)** cuelgan: 3rd person plural, present indicative *(colgar)* - **(10)** recomienda: 3rd person singular, present indicative *(recomendar)* - **(11)** apuestan: 3rd person plural, present indicative *(apostar)* - **(12)** acuérdense: imperative, 3rd person plural, present subjunctive *(acordarse)* - **(13)** difiero: 1st person singular, present indicative *(diferir)* - **(14)** encierre: 1st or 3rd person singular, present subjunctive *(encerrar)* - **(15)** defiendas: 2nd person singular, present subjunctive *(defender)* - **(16)** conduélase: imperative, 3rd person singular, present subjunctive *(condolerse)* - **(17)** envuelvan: 3rd person plural, present subjunctive *(envolver)* - **(18)** volvierais: 2nd person plural, imperfect subjunctive *(volver)* - **(19)** sintamos: 1st person plural, present subjunctive *(sentir)* - **(20)** revolvisteis: 2nd person plural, preterite *(revolver)*.

t) **(1)** sentís: 2nd person plural, present indicative *(sentir)* - **(2)** revolvías: 2nd person singular, imperfect indicative *(revolver)* - **(3)** discernís: 2nd person plural, present indicative *(discernir)* - **(4)** segaron: 3rd person plural, preterite *(segar)* - **(5)** llueve: 3rd person singular, present indicative *(llover)* - **(6)** huela: 1st or 3rd person singular, present subjunctive *(oler)* - **(7)** encomendaron: 3rd person plural, preterite *(encomendar)* - **(8)** vuelo: 1st person singular, present indicative *(volar)* - **(9)** aprobabas: 2nd person singular, imperfect indicative *(aprobar)* - **(10)** encuentres: 2nd person singular, present subjunctive *(encontrar)* - **(11)** asolaban: 3rd person plural, imperfect indicative *(asolar)* - **(12)** comprobaré: 1st person singular, future *(comprobar)* - **(13)** disuena: 3rd person singular, present indicative *(disonar)* - **(14)** sintieses: 2nd person singular, imperfect subjunctive *(sentir)* - **(15)** renovamos: 1st person plural, imperfect indicative *(renovar)* - **(16)** huelga: 3rd person singular, present indicative *(holgar)* - **(17)** resollaras: 2nd person singular, imperfect subjunctive *(resollar)* - **(18)** pensemos: 1st person plural, present subjunctive *(pensar)* - **(19)** mordía: 1st or 3rd person singular, imperfect indicative *(morder)* - **(20)** esfuérzate: 2nd person singular imperative *(esforzar)*.

u) **(3)** envolver - **(5)** recordar - **(8)** soñar - **(10)** soler - **(12)** mostrar - **(13)** divertir - **(14)** sentir - **(16)** preferir - **(17)** costar - **(19)** demostrar - **(20)** pedir.

v) **(1)** ¡ven! - **(2)** lo harás - **(3)** pidió - **(4)** concluyeron - **(5)** que haya escrito - **(6)** enciendo - **(7)** ¡descansa! - **(8)** pondrá - **(9)** saldrán - **(10)** ¡ vete! - **(11)** levantémonos - **(12)** condujeron - **(13)** tengo - **(14)** querríamos - **(15)** aléjate, aléjese, aléjense, alejaos - **(16)** vuelvo - **(17)** ¡ párate! - **(18)** pongo - **(19)** vuelve - **(20)** te despiertas.

w) **(1)** pediría - **(2)** muestran - **(3)** nos quedaremos - **(4)** cierras - **(5)** gastabais - **(6)** digo - **(7)** se callaron todos - **(8)** ¡ suelta! - **(9)** quitaremos - **(10)** que seas - **(11)** hago - **(12)** sé - **(13)** se ha levantado - **(14)** trae - **(15)** ¡ siéntate ! - **(16)** han muerto - **(17)** vengo *or* voy - **(18)** que pongan - **(19)** distingo - **(20)** resuelve.

x) **(1)** A vosotros, os gustan - **(2)** A ti, te encanta - **(3)** A ellos, les ilusiona - **(4)** A usted, se le ocurren - **(5)** A mí, se me antoja - **(6)** A nosotros, nos da ganas de - **(7)** A ustedes, se figuran que . . . - **(8)** A ella, le da vergüenza - **(9)** A los niños, les dan pena - **(10)** A él, le duelen.

y) **(1)** dicho - **(2)** dispuesto - **(3)** escrito - **(4)** cubierto - **(5)** deshecho - **(6)** devuelto - **(7)** hecho - **(8)** muerto - **(9)** roto - **(10)** puesto - **(11)** impreso - **(12)** descubierto - **(13)** abierto - **(14)** propuesto - **(15)** resuelto - **(16)** visto - **(17)** provisto - **(18)** frito - **(19)** bendito - **(20)** distinguido.

10. THE VERB 'TO BE'

a) (1) son - (2) eres, soy - (3) sois - (4) somos - (5) es - (6) está - (7) están, estamos - (8) está - (9) estamos - (10) son.

b) (1) somos - (2) es - (3) están - (4) está - (5) son - (6) estoy - (7) están - (8) es - (9) son - (10) son.

c) (1) es - (2) está - (3) estáis - (4) son - (5) eres - (6) están - (7) soy - (8) están - (9) estoy - (10) somos.

d) (1) Soy yo - (2) Mi santo es el diez del enero - (3) Son de Cataluña - (4) Si, estamos bien - (5) Mis colores preferidos son el rojo y el negro - (6) Estamos a quince de agosto - (7) Somos treinta - (8) Vamos al campo - (9) No estoy en ningún partido político - (10) Sí, lo estoy.

e) (1) Estamos - (2) Es - (3) Estamos - (4) Fueron - (5) está - (6) está - (7) está - (8) fue (9) estaba - (10) está - (11) está - (12) es - (13) es - (14) era - (15) es - (16) son - (17) estaban - (18) es - (19) es - (20) fueron.

f) (1) sois - (2) es - (3) estoy - (4) Estás - (5) es - (6) están - (7) es, es - (8) está - (9) estaréis - (10) Estaos - (11) es - (12) es - (13) son - (14) son - (15) Estás - (16) Son - (17) son - (18) está - (19) está - (20) Son.

g) (1) está - (2) es - (3) estáis - (4) está - (5) está - (6) estáis - (7) estamos - (8) Está - (9) estuvo - (10) está - (11) Está - (12) está - (13) estáis - (14) Estamos - (15) están - (16) es - (17) fue -(18) fue - (19) están - (20) Están.

h) (1) está - (2) está - (3) está - (4) está - (5) está - (6) está - (7) es - (8) está - (9) Es - (10) Es - (11) es - (12) es - (13) Es - (14) está - (15) es - (16) está - (17) son - (18) Está - (19) Es - (20) Está.

i) (1) fue - (2) están - (3) fue - (4) es - (5) Estamos - (6) sois ... Somos - (7) Son - (8) está - (9) Estás - (10) están - (11) estás ... Estamos - (12) Están - (13) Estáis - (14) está - (15) es - (16) es - (17) Son - (18) Está ... estoy - (19) son - (20) Es.

j) (1) es, son, estoy, estoy - (2) soy, estés, es, es, es, es, es - (3) estabas, estabas - (4) es, es, es, es, es, son, eres - (5) es - (6) estoy, está. son - (7) son, son, son, están - (8) estoy, estoy - (9) estoy - (10) estoy, estéis.

k) (1) Andalucía es una región en el sur de España - (2) El coche de tu padre es gris - (3) Esta puerta es de vidrio - (4) Sois chilenos pero venís de Cuba - (5) Esta casa no es suya - (6) Era la una de la

363

noche cuando se marcharon - **(7)** Es ingeniero en una gran empresa - **(8)** Es necesario hacerlo hoy mismo - **(9)** Creo que el español
es muy fácil de aprender - **(10)** Tenías los ojos rojos -
(11) Su vestido era amarillo - **(12)** La cerradura fue rota por los
ladrones - **(13)** Fue acogida con mucho cariño - **(14)** Las vendimias
fueron estropeadas pot el mal tiempo - **(15)** Cuando entraste en el
desván, viste que el tragaluz estaba roto - **(16)** Los paquetes
pueden ser enviados por correos - **(17)** El palacio fue edificado en
1492 - **(18)** Los Alpes están en la frontera franco - italiana -
(19) Estamos en contra de la contaminación - **(20)** El error está en
(*or* es debido a) la mala acústica.

11. THE VERB 'TO HAVE'

a) **(1)** He - **(2)** tenía - **(3)** Has tenido - **(4)** Habrán tenido -
(5) Tenía - **(6)** Tendrías que - **(7)** Tenéis - **(8)** No había - **(9)** Tengo -
(10) Hubieron.

b) **(1)** Ha recorrido el Madrid antiguo - **(2)** Tenía 24 años cuando se
casó - **(3)** Esta mañana hemos tomado el autobús - **(4)** Nunca
tienes dinero contigo - **(5)** Lo hemos visto en un café - **(6)** Habéis
viajado mucho - **(7)** Hace unos años tenía una finca en Galicia -
(8) Este teatro no tiene bastantes localidades - **(9)** Le ha escrito
para anunciar su llegada - **(10)** Han elegido callarse - **(11)** Sólo
teníamos que cruzar la calle para estar en la playa - **(12)** Hablo
del niño que tenía un papagayo - **(13)** No les dijiste que él había
muerto - **(14)** Ya no tiene muchos empleados esta empresa -
(15) Esta avenida tiene numerosas librerías - **(16)** Nadie tiene sus
señas - **(17)** Tienen algunas horas para reflexionarlo -
(18) No tiene todos los discos del cantante - **(19)** Tengo varias
estátuas precolombinas - **(20)** Su piso tiene pocos muebles.

c) **(1)** Nuestro vecino tiene un coche nuevo - **(2)** ¿Tiene los medios de
marcharse? - **(3)** Le he llamado varias veces - **(4)** Habían ido a
visitar la catedral - **(5)** No tienes ningún dato que darles -
(6) Tengo mucho que hacer - **(7)** ¿Has comprado su última novela?
- **(8)** Tenemos muchas fotos de ellos - **(9)** En esta cafetería, no
tienen muchos camareros - **(10)** Habíamos seguido sus consejos.

12. THE SUBJUNCTIVE

a) **(1)** duerman - **(2)** estés - **(3)** tenga - **(4)** haya - **(5)** sepan - **(6)** prefiera - **(7)** encuentre - **(8)** mientan - **(9)** te arrepintieras - **(10)** volvieran - **(11)** te pida - **(12)** se despidiera - **(13)** te enfurezcas - **(14)** conociera - **(15)** encuentren - **(16)** juegue - **(17)** sienta - **(18)** muerda - **(19)** hayan - **(20)** apostaras.

b) **(1)** vuelvan, volvieran - **(2)** lo hagas, lo hicieras - **(3)** lo pida, lo pidiera - **(4)** duerma, durmiera - **(5)** nos levantemos, nos levantáramos - **(6)** os riáis, os rierais - **(7)** conduzcan, condujeran - **(8)** vayan, fueran - **(9)** salgan, salieran - **(10)** lo diga, lo dijera.

c) **(1)** vino - **(2)** venga - **(3)** viene - **(4)** viniera - **(5)** vino - **(6)** viene - **(7)** venga - **(8)** viniera - **(9)** me encuentre - **(10)** me viera.

d) **(1)** salgas - **(2)** salieras - **(3)** salgas - **(4)** lo sepas - **(5)** lo supieras - **(6)** vuelva - **(7)** volviera - **(8)** vuelva.

e) **(1)** corran - **(2)** haya comido, pruebe - **(3)** tuviera - **(4)** aprobaras - **(5)** me guste - **(6)** él vuelva - **(7)** la conocieran - **(8)** tuvieras - **(9)** la absuelvas - **(10)** sintáis - **(11)** duermas - **(12)** le quisieran - **(13)** tenga - **(14)** sea - **(15)** comas - **(16)** vaya - **(17)** la protejan - **(18)** te pregunten - **(19)** sepan - **(20)** tome.

f) **(1)** se presentase - **(2)** vengan, pase - **(3)** atienda - **(4)** llegue - **(5)** estés - **(6)** conozcáis - **(7)** hable - **(8)** pase - **(9)** desayune - **(10)** leas - **(11)** vean - **(12)** viva - **(13)** interrumpieran - **(14)** comiera - **(15)** terminarais - **(16)** trajeran - **(17)** viviera - **(18)** quisiera - **(18)** quisiera - **(19)** acompañara - **(20)** divirtiera.

g) **(1)** deje - **(2)** tuvierais - **(3)** redujéramos - **(4)** esperaran - **(5)** viniera - **(6)** tomaras or tomes - **(7)** siguiera - **(8)** esté - **(9)** dijera - **(10)** asomáramos - **(11)** comprendieran - **(12)** fuméis - **(13)** duerman - **(14)** salieran - **(15)** tuvieran - **(16)** acoja - **(17)** seáis - **(18)** destruyamos - **(19)** eligiera - **(20)** tenga.

h) **(1)** Más vale que lo hagas mañana - **(2)** Sería justo que fuera castigado - **(3)** Es probable que vaya a marcharse - **(4)** Era sorprendente que les invitaras - **(5)** Será imprescindible que les escucháramos - **(6)** Ya es hora de que se vaya - **(7)** Sería importante que intervinieras - **(8)** Es extraño que no haya contestado - **(9)** Sería urgente que se mejorara - **(10)** No está bien que no los reciba.

i) **(1)** No puede trabajar sin que le interrumpas - **(2)** Te llamo para que estés informado - **(3)** Es difícil corregirla, tanto más cuanto

no la conocemos - **(4)** Hablaba de tal modo que nadie podía
seguirle - **(5)** Para que todo salga bien será preciso ser objetivo -
(6) Han traído sus libros para que los vendaís - **(7)** Después de
leer, ya podrás divertirte - **(8)** En cuanto esté aquí, le informaré -
(9) Leeré los documentos a medida que los vaya recibiendo -
(10) Aunque hubiera hablado en voz alta, no le hubieran oído.

j) **(1)** Nos encanta que venga - **(2)** Siento que no haya triunfado - **(3)**
Me parecía importante que te responsabilizaras - **(4)** Te gustaría
que todos te obedecieran - **(5)** Les precuparía preciso no encontrase
alojamiento - **(6)** Le molestará que no les acompañe - **(7)** He
deseado que volváis a veros - **(8)** Nos alegramos de que tengas tu
permiso de conducir - **(9)** Sería una lástima que vacilarais -
(10) Sentía que no estuvieran atentos.

k) **(1)** Te pido que comas en casa - **(2)** Le había aconsejado que
llamaran - **(3)** No crees que se ocupe de ellos - **(4)** Habría querido
que te quedaras ahí - **(5)** Hemos aconsejado que comprara esta
marca - **(6)** Me pedirán que te lo diga - **(7)** Vuestra madre prefiere
que os pongáis pantalón y camisa - **(8)** Le ha impedido que haga
una tontería - **(9)** Su jefe le ordenará que dispare -
(10) No les permiten que fumen - **(11)** No creía que emprenderan
este viaje - **(12)** Preferiría que pasarais las vacaciones en el
campo - **(13)** Le encargarás que rellene estas hojas -
(14) Te digo que vengas en seguida - **(15)** Te rogaba que
tuvieras paciencia - **(16)** Te aconsejamos que des pruebas
de ello - **(17)** Desearía que tomara unas vacaciones -
(18) Les dirá que conduzcan con prudencia - **(19)** Le aconsejaste
que no mintiera - **(20)** Les ha pedido que guarden el correo.

l) **(1)** Mi padre quiere que le acompañes - **(2)** Es necesario que
cerremos las ventanas - **(3)** Creía que prepararas la cena -
(4) Les recomendarás que lean antiguos autores - **(5)** No quería
que lo hiciera - **(6)** Te pedirá que vayas a nadar con ella -
(7) Temía que no estuvieras en casa - **(8)** Si no vinieras,
les daría lástima - **(9)** Sería deseable que tomarais vuestros
billetes - **(10)** No creo que lo veas. - **(11)** Insiste en que vayas a
ver a un médico - **(12)** Nos alegrábamos que ustedes también
fueran invitados - **(13)** Está muy bien que obedezcas -
(14) Le aconsejaríamos que tomara el coche - **(15)** Nadie
lo creerá - **(16)** Te han aconsejado que lo pases todo a máquina -
(17) Sientes que no te hayan transmitido el documento -
(18) Les escribiréis para que no se preocupen - **(19)** Le encantaría
que ella aprobara todos los exámenes - **(20)** Desearíamos que se
instalaran a orillas del mar.

13. SEQUENCE OF TENSES

a) (1) Insistió, hiciéramos - (2) Dudé, acertara - (3) Era probable que hubieran llegado - (4) Era inútil que se lo devolviera - (5) Sentí mucho que no hubiera ganado - (6) No pude admitir que no te escucharan - (7) Quise que se recuperara - (8) Nos extrañó mucho que no contestaran - (9) Estuvimos *or* Estábamos satisfechos con tal que aprobaran - (10) Te esperé hasta que me llamaste - (11) Le rogué que se despidiera - (12) Busqué a alguien que me aconsejara - (13) Me temí *or* temía que no estuvieran - (14) Te avisó a fin de que tomaras conciencia de esto - (15) Les pidió que trajeran sus discos - (16) Era normal que celebraran el suceso - (17) Deseaba que se tranquilizara - (18) Les pareció *or* parecia raro que salieran tan tarde - (19) Nos gustó que vinieran a vernos - (20) No soportaron que hicieran tanto ruido.

b) (1) haya - (2) me ayudaras - (3) repitieras - (4) contestara - (5) puedan - (6) pensara - (7) se escapara - (8) pongan - (9) consigáis - (10) viviera - (11) disfrutaran - (12) se vistieran - (13) vieran - (14) haya - (15) rindiera - (16) quiera - (17) conociera - (18) llamemos - (19) ha - (20) atribuyeran.

c) (1) siguierais - (2) se rinda - (3) calienta - (4) escoge, quieras - (5) restituya - (6) pertenece - (7) repitas - (8) vuelvan - (9) pongan - (10) haya - (11) trajera - (12) vengáis, demos - (13) adquirieras - (14) corrígelo - (15) sepas - (16) atienda - (17) sea - (18) que apruebes - (19) almuerce - (20) le animen.

d) (1) lo hagas - (2) es - (3) han - (4) me voy - (5) te lo diga - (6) los supieras - (7) le comprendiera - (8) quédate - (9) los veáis - (10) lo deseaba - (11) lo hace - (12) vente - (13) viajaba - (14) estaba - (15) salen - (16) oyera - (17) me infomara - (18) quieras - (19) podáis - (20) vuelvas.

e) (1) amenazaran - (2) empeñes - (3) salgas - (4) vaya - (5) cogiera - (6) estuviera - (7) insistiera - (8) sea - (9) pegan - (10) contarais - (11) fueran - (12) colgó - (13) hagan - (14) puedan - (15) haya - (16) haga - (17) me guste - (18) te acuestes - (19) obtenga - (20) excluyan.

f) (1) Veo que no somos bienvenidos - (2) Me enteré de que llegasteis tarde - (3) Nunca había notado que era raro - (4) No sabíamos que había pinos en esa región - (5) Lo que tú dices no está muy bien admitido - (6) No cree que los conozcáis - (7) Me imagino que todos son felices - **(8)** Parece que hace buen tiempo - **(9)** Supone que han hecho sus deberes - **(10)** No me parecía que hiciese tanto frío el año pasado - **(11)** No se imaginaba que tuviese usted dinero - **(12)** No creía que lo diríais - **(13)** No prometen que to recibirán - **(14)** No pensábamos que todos tuvieran la misma opinión - **(15)** No era normal que protestaran - **(16)** Les mandas que se queden quietos - **(17)** Dudaba usted que se presentara - **(18)** Sería interesante que participaras en las investigaciones - **(19)** Me alegro que haya tenido buen viaje - **(20)** Te dijimos que no la escucharas.

g) **(1)** se pongan - **(2)** ordenarais - **(3)** vayamos - **(4)** la despertaras - **(5)** subiera - **(6)** te calles - **(7)** salieran - **(8)** vinieran - **(9)** hayan - **(10)** me molesten - **(11)** abramos - **(12)** interrumpiera - **(13)** se reúnan - **(14)** se instalen - **(15)** estuvieras - **(16)** concluyera - **(17)** se acordara - **(18)** leyeran - **(19)** asistieran - **(20)** haya.

h) **(1)** se vayan - **(2)** oculte - **(3)** hayamos - **(4)** hiciera - **(5)** comen - **(6)** se muden - **(7)** saque - **(8)** apruebes - **(9)** cueste - **(10)** volviera - **(11)** paguen - **(12)** tengamos - **(13)** haga - **(14)** durmieran - **(15)** fuera - **(16)** nades - **(17)** fumara - **(18)** hiciéramos - **(19)** acompañaras - **(20)** se juntaran.

i) **(1)** miras - **(2)** vuelvan - **(3)** se hubiese *or* se hubiera - **(4)** vayas - **(5)** sabéis - **(6)** avisara - **(7)** se marchó - **(8)** den - **(9)** vayas - **(10)** pudierais - **(11)** se enterara - **(12)** destacan - **(13)** suene - **(14)** funcione - **(15)** tenga - **(16)** relajes - **(17)** haya - **(18)** perjudicara - **(19)** practiquéis - **(20)** insistan.

14. THE IMPERATIVE

a) **(1)** Siéntense - **(2)** Vete - **(3)** Póngaselo - **(4)** Sé - **(5)** Pensadlo - **(6)** Despiértense - **(7)** Di - **(8)** Tengamos - **(9)** Salga - **(10)** Haz.

b) **(1)** no te sientas, no se sienta, no nos sintamos, no os sintáis, no se sientan - **(2)** no te pruebes, no se pruebe, no nos probemos, no os probeis, no se prueben - **(3)** no te conduelas, no se conduela, no nos condolamos, no os condoláis, no se conduelan - **(4)** no te vuelvas, no se vuelva, no nos volvamos, no os volváis, no se vuelvan - **(5)** no te esfuerces, no se esfuerce, no nos esforcemos, no os esforcéis, no se esfuercen - **(6)** no te pasees, no se pasee, no nos paseemos, no os paseéis, no se paseen - **(7)** no te arrepientas; no se arrepienta, no nos arrepintamos, no os arrepintáis, no se arrepientan - **(8)** no te vistas, no se vista, no nos vistamos, no os vistáis, no se vistan - **(9)** no te asomes, no se asome, no nos asomemos, no os asoméis, no se asomen - **(10)** no te despiertes, no se despierte, no nos despertemos, no os despertéis, no se despierten.

c) **(1)** siéntate, siéntese, sentémonos, sentaos, siéntense - **(2)** reúnete, reúnase, reunámonos, reuníos, reúnanse - **(3)** duérmete, duérmase, durmámonos, dormíos, duérmanse - **(4)** muévete, muévase, movámonos, moveos, muévanse - **(5)** cáete, cáigase, caigámonos, caeos, cáiganse - **(6)** échate, échese, echémonos, echaos, échense - **(7)** vete, váyase, vámonos, idos, váyanse - **(8)** diviértete, diviértase, divirtámonos, divertíos, diviértanse - **(9)** ríete, ríase, riámonos, reíos, ríanse - **(10)** acuérdate, acuérdese, acordémonos, acordaos, acuérdense.

d) **(1)** no contéis - **(2)** no nos durmamos - **(3)** que no traiga - **(4)** no digas - **(5)** no vuelvan - **(6)** no te tengas - **(7)** no hagas - **(8)** no busquéis - **(9)** no sueñes - **(10)** no huyan.

e) **(1)** ve - **(2)** corra - **(3)** no te quedes ahí - **(4)** ven - **(5)** di - **(6)** pon la mesa - **(7)** no hagas caso - **(8)** no lo sientas - **(9)** no te molestes - **(10)** sal - **(11)** sé - **(12)** no os mováis - **(13)** sé bueno - **(14)** siéntate - **(15)** levántate - **(16)** no te duermas - **(17)** sentémonos - **(18)** lávate las manos - **(19)** espérenme - **(20)** no os paseéis.

f) **(1)** Veamos eso - **(2)** Pruébate esta falda plisada - **(3)** Vete a su casa - **(4)** Dedicaos a vuestros estudios - **(5)** No te tiñas el pelo de marron - **(6)** Cámbiese, vístase - **(7)** Empecemos - **(8)** Perdone la molestia pero necesito una infomación - **(9)** Vamonos - **(10)** Ponte esta camisa, te sentará bien - **(11)** No lleves moneda - **(12)** No nos apresuremos, no nos toca - **(13)** Ten paciencia - **(14)** Sal a verlos -

(15) Dile la marca del coche - (16) No atravieses con el semáforo verde - (17) idos - (18) No se equivoquen de carretera -
(19) No emprendamos la carrera - (20) Sirvanse ustedes abrochar los cinturones.

g) (1) No caigamos - (2) Traelo - (3) No los distribuyáis -
(4) Ten dinero - (5) No te asomes a la ventana - (6) Corrige el problema - (7) Sal al jardin - (8) ríamonos - (9) No conduzcas rápido - (10) No sigáis - (11) Construyamos la carretera - (12) Traduce este texto - (13) Enciende la calefacción - (14) No andes descalzo - (15) Instruios - (16) No nos pongamos nerviosos - (17) Pide *or* Pregunta *or* Ruega - (18) Escojan - (19) Vístete - (20) Vistámonos.

15. THE PASSIVE

a) **(1)** El empleado no recibió el paquete - **(2)** Construyeron -
(3) Plantaron - **(4)** Le pusieron - **(5)** El arquitecto ideó el plano -
(6) Unos aficionados publicaron esta obra - **(7)** El público aplaude
al cantante - **(8)** El alcalde cerró varias escuelas - **(9)** El director
abrió el almacén - **(10)** Los diputados eligieron al presidente.

b) **(1)** fue escrita - **(2)** se sirve - **(3)** se recibían a, cran recibidos
alumnos - **(4)** fue cerrado, se cerró - **(5)** será enviado, se enviará -
(6) fue comprado - **(7)** fue detenido - **(8)** es dado - **(9)** fue cegado -
(10) es protegido.

c) **(1)** La mayoría de la problación lo eligió presidente de la
república - **(2)** Los jóvenes ven mucho esta película - **(3)** Lo
aplaudieron todos - **(4)** Los vecinos ayudaron al niño - **(5)** Los
bomberos apagaron el incendio - **(6)** Le avisaron sus amigos -
(7) Un loco mató al cantante - **(8)** Tus padres te ofrecerán el disco -
(9) El conserje cierra el palacio - **(10)** La asistenta limpia la casa.

d) **(1)** Hace una semana, mandaron la carta - **(2)** Antes de dejar la
sala, abrieron la ventana - **(3)** A todos les fue comunicada la
noticia - **(4)** Allí construyeron varios edifícios - **(5)** Se estableció un
régimen liberal - **(6)** Programaron unas elecciones para la
primavera - **(7)** Promulgaron unas leyes - **(8)** Se vendió muy cara
la obra maestra de Velázquez - **(9)** Un cazador mató al ciervo -
(10) La sala está vacía - **(11)** Lo hirió una máquina -
(12) Ha sido recibido por un autor famoso - **(13)** Todas las cajas
están cerradas - **(14)** Están muy sucias las aceras - **(15)** El policía
las detuvo - **(16)** Nos acogió nuestro huésped - **(17)** Este cuadro no
lo firmó el artista - **(18)** Está silenciosa la casa - **(19)** Están
marchitas las flores - **(20)** Lo aprobó el jurado.

16. THE GERUND

a) **(1)** Estoy haciendo - **(2)** Sigue llorando - **(3)** Iba subiendo - **(4)** Estabas comiendo - **(5)** va mejorando - **(6)** va creciendo - **(7)** Anda buscando - **(8)** Andábamos proyectando - **(9)** No estabas diciendo - **(10)** Ya vas siendo.

b) **(1)** estaba **(2)** estaba - **(3)** seguía - **(4)** estaba - **(5)** seguía - **(6)** seguías - **(7)** estabais - **(8)** seguía - **(9)** va - **(10)** van.

c) **(1)** Se marcharon ya que pensaban que descansaba - **(2)** Se entendía de lo que se trataba al leer las instrucciones - **(3)** Ya que no hay ruta, tendremos que inventarla - **(4)** Los habéis visto hacer los deberes - **(5)** Le ofreces un buen regalo aunque no lo merece - **(6)** Pensaba que no irías, así que no sacó las entradas - **(7)** En cuanto amaneció se levantaron - **(8)** Mientras se paseaba, sacó fotos - **(9)** Se las arregla trabajando - **(10)** Iba dirigiéndose hacia ellos.

17. CONDITIONS

a) (1) edificarán - (2) dolerían - (3) estimarán - (4) sería - (5) olvides - (6) tendría - (7) seríamos - (8) podrían - (9) dolerían - (10) sería.

b) (1) viajaría - (2) podrías - (3) te habrías - (4) saldrías - (5) perderías - (6) ganarían - (7) tendría - (8) emprendería - (9) entablarían - (10) irías.

c) (1) Si no quieres tener problemas, cállate - (2) Si éste no te gusta, puedes tomar otro - (3) Si viene mañana, lo verá - (4) Si metéis ruido, se quejarán los vecinos - (5) Si tenéis frío, meteos en casa - (6) Si salen temprano, pasarán a veros - (7) Si voy al teatro, te traeré el programa - (8) Si conoce su dirección, enséñenosla - (9) Si sabes tus lecciones, aprobarás el examen - (10) Si se reúne con ellos, con ellos volverá - (11) Si disuelven las Cortes, nuevas elecciones habrá - (12) Si te vistes de prisa, llegarás a la hora - (13) Si no discernimos sus intenciones, tendremos dificultades - (14) Si distribuyen premios, a él le darán uno - (15) Si no abrís la puerta, la romperán - (16) Si vamos a despedirnos de ellos, nos quedaremos a cenar - (17) Si vuelcas el vaso, tendrás que limpiar la mesa - (18) Si se derrite la nieve, no podrán esquiar más - (19) Si se cuela, no estará contenta la gente - (20) Si te adaptas, sería más fácil para ti.

d) (1) Si conociera su dirección, podría escribirle - (2) Si condujerais menos rápido, veríais el paisaje - (3) Si durmiéramos más, no estaríamos tan cansados - (4) Si se sentara bien, no le dolería la espalda - (5) Si nevara, podríamos esquiar - (6) Si conociéramos las leyes, tendríamos menos problemas - (7) Si lo supieras, se lo dirías - (8) Si no saliera tanto, sacaría mejores notas - (9) Si hiciera buen tiempo, podríamos broncearnos - (10) Si lloviera, nos mojaríamos - (11) Si os acostarais más temprano, estaríais más descansados - (12) Si les dijéramos la verdad, estarían decepcionados - (13) Si me lo pidieras, lo haría - (14) Si fuerais más numerosos, jugaríais a las cartas - (15) Si tuviera tiempo, iría con vosotros - (16) Si tuviera dinero, viajaría a menudo - (17) Si saliéramos con ellos, nos divertiríamos - (18) Si te pusieras este jersey, no pasarías frío - (19) Si viviera en el campo, menos contaminación tendría - (20) Si les llamarais, os dirían que están listos.

e) (1) Si hubieras desobedecido, habrías sido castigado - (2) Si hubiera nacido un año antes, no habría hecho el servicio militar - (3) Si os hubiérais hecho ricos, habríais ayudado a vuestros padres - (4) Si se hubieran quedado más tiempo, le habrían encotrado - (5) Si le hubiera regalado un disco, eso le habría dado

mucha alegría - **(6)** Si ese país tuviera más cereales, no sería
deficitario - **(7)** Si hubieras reducido tu tren de vida, no tendrías
deudas ahora - **(8)** Si se hubiera arrepentido, todos le habrían
perdonado - **(9)** Si ella hubiera conseguido convencerle, yo habría
estado satisfecha - **(10)** Si les hubiera echado de menos, habría
vuelto - **(11)** Si hubiéramos visto esta película, habríamos podido
hablar de ella - **(12)** Si les hubiera escrito, habrían estado
encantados - **(13)** Si hubiera regresado para verla, habría sido
muy feliz -
(14) Si nos hubiera dicho de qué se trataba, no nos habríamos
sorprendido - **(15)** Si hubiera hecho su trabajo, habría podido
salir - **(16)** Si nos hubieran visto, nos habrían esperado - **(17)** Si os
hubierais disfrazado, a lo mejor habríais recibido un premio -
(18) Si no te hubieras roto la pierna, habrías podido practicar
deporte - **(19)** Si hubiéramos devuelto la casete, nos habrían
devuelto el dinero - **(20)** Si hubiera puesto la mesa, se habrían
tranquilizado.

f) (1) Si almorzáramos más temprano, aprovecharíamos la tarde -
(2) Si apostaras, ganaría yo - **(3)** Si aprobara el examen, estaría
aliviado - **(4)** Si lo consolara, tendría más ánimo - **(5)** Si pensaras
más en tu porvenir, olvidarías tu duelo - **(6)** Si renováramos el piso
sería mas cómodo - **(7)** Si intercambiaran direcciones, se cartearían
- **(8)** Si les hiciera un favor, podrían contar con usted - **(9)** Si
hiciera ejercicios, le entrarían ganas de trabajar -
(10) Si corrigiera sus deberes, comprenderían sus errores -
(11) Si me vistiera de traje de etiqueta, entraría en el casino -
(12) Si nos atendieran rápido, regresaríamos pronto -
(13) Si descubrieran nuevos vestigios, los expondrían -
(14) Si se derritiera la nieve, tendríamos que marcharnos
de nuevo - **(15)** Si el gobierno exilara al rey, estaría decepcionado el
pueblo - **(16)** Si tomaras el metro, no llegarías tarde -
(17) Si eligiéramos a un nuevo presidente, sufriría cambios la
Bolsa - **(18)** Si encuentras la solución, llámeme por teléfono -
(19) Si dijera menos tonterías, la creeríamos - **(20)** Si hubiera más
justicia, la gente estaría satisfecha.

g) (1) De habérmelo dicho, lo habría hecho - **(2)** De ser su padre -
(3) De haber tenido - **(4)** De haberlo sabido - **(5)** De tener -
(6) De alcanzar - **(7)** De dormir - **(8)** De soltar - **(9)** De llover -
(10) De nevar.

18. OBLIGATION

a) **(1)** tiene que - **(2)** debe - **(3)** debemos - **(4)** Tienes que - **(5)** hay que - **(6)** Hemos de - **(7)** tengo que - **(8)** Hay que - **(9)** he de - **(10)** tienes que.

b) **(1)** Han de - **(2)** Es menester - **(3)** Hace falta - **(4)** Tendríamos que - **(5)** Tenías que - **(6)** Tuviera que - **(7)** Hará falta - **(8)** Es necesario - **(9)** tengan - **(10)** Tenéis que.

c) **(1)** hay que - **(2)** debe - **(3)** tienen que - **(4)** tenía que - **(5)** tenían que - **(6)** has de - **(7)** Tengo que - **(8)** No hay que - **(9)** tienes que - **(10)** hay que.

d) **(1)** Debéis devolver lo que no os pertenece - **(2)** Es preciso intervenirla - **(3)** Se ha de respetar el código - **(4)** Cada noche tiene que estudiar - **(5)** Deben respetar al vecindario - **(6)** Hará falta mucha paciencia para aguantarlos - **(7)** Necesitan ropa limpia - **(8)** Se debe ser amable con todos - **(9)** No tienes que leer sin comprender - **(10)** Es preciso que escriba mejor - **(11)** Hay que llamar varias veces al timbre si quieres que te oigan - **(12)** No debe vestirse de esta manera - **(13)** No habrían de ser tan insolentes - **(14)** Este niño no habría debido alejarse de sus padres - **(15)** No tienes que trasnochar - **(16)** ¡ Qué se debe hacer ? - **(17)** Era preciso que no mezclara los medicamentos - **(18)** No debéis arrancar las hojas de los libros - **(19)** Es menester que se comporten como todos - **(20)** Tienes que avisarlos.

19. THE INFINITIVE

a) **(1)** al aparecer - **(2)** al penetrar - **(3)** al verse - **(4)** al encontrarlo -
(5) al ponerse a hablar - **(6)** al volver - **(7)** al recibir -
(8) al asomarse - **(9)** al dar clase - **(10)** al leer.

b) **(1)** Asistieron a la ceremonia sin saludar a nadie - **(2)** De haber
escuchado la conferencia, estarían al tanto de las novedades -
(3) Al subir al desván, se cayó - **(4)** Toca el piano sin mirar la
partitura - **(5)** Al llegar, notó el cambio - **(6)** Al salir de su casa, se
dió con un coche - **(7)** Tienen la casa hecha una verdadera ruina,
por no ocuparse de ella - **(8)** Le acusaron por haber robado muchas
cosas - **(9)** Tuvo un accidente por no haber visto el semáforo -
(10) Aprobaron el presupuesto sin tener en cuenta
las consecuencias.

20. THE VERB 'TO BECOME'

a) **(1)** Se hace - **(2)** se hizo - **(3)** llegó a ser - **(4)** se hace - **(5)** volviéndose - **(6)** se vuelven - **(7)** se convirtió en - **(8)** llega a ser - **(9)** se transforma - **(10)** llegaron a ser.

b) **(1)** se pone - **(2)** se ha vuelto - **(3)** se hizo - **(4)** se volvió - **(5)** se convierte en - **(6)** se puso - **(7)** se hizo - **(8)** se volvió - **(9)** se hicieron - **(10)** se volvió - **(11)** se pone - **(12)** se convierte en - **(13)** hagáis - **(14)** ponerse - **(15)** se convirtió en - **(16)** se hizo - **(17)** se hizo - **(18)** se vuelve - **(19)** se volvieron - **(20)** se hace.

c) **(1)** Se hace - **(2)** Te vuelves - **(3)** se hizo - **(4)** Se pone - **(5)** se convirtió en - **(6)** llegaron a ser - **(7)** Se vuelve - **(8)** se convierte - **(9)** te pongas - **(10)** llegó a ser.

d) **(1)** Este profesor se ha vuelto muy severo - **(2)** Os habeis hecho ricos - **(3)** Te volverás muy fuerte si haces deporte - **(4)** Este país se ha vuelto una gran potencia económica - **(5)** Esta casa se ha convertido en un museo - **(6)** Al enterarse de la noticia se puso nerviosa - **(7)** Desde que hacemos yoga, nos hemos vuelto más tranquilos - **(8)** El golf llega a ser un deporte de moda - **(9)** Se hicieron amigos durante el crucero - **(10)** Se pone rojo cuando corre - **(11)** Se vuelve agresivo cuando la gente no está de acuerdo con él - **(12)** Al hacernos mayores, nos volvemos más serios - **(13)** Este perro abandonado se convirtió en una verdadera fiera - **(14)** Este negocio vino a ser una verdadera empresa - **(15)** Un día, esta estatua se transformará en un monumento - **(16)** No te vuelvas impaciente - **(17)** Esta discoteca se ha puesto muy de moda - **(18)** Vivir con ellos viene a ser una tarea - **(19)** Si hubiera más coches, eso vendría a ser una pesadilla - **(20)** Se volvieron verdaderos aficionados a la música.

21. TO GET, TELL SOMEONE TO DO SOMETHING

a) **(1)** mandó - **(2)** mandes - **(3)** Le mandaron - **(4)** No le mande -
(5) mandaron - **(6)** mandará - **(7)** Os mandaban -
(8) Te mandarán - **(9)** mandaban - **(10)** mandó.

b) **(1)** Mandé que te trajeran café - **(2)** Mandas planchar la ropa -
(3) Les manda obedecer - **(4)** Le mandáis poner la mesa -
(5) Les mandamos traducir el texto - **(6)** Le mandaste limpiar los
cristales - **(7)** Te manda leer muchos libros - **(8)** Te mandan vaciar
el desván - **(9)** Nos mandarás ordenar la habitación -
(10) Le mandará escribirlo a máquina.

22. ADVERBS

A. ADVERBS OF PLACE

(1) aquí - (2) lejos - (3) en - (4) dentro - (5) Fuera - (6) Cerca -
(7) debajo - (8) en ninguna parte - (9) encima - (10) Abajo.

B. ADVERBS OF TIME

(1) Ahora - (2) Todavía - (3) Aún - (4) Luego - (5) Mañana -
(6) pronto - (7) Siempre - (8) acto seguido - (9) Dentro de poco -
(10) Ahora.

C. ADVERBS OF MANNER

a) (1) cordialmente - (2) penosamente - (3) claramente -
(4) superficialmente - (5) espontáneamente - (6) alegremente -
(7) lentamente - (8) audazmente - (9) facilmente -
(10) frecuentemente.

b) (1) Quiere irse en seguida, no va a esperarte - (2) Nos saludó
cortesmente - (3) Ya lo decía yo - (4) Seguramente, irá -
(5) Ya voy - (6) Se instalaron cómodamente - (7) Habla clara y
distintamente - (8) Desgraciadamente, no puede venir nadie -
(9) Ya no va - (10) Pienso luego soy - (11) Entraron
silenciosamente - (12) El problema se complica extremadamente - (13) Estoy citado para pasado mañana - (14) Se me
cayeron
encima - (15) Fue herido levemente - (16) Condujeron muy de
prisa - (17) Vive intensamente - (18) Se comportan
peligrosamente - (19) Siempre contestamos cortésmente -
(20) Miraba tristemente la foto.

c) (1) de prisa - (2) con gravedad - (3) a hurtadillas -
(4) con gusto - (5) de buena gana - (6) de verdad - (7) en público
- (8) con rapidez - (9) Desgraciadamente - (10) con claridad.

d) (1) rápido - (2) temprano - (3) mucho - (4) después - (5) alli -
(6) detrás - (7) fuera - (8) poco - (9) cerca - (10) raras veces.

23. PREPOSITIONS

a) **(1)** de - **(2)** Desde - **(3)** de - **(4)** De - **(5)** de - **(6)** Desde - **(7)** desde - **(8)** de - **(9)** Desde - **(10)** Desde.

b) **(1)** En - **(2)** A, en - **(3)** a - **(4)** en, a - **(5)** En - **(6)** a, en - **(7)** A **(8)** A - **(9)** a - **(10)** en.

c) **(1)** de - **(2)** de - **(3)** sobre - **(4)** de, a - **(5)** sin - **(6)** a por - **(7)** para - **(8)** en - **(9)** a - **(10)** en.

d) **(1)** a - **(2)** en - **(3)** Según - **(4)** delante de - **(5)** Antes de - **(6)** dentro de - **(7)** después - **(8)** debajo de - **(9)** ante - **(10)** encima de - **(11)** por - **(12)** a - **(13)** de - **(14)** con - **(15)** con - **(16)** de, en - **(17)** a - **(18)** en - **(19)** a - **(20)** de.

e) **(1)** con - **(2)** En, en - **(3)** a - **(4)** por - **(5)** con, para - **(6)** al - **(7)** por - **(8)** Por - **(9)** para - **(10)** Por - **(11)** de - **(12)** de - **(13)** En - **(14)** sin - **(15)** a - **(16)** por - **(17)** a, para - **(18)** a, en - **(19)** a - **(20)** en.

f) **(1)** en - **(2)** a - **(3)** de - **(4)** por - **(5)** en - **(6)** en - **(7)** de - **(8)** de - **(9)** de - **(10)** por - **(11)** sin - **(12)** De - **(13)** para - **(14)** ante - **(15)** para con - **(16)** a - **(17)** con - **(18)** en - **(19)** en, antes de - **(20)** después de.

g) **(1)** A los doce años abandonó la casa - **(2)** En el café, siempre se sienta en la barra - **(3)** Puedes ir andando, a caballo, en coche - **(4)** Ayer entrastéis en Segovia - **(5)** Que yo sepa, murió al día siguiente - **(6)** Volvimos tres días más tarde - **(7)** Dos veces al día baja al buzón - **(8)** Salió a por el periódico - **(9)** Le convocó el director - **(10)** Frente a tantas responsabilidades, abdicó - **(11)** Bajo el reino de Felipe IV era el siglo de oro - **(12)** Son atentos con todos - **(13)** Este vestido es de algodón - **(14)** El chico de ojos azules es amigo de la familia - **(15)** Se pronunciaron contra ese proyecto de ley - **(16)** En España se suele comer a eso de las tres de la tarde - **(17)** De niño soñaba mucho - **(18)** Los precios han subido del diez por ciento - **(19)** Vinieron quinientas personas por lo menos - **(20)** No obedeces a sus ordenes.

h) **(1)** Por - **(2)** Por - **(3)** a *or* por - **(4)** por - **(5)** por - **(6)** por - **(7)** Por - **(8)** Por - **(9)** por - **(10)** Por - **(11)** por - **(12)** por - **(13)** por - **(14)** para - **(15)** Por - **(16)** por - **(17)** por - **(18)** por - **(19)** por - **(20)** Para.

i) **(1)** Lo hizo por necesidad - **(2)** Cometiste ese error por estar cansado - **(3)** Nos hemos reunido para repasar los apuntes - **(4)** Va a cambiar ese disco por otro - **(5)** Tal cambio sería bienvenido para Chile - **(6)** No es para comer - **(7)** Fue atropellado por un coche - **(8)** Siguió este curso para ser ingeniero - **(9)** Le regañaron sus padres por haber mentido - **(10)** Se interesa por la política.

24. CONJUNCTIONS

a) **(1)** que - **(2)** como - **(3)** que - **(4)** como - **(5)** que -
(6) que - **(7)** que - **(8)** como - **(9)** pero - **(10)** pues - **(11)** No, ni -
(12) que - **(13)** como - **(14)** por lo tanto - **(15)** sino - **(16)** sino -
(17) siquiera - **(18)** más que - **(19)** ya que - **(20)** entonces.

b) **(1)** sino - **(2)** pero - **(3)** por lo tanto - **(4)** sin embargo -
(5) o - **(6)** así - **(7)** En lo tocante a - **(8)** Por fin - **(9)** a pesar de -
(10) Ante todo.

25. DURATION

a) **(1)** Están trabajando en esta tienda desde hace dos meses -
(2) Se fue desde hace un año - **(3)** Llevo seis meses sin ir al cine -
(4) Llevan cinco años estudiando en España - **(5)** Hace media hora
que le aguardo - **(6)** Llevaba mucho tiempo con ellos - **(7)** Hacía
seis meses que estaban edificando la casa - **(8)** Llevaba una hora y
media hablando por teléfono - **(9)** Lleva sin llover desde el invierno
pasado - **(10)** Llevan mucho tiempo advirtiéndole.

b) **(1)** Las mujeres llevan años luchando por la igualdad de derechos -
(2) Llevo mucho tiempo sin verte - **(3)** Llevan meses sin trabajar -
(4) Lleváis tiempo sin ir a misa - **(5)** Lleva dos años yendo al
dentista - **(6)** En setiembre, hará cuatro años que va al mismo
instituto - **(7)** Llevo semanas sin salir - **(8)** Lleva una semana sin
lavarse el pelo - **(9)** Llevaba algunas horas esperándole -
(10) Llevan un año sin hablarse.

26. NUMBERS

a) **(1)** mil cuatrocientos noventa y dos - **(2)** mil seiscientos cincuenta y seis - **(3)** dos, tres - **(4)** mil novecientos treinta y ocho - **(5)** mil novecientos treinta y siete - **(6)** mil novecientos cincuenta y nueve - **(7)** tres años - **(8)** mil novecientos setenta y ocho - **(9)** mil novecientos treinta y seis - **(10)** veintitrés de febrero.

b) **(1)** Estamos a uno de agosto - **(2)** Eran quince en clase - **(3)** Había miles de gente en las manifestaciones - **(4)** De aquí a tu casa en autobus hay veinte paradas - **(5)** Eres el quinto niño - **(6)** El alfabeto inglés consta de veintiséis letras - **(7)** Compré seis discos para su cumpleaños - **(8)** Cada día sois diez en la mesa - **(9)** La biblioteca de este señor tiene tres mil libros - **(10)** Este comerciante vende cinco metros de tela por cinco mil pesetas - **(11)** Cecilia tiene dos veces la edad que su hija - **(12)** Tienes bastante dinero con diez mil pesetas - **(13)** El verano del setenta y seis fue muy cálido - **(14)** Han cobrado unos millones, tocándoles el gordo - **(15)** Su dirección es: calle Veracruz número dos, Madrid - **(16)** América fue descubierta en mil cuatrocientos noventa y dos - **(17)** El uno de noviembre es la fiesta de Todos los Santos - **(18)** El treinta y uno de diciembre es una noche de fiesta - **(19)** La guerra civil española fue de mil novecientos treinta y seis a mil novecientos treinta y nueve - **(20)** En Sevilla la temperatura sube hasta treinta grados en el mes de mayo.

c) **(1)** Este coche cuesta diez mil dólares - **(2)** Nunca eres primero, sino segundo - **(3)** Esta empresa tiene una treintena de empleados - **(4)** Siempre les han gustado "las Mil y Una Noches" - **(5)** Las tres cuartas partes de la gente estaban en contra de esta ley - **(6)** Este libro antiguo vale varios miles de pesetas - **(7)** Tarda media hora en aparcar - **(8)** En este teatro hay un millar de personas - **(9)** Alfonso Trece era abuelo del Rey Juan Carlos - **(10)** Llama al noveno piso.

d) **(1)** Al cumplir los veinte años, invitó a una treintena de amigos - **(2)** Sólo me quedan unos miles de pesetas - **(3)** Celebró sus cien años - **(4)** A los quince años se fue a América - **(5)** Le habéis regalado trece rosas - **(6)** Esta estantería consta de unos cien libros - **(7)** Los precios han subido del diez por ciento - **(8)** Si uno quiere enseñar bien un idioma no debía tener más que doce alumnos en la clase - **(9)** Sólo tomas cincuenta gotas de este medicamento - **(10)** A las siete es cuando se levanta la familia.

Index
to
Exercises